D0278748

VALUES, VISIONS AND VOICES

An Anthology of Socialism

EDITED BY

GORDON BROWN
AND
TONY WRIGHT

RESEARCH EDITOR CAROLINE DANIEL

MAINSTREAM
PUBLISHING

Introduction copyright © Gordon Brown and Tony Wright, 1995
All rights reserved
The moral right of the authors has been asserted

First published in Great Britain in 1995 by
MAINSTREAM PUBLISHING COMPANY (EDINBURGH) LTD
7 Albany Street
Edinburgh EH1 3UG

ISBN 1 85158 731 4

No part of this book may be reproduced or transmitted in any form or
by any means without written permission from the publisher, except by
a reviewer who wishes to quote brief passages in connection with a
review written for insertion in a magazine, newspaper or broadcast

A catalogue record for this book is available from the British Library

Printed and bound by Butler & Tanner Ltd, Frome

CONTENTS

Gordon Brown and Tony Wright, *Introduction*   13

HUMAN EQUALITY

G.D.H. Cole, *Equal Worth*   32
Robert Burns, *A Man's a Man for A' That*   32
Percy Bysshe Shelley, *Man Behind the Mask*   34
D.H. Lawrence, *Each Man Shall Be Himself*   34
William Thompson and Anna Wheeler,
   An Appeal for Equal Respect   35
Matthew Arnold, *The Instinct for Equality*   36
Raymond Williams, *Equality of Being*   37
Bernard Crick, *The Character of a Moderate Socialist*   38
Sir Thomas More, *The Unjust Public Weal*   40
John Ball, *Sermon to the People*   40
Jonathan Swift, *The Use of Money*   41
Sir Francis Bacon, *Money is Like Muck*   41
Gerrard Winstanley, *The Earth is Ours*   42
Robert Tressell, *The Ownership of Air*   43
Anonymous, *Warning to Masters and Owners*   43
Anonymous, *Stealing the Common*   44
Idris Davies, *The Angry Summer*   44
Frank Betts, *The Pawns*   46
Charles Dickens, *The Divided Society*   47
William Blake, *Holy Thursday*   48
H.G. Wells, *This Misery of Boots*   48
George Bernard Shaw, *Inequality Fosters Despair*   50
George Orwell, *Revolt Against Privilege*   51
George Orwell, *Class Distinctions*   51
D.H. Lawrence, *The Oxford Voice*   52
Raymond Williams, *Culture is Ordinary*   53
Peter Townsend, *A Classless Society*   54

FAIRNESS IN ECONOMIC DISTRIBUTION

George Bernard Shaw, *How Much is Enough?* 58
Robert Tressell, *What is Poverty?* 60
George Lansbury, *Attacking Poverty* 61
William Morris, *Equality of Condition* 62
E.F.M. Durbin, *A New and Better Society* 63
Douglas Jay, *Minimum Practicable Inequality* 64
R.H.S. Crossman, *Fair Shares* 66
Joe Batey, *The Plea of Labour* 67
Edward Carpenter, *The Dignity of Human Labour* 67
Julian le Grand, *Equality and Fairness* 68
Anthony Crosland, *How Far Towards Equality?* 71
Hugh Gaitskell, *Opportunity for All to Develop* 72
Social Justice Commission, *Equality of Opportunity* 73
Bernard Williams, *The Idea of Equality* 74
T.H. Marshall, *Equality of Status* 74
Bernard Crick, *Creating an Egalitarian Society* 75
Raymond Plant, *Why Do Inequalities Matter?* 77
Neil Kinnock, *Should We Abandon Equality?* 79
R.H. Tawney, *Equality* 81

FREEDOM: A PRACTICAL LIBERTY

Percy Bysshe Shelley, *What Art Thou Freedom?* 88
William Blake, *London* 91
J.B. Priestley, *A Great Country?* 91
Charles Kingsley, *Freedom to Rise?* 92
Charles Dickens, *The Poor Will Always Be With Us* 93
Walter Greenwood, *Hanky Park* 95
J.B. Priestley, *Rusty Lane* 95
Ronald Murphy, *Slagtips* 96
Bill Douglas, *We Will Be Free* 97
John Stuart Mill, *Whose Responsibility?* 99
Robert Blatchford, *Merrie England* 100
William Cobbett, *Lancashire Girls* 103
John Elliott McCutcheon, *The Hartley Colliery Disaster* 103
Neil Kinnock, *The Need for a Platform* 104
James Maxton, *The Will to Socialism* 105
J.B. Priestley, *Why?* 106
L.T. Hobhouse, *The State as Enabler* 106
Fred Henderson, *Positive Liberty* 109

John Maynard Keynes, *A Question of Development*   110
Clement Attlee, *Liberty for All*   110
William Temple, *Extending Choice*   112
Harold J. Laski, *Justice is the Twin-sister of Freedom*   113
R.H.S. Crossman, *Enlarging Freedom of Choice*   115
R.H. Tawney, *We Mean Freedom*   116
Barbara Wootton, *Arguing for Freedoms*   118
Richard Titmuss, *Entering Gift Relationships*   120
Raymond Plant, *Emancipating Individuals*   121
Roy Hattersley, *What We Stand for is Freedom*   122
Independent Labour Party Declaration   124

THE INDIVIDUAL AND FREEDOM

Anthony Crosland, *Open-air Cafés*   128
John Smith, *Freedom is a Moral Goal*   130
T.H. Green, *Liberation for the Common Good*   132
Ramsay MacDonald, *Developing Individuality*   133
Robert Tressell, *The Socialist Van*   133
Oscar Wilde, *Socialism Enhances Individualism*   135
John Mortimor, *Oscar Wilde Remembered*   136
R.H. Tawney, *Capitalism and Religion*   137
E.P. Thompson, *Human Potential*   138
William Morris, *The Rebirth of Society*   139
George Orwell, *Earthly Paradise*   140
William McIlvanney, *Socialism and Humanity*   141
Arnold Wesker, *Full of Living*   142
J.A. Symonds, *These Things Shall Be*   142
Rex Warner, *Future*   143
William Blake, *Jerusalem*   144

COMMUNITY

Neil Kinnock, *No Such Thing as Society*   146
John Stuart Mill, *Private War*   146
Bishop Westcott, *Socialism versus Individualism*   147
Alan Bleasdale, *Looking After Number One*   148
Dennis Potter and Melvyn Bragg, *An Interview*   149
Brian Barry, *Private Solutions?*   151
Raymond Williams, *Thinking Socially*   152
Herbert Morrison, *Call for Fellowship*   154
William Temple, *Social Fellowship*   154

Sidney Webb, *Fellowship is Life*   155
J.M. Ludlow, *Partnerships*   156
Maureen, *What the World Needs*   157
Anonymous, *Community*   158
Sidney Webb, *Thinking in Communities*   159
Ramsay MacDonald, *Community Consciousness*   159
Glenda Jackson, *Everybody's School*   160
Robert Tressell, *Community Responsibility*   160
T.H. Marshall, *Citizenship versus a Class System*   161
David Marquand, *Community Loyalty*   162
Richard Hoggart and Raymond Williams, *Working-Class Attitudes*   162
Peter Townsend, *War Solidarity*   164
Anne Phillips, *Fraternity*   166

DEVELOPING A COMMON PURPOSE

G.D.H. Cole, *Defining the Community*   170
R.H. Tawney, *Organising on the Basis of Function*   171
Sidney Webb, *The Individualist Town Councillor*   174
John Stuart Mill, *Changing the Individualist Culture*   175
G.D.H. Cole, *The State and Sovereignty*   177
Robert Owen, *A New View of Society*   178
William Morris, *How I Became a Socialist*   179
William Temple, *Objectives for Citizens*   180
Richard Titmuss, *Generosity Towards Strangers*   181
A.H. Halsey, *A Fraternal Society*   182
E.P. Thompson, *Writing by Candlelight*   183
David Marquand, *Active Citizenship*   184
Sheila Rowbotham, *A Self-Help Community*   185
Commission on Social Justice, *Making a Good Society*   185
Herbert Morrison, *Defending Co-operation*   188
Anonymous, *If it Wisnae for the Union*   189
Alan Bleasdale, *Acting for Others*   190
Socialist Sunday Schools, *The Socialist Ten Commandments*   191
Hamish Henderson, *Freedom Come All Ye*   192
Idris Davies, *Tonypandy*   193
Jennie Lee, *Our Banner*   194
J.B. Priestley, *The English Spirit*   195

DEMOCRACY

The Putney Debates, *The Right to Vote* 198
Thomas Paine, *Natural Rights* 199
William Wordsworth, *The Will of All* 201
Joseph Priestley, *The Happiness of All* 202
First Chartist Petition, *Demand for the Vote* 202
William Cobbett, *Parliamentary Reform* 204
William Lovett, *Democracy and Representation* 205
Mary Wollstonecraft, *The Representation of Women* 206
Harriet Taylor Mill, *Women and the Vote* 207
James Keir Hardie, *Votes for Women* 208
John Strachey, *Debts to the Past* 209
Sidney Webb, *The Importance of Consent* 209
Sidney Webb and Beatrice Webb, *Informing the Electorate* 210
Ramsay MacDonald, *The Consent of Active Minds* 211
Michael Foot, *My Kind of Party* 212
Aneurin Bevan, *Democratic Socialism* 213
Neil Kinnock, *Democratic Socialism – A Rational Choice* 213

DEMOCRACY AND THE ECONOMY

John Stuart Mill, *Assessing Property* 216
William Morris, *The Damage Caused by Profit* 217
Sidney Webb and Beatrice Webb, *Extending Socialisation* 218
G.D.H. Cole, *Controlling the Machine* 219
Anthony Crosland, *Aims of Democratic Socialism* 220
John Maynard Keynes, *The End of Laissez-faire* 221
Michael Young, *Economic Democracy* 221
Aneurin Bevan, *Democratic Control of the Economy* 223
James Keir Hardie, *Control over Property* 223
G.D.H. Cole, *Self-Government in Industry* 224
Aneurin Bevan, *Public and Private Property* 226
George Orwell, *Centralised Ownership* 227
Anthony Crosland, *Public and Private Ownership* 227
John Strachey, *Last-stage Capitalism* 228
Douglas Jay, *Attacking Unearned Incomes* 230
Alan Ryan, *Capitalism and Authority* 231
David Marquand, *The Public Good* 232
Will Hutton, *A Return to Responsibility* 233
Peter Shore, *In the Room at the Top* 235

DEVOLVING POWER

R.H. Tawney, *The Desire for Results*   238
E.F.M. Durbin, *Defence of Democracy*   239
Neil Kinnock, *Democracy and Power*   240
Tony Benn, *Technology and Democracy*   242
Michael Meacher, *Empowering People*   243
G.D.H. Cole, *Diffusing Power*   244
James Maxton, *If I Were a Dictator*   244
Raymond Williams, *Power in the Base*   245
Paul Hirst, *The Pluralist State*   246
G.D.H. Cole, *Active Citizenship*   247
Sheila Rowbotham, *The Women's Movement*   250
Louis MacNiece, *The Next Day I Drove by Night*   251
William Morris, *Looking Forward*   252

Copyright Acknowledgments   255

PREFACE

At a time when those of us in the Labour Party are setting out our basic values and beliefs, it seemed an appropriate moment to bring together a collection of material from our socialist tradition in Britain. We hope this will be of value and interest to everyone in the Labour Party, in identifying its enduring socialist themes through the voices of some of those who have best articulated them. We also hope it will attract others who feel they want to be associated with the kind of values represented here.

This book would not have been possible without the enthusiasm and commitment of a number of people in meeting an impossible timetable. We are grateful to all those colleagues and friends who responded so readily to our request for suggested items for inclusion, even if we have not been able to include them all. We thank (with apologies for any omissions):

Janet Anderson, Lord Archer of Sandwell, Stuart Bell, Tony Blair, David Blunkett, Paul Boateng, Chris Bryant, Anne Campbell, Ronnie Campbell, Jamie Cann, Baroness Castle, David Clark, Peter Clarke, Tom Clarke, Harry Cohen, Robin Corbett, Bernard Crick, Richard Eyre, Baroness Falkender, Steven Fielding, Eleanor Fishman, Nina Fishman, Maria Fyfe, Lord Glenamara, Julien le Grand, Bruce Grocott, Peter Hain, Lord Healey, John Heppell, Paul Hirst, George Howarth, Lord Howell, Kim Howells, Adam Ingram, Lady Irvine, Lord Jay, Lord Jenkins of Putney, Lord Judd, Jane Kennedy, Lord Kennet, Peter Kilfoyle, Ken Livingstone, Lord Longford, John McAllion, Graham McCann, George McMaster, David Marquand, Andrew Miller, Paul Murphy, Lord Murray, Martin O'Neill, Lord Oram, Lord Parry, Eleanor Phillips, Rhiannon Phillips, Ben Pimlott, Nick Raynsford, Raphael Samuel, Lord Sefton of Garston, Rachel Squire, Wilf Stevenson, Lord Taylor of Gryfe, Pat Thane, Stephen Timms, Nick Tiratsoo, Boyd Tonkin, Harold Walker, Lord Wilson of Rievaulx, and Sue Woodward.

We particularly want to record our thanks to our researcher, Caroline Daniel, who did the real work. She has worked tirelessly to meet demands that should never have been placed upon her. The book could not have been produced without her and we are immensely grateful.

Finally, we are grateful to Bill Campbell and Mainstream for their commitment to the project – and for being the kind of publisher that can make the impossible happen.

Gordon Brown
Tony Wright

Gordon Brown and Tony Wright
INTRODUCTION

This book celebrates the socialist tradition in Britain. It seeks to show that fundamental socialist values endure and continue to inspire, which is why they should be clearly reflected in both the Labour Party constitution and in Labour Party policy.

The British socialist tradition is rich, vigorous and includes many of the most intelligent voices heard in the land. While these voices may differ in their emphasis, what unites them is the sense of socialism as a project of human emancipation. They believe, as we do, that socialism offers the best account of the good society that has been framed by the human mind and imagination.

Nor should this vision be set apart from the daily political battles and the running debates on policy. Politics is more than a struggle for office and power, a perpetual game between the 'ins' and 'outs' in which principles are simply the servants of ambition. There are competing visions at issue, rooted in fundamentally different values and sharply contrasting understandings of the human condition. Clarity about the framework of values and principles within which and against which our politics is conducted is crucially important: it should inform every detail of policy, ensuring our approach is principled rather than opportunist. Of course, politics is often difficult and intractable. The world with which it deals is complex and rapidly changing. It would be easy to conclude that human ambitions should be attenuated in the face of problems that defy our reach and mock our grasp. Yet this would be an evasion and an abdication.

Socialism stands for the historic attempt by human beings acting together to transform society on the basis of certain values; and that attempt remains as important and relevant as ever. Indeed, the present condition of the world – poverty, ecological degradation, injustice and conflict – gives it a new urgency. This is the answer to those who argue that the historic tasks of the Left in Europe have been completed, that free market ideology has been triumphant, that all the basic aims of the early socialists – the project of emancipation – can be achieved within the confines of a sovereign free-market economics and that we have now reached the end of ideology, or even – as some put it – the end of history.

The removal of poverty, unemployment and injustice have always been and remain central to our aspirations and cannot be fully accomplished without a major reordering of society. Yet our aspirations have always been even more ambitious than that. At root, our objective is that individuals should have the opportunity to realise their potential to the full – enabled to bridge the gap between what they are and what they have it in themselves to become – and our distinctive argument is that the strength of society, the community acting as a community, is essential not only to tackle all the entrenched interests and accumulations of power that hold people back, but also positively to intervene to promote the potential of each of us. This belief frames our values of equality, community and democracy.

So it is vital to have an active sense of what these core socialist values are; and of the way in which they combine to form the socialist political vision. We also need to set them down with clarity and with confidence. Perhaps the most distinctive feature of British socialism historically has been its insistence on the moral basis of politics. A century ago this kind of ethical socialism may have looked like an aberration in terms of general socialist doctrines, but it has been triumphantly vindicated. Under the sway of a crude form of Marxism many socialists allowed themselves to succumb to the delusion that socialism was primarily a science of society, or that history was on its side and predetermined, or that it belonged only to one class. These errors of theory produced even greater errors of practice. Yet the best British socialists always insisted that, at bottom, socialism was a matter of moral choice. Socialism has always been, at root, more an ethic of society than an economic doctrine. It has stood for universal values and general emancipation.

Indeed, as the extracts included in this anthology show, there are three important propositions at the centre of the socialist ethic. The first is a belief that individual potential is far greater than could be realised in a wholly capitalist society. The second is a belief that individuals are not just self-centred, but also co-operative and that different social arrangements could better reflect the individual as a member of society. The third is a belief not only that individuals thrive best in a community and that the potential of the individual is enhanced by membership of a community, but also that a strong community – acting positively as a community to create opportunities for all – is essential for the advancement of individual potential.

Of course there are economic as well as moral reasons for advancing the new politics of potential and therefore a non-socialist concerned about liberty or economic efficiency might wish to accept our case. But when the Right assert that individuals are wholly self-seeking, best off left to their own devices, more held back by society than helped by it and that the less government – in effect , the fewer responsibilities of the community – the better, we as socialists should be confident about asserting a different view. Individuals are not just self-seeking but share moral and cultural commitments. They think of themselves not simply as competitors in a marketplace but also as part of a community. They also understand the need for the community to act on their behalf; to make provision for safeguards and services which individuals cannot of themselves ensure; and to offer them opportunities to develop their potential to the full. We can therefore reject the view that pits selfishness against altruism and suggests that individuals cannot both pursue their own interests and share moral commitments.

Far from being outdated, these ethical principals – of a community empowering the individual and developing his or her potential – are still as relevant as before. When Crosland wrote about socialism in the 1950s, he began by arguing that socialists had always been motivated by a number of different aspirations, and listed them: an abhorrence of poverty; a wider concern for social welfare; a belief in equality and the classless society; a rejection of competitive antagonism and an ideal of fraternity and co-operation; and protest against the inefficiencies and waste of capitalism.

The point in listing them again now is to show how our basic objectives are wider, more comprehensive and more universal than the relief of poverty – central though that remains to any socialism. Today we would also need to add further to Crosland's list, with particular reference to: the improvement and care of the environment, a recognition that any debate about who controls what should always be carried out within the context of the impact of production and economic arrangements on the environment as a whole; and recognition of the rights and aspirations of women.

What this also demonstrates is that our objectives should never have been confused merely with a commitment to nationalisation, at best a means and certainly not an end. For the whole basis of socialist theory has never been the nationalisation of this institution or that, but the liberation of individual potential through mobilising the power of community. In the early years of the Labour Party's history, the realisation of potential necessarily meant the immediate demand for the relief of poverty, homelessness and squalor. It is a shameful fact that these demands have still to be met on behalf of millions of our citizens today. In the middle of the century, the realisation of potential required the creation of new rights to health care, education, social security and work, also rights still to be realised adequately for all our citizens.

Now we have an even more ambitious view of what it takes to realise the highest aspirations for everyone. Central to this is the recognition that the success and failure of an economy depend on access to knowledge more so than access to capital. Individual liberation as well as economic progress arises from the enhancement of the value of labour rather than the abolition of private capital.

These views have always been connected to a further insight. A society might choose self-regarding individualism instead of socialism, but what it could not do was to escape the consequences of the choice it made. The years since 1979 in Britain stand as testimony to this fundamental point. For a time an ideology of possessive individualism, repudiating values of equality and social justice, seemed to carry all before it. It promised that a good society, with benefits for all, could be created on this basis. The enhanced wealth of the few would trickle down into the pockets of the poor. Yet the real consequences are all around us in decay, division and disorder. These are less the fruits of failure of policies than the necessary consequences of their success.

It has been possible to create a society of widening inequalities, the evidence for which has now been confirmed in a number of authoritative studies as well as by daily observation. What it has not been possible to do, though, is to produce the benevolent consequences promised. For what has taken place is not a benign trickle down but a malign trickle up, in which the effects of poverty, unemployment, alienation and despair have not been conveniently confined to those who are their direct victims but have pushed their way into the lives of everyone in society. There is, literally, no hiding-place from this kind of politics. What socialists have always known has now received its definitive demonstration, not in the positive way that comes from a commitment to general social improvement for all but in the negative effects of widening inequalities and divisions. A fair society and a prosperous economy go together. Social justice and economic efficiency are not mutually exclusive but inextricably linked. Growth, to be sustained, must be shared.

It is not possible to create a good society on the basis of bad morals. Any attempt to do so will not only fail, but will bring with its failure consequences of the most appalling kind. One kind of future is now glimpsed in those enclaves of the affluent in the United States which have turned themselves into fortresses, physically guarded and protected against the human sea of insecurity around them. But that is the end of society, not a kind of society. The culture of contentment turns out to be an illusion, for what it cannot deliver is contentment itself. Western societies are less characterised by contentment achieved as by potential frustrated. Those who preach the merits of widening inequalities and deepening insecurities cannot escape the consequences of what they advocate. Some socialists in the past may have been too ready to believe that the human potential for improvement (stretching even to perfectibility) was the malleable product of a benign social environment, but what they were not wrong about was the nature of the connection between a people and its politics. A decent society has to be embedded in the solid foundations of practical decency.

This is what socialism has always stood for. At its best it has had its eyes on the stars while having its feet planted firmly on the ground. Its early pioneers understood that the path to human emancipation led serious reformers to attend to the condition of the sewers. Socialists were not required to believe that their fellow citizens were imbued with moral properties of an unlikely kind, but that socialism offered to most people the prospect of practical advantage. What was morally right was also socially and economically useful. That insight remains, fusing the moral argument with the practical claim. Social justice *does* combine with economic efficiency.

This is a reminder of the extent to which socialism has been both a moral doctrine and an empirical analysis. Both are indispensable. It is necessary to engage with the world morally and intellectually, never more so than now. You have to know *why* you want to change the world; but you also have to understand that world in order to know *how* to change it. There should be no doubt that socialism is primarily an ethical doctrine; but its moralism should also be severely practical. Again, British socialism at its best has fused these dual insights into a powerful and impressive combination.

It has also sustained a dual focus on efficiency and equality (and, as has been seen, on their relationship). The central argument here is that an unregulated market economy was incapable of delivering either a decent economy or a decent society. Capitalism had to be socialised in the public interest. The conditions of both production and distribution had to be attended to. People had to be protected from both the economic malfunctions and the social consequences of a capitalism red in tooth and claw. The arguments of today may seem far removed from some of these socialist arguments from a century ago, before the social democratic revolutions of Keynes and Beveridge, but in fact there is a striking continuity.

There may no longer be a belief that centralised state planning is the only alternative to market failures, or that the infirmities of a capitalist economy can only be corrected by public ownership. These were historic attenuations of the socialist vision, even though they were sometimes erected into articles of faith (if not of practice). The preoccupation with ownership alone represented a classic inversion of ends and means, historically understandable but morally and intellectually deficient. It confused the underlying purposes and values of socialism with what was, at most, one means towards their realisation. The monstrous tyranny of the command economy should have removed any residual confusion on this matter of socialism-as-ownership. In practice, British socialism adopted the entirely sensible course of applying public ownership to natural monopolies, market breakdown and essential public services, but this did not prevent a long delay in bringing its doctrine in line with its practice. It is this confusion of ends and means that has been finally, and historically, attended to in Labour's constitutional changes.

One hundred years ago it could also be thought that, for the individual to have some control over the productive process in the public interest, the only possible solution was expropriation of the means of production. Similarly, it could also be held that this assertion of the public interest inevitably conflicted with the continued existence of markets. It is now well understood that neither of these conclusions necessarily follows from the recognition of a public interest. For it is quite clear that power can concentrate at the expense of individuals within the State as well as within private capital and that the State can, like private capital, be a vested interest.

But what is also clear about markets is that while they can be and in important respects are in the public interest, their operation is not to be identified with public interest, for they can produce unfairness, monopoly, waste and inefficiency as well as undervaluing skills and the environment. So while the public interest clearly does not require the abolition of markets, what it does require is that we take active and energetic steps to ensure that markets really do operate in the public interest. The key question today is not whether we abolish markets but how we set standards in a way that ensures that markets work in the public interest.

One hundred years ago capital was clearly in a position to exploit labour and again the answer seemed to be that the public interest was advanced by abolishing, or at least by controlling, private capital. Now most would accept that the real answer to capital exploiting labour in the interests of a few is to create the circumstances in which capital is not, somehow, abolished, but where labour can use capital, as a commodity, and do so in the public interest.

This goes far beyond what is called 'the managerial revolution'. Fifty years ago the managerial revolution recognised that in the organisation of the standard company a separation had taken place between the function of owner and the function of manager, and that the manager performed a different role from the owner of capital. Now the skills revolution rather than just the managerial revolution is upon us. While capital remains an essential ingredient for the success of an individual company, it should be treated as a commodity like plant and machinery rather than the directing force of our economy. We should recognise that now it is the skills of all the workforce that are the key to economic progress.

If this analysis is right, socialist theory fits the economic facts of the 1990s more than the 1890s. The foundation of modern economic success – and individual prosperity for all – is expanding individual economic opportunity and in this way modernising the industrial base. In other words, our basic values – the community empowering the individual – require an economic policy for enhancing the value of labour.

Yet while our ability to succeed depends on knowledge rather than capital our economic institutions are based on capital rather than knowledge. The challenge therefore is to rebuild our economic institutions around enhancing the value of labour rather than the primacy of capital. The important conclusion we reach from this is that Labour's basic century-old case – that we can enhance the value of labour as the key to economic prosperity – is now realisable in the modern economy.

So it is still possible to affirm an underlying continuity of approach. For what the early socialists in Britain were arguing, was that the economy should be organised and run in the public interest and not merely in the private interests of those who happened to possess economic power. The corollary of this was that there was a large and vigorous role for an active and intelligent state. The nature of this role will necessarily change over time – government may be partner, catalyst, enabler, financier or simply regulator, rather than owner, employer or manager only; just as government may be local and international as well as national. But what does not and should not change is the public interest perspective. This is what sustains the continuity of the socialist economic argument and differentiates it from those who are enslaved by the tyranny of the market.

It is possible to be enslaved by the tyranny of the State and of the market: the modern democratic socialist wants to be enslaved by neither. The public interest task today is to use the power of the community to make a market economy work efficiently and responsibly in the public interest. In a global market, this will also require concerted action beyond the level of the national state to provide a framework for employment, growth and environmental sustainability; but socialists have long understood the importance of internationalism. The making of new international economic institutions is a major challenge that lies ahead of us. We also require vigorous domestic activity too, for a modern economy – as we suggest above – depends crucially upon the quality of its human capital and that quality has to be energetically nurtured. We should equip people to succeed in the modern global market place. The traditional weaknesses of the British economy – above all, the triumph of short-term finance over long-term investment – are still waiting to be remedied.

There is a huge agenda here, but at its centre is a modern state engaging in active partnerships in pursuit of public interest objectives. Public and private, state and market, capital and labour, national and international: these are the components of a modern partnership economy. There is also an integration of economic and social objectives, for what is involved is not merely a kind of economy but a kind of society. It grows out of and expresses the political culture of western Europe, to which British socialism has made a distinctive contribution and from which the ideological zealots of 'new' British conservatism want to effect a rupture in their pursuit of an Americanised model of market deregulation. There is a real choice involved here, with momentous implications for the fabric and character of our society. The old economic antinomy between capitalism and socialism as forms of ownership finds its modern expression in the choice between responsibility and irresponsibility, social market and unsocial market, a stakeholder economy and footloose capitalism.

These issues also illuminate further the matter of ends and means for socialists. Socialists should be resolutely fundamentalist about ends, for these are the permanent furniture of beliefs and values constituting what socialism is. These basic values may be distinguished from aims, despite their intimate connection, in the sense that equality is a value and the removal of unjustifiable inequalities a derivative aim. Aims in turn need translation into the hard currency of means through the practical business of policies and programmes.

The perennial and proper task is to combine a root and branch radicalism about values with a pragmatic ingenuity about their application in ever-changing circumstances. That is the condition for any serious political engagement at all, though one kind of socialist will always prefer a recitation of old verities to the rigours of new thought. All socialists must be both radicals and permanent revisionists, constantly exploring how their enduring values can find fresh resonances and applications. Thus the task of finding a socialism 'for today' is not a species of betrayal, but a process of active renewal.

Yet values provide the rock of reference, against which applications and derivations must be measured. They are the focus of the material collected here, for the purpose is to illuminate the socialist political vision of which they are its constituent parts. Of course, these core values, which we identify and discuss below, are not without their difficulties. All values and concepts are contested and none more so than the political vocabulary of equality, freedom and the rest. The task is to distinguish the particular socialist resonances among this general mood music of western political thought. The further task is to emphasise that, while it may be convenient to identify a number of core values, it is the nature of their integration that gives the defining character to the socialist vision. It is not the values separately but the nature of their interaction that makes socialism what it is. For example, the British socialist tradition has been distinguished by a particular (and powerful) argument about the interconnectedness of freedom and equality. In looking at the parts, the purpose is to illuminate the whole. All categories are somewhat arbitrary, including the ones used here, but the cumulative force defines a project worth living for.

Equality: a Society of Equals

A society of equals: the phrase comes from William Morris and goes to the heart of the socialist political vision. Endlessly misunderstood and contested, equality is an elemental socialist value. It is rooted in a belief, in an original and primary sense, in the equal worth of all individuals. Its flavour is caught by Burns with his 'a man's a man for a' that', just as it is heard in the memorable exchange from the Putney debates of the 1640s when it is proclaimed that 'the poorest he that is in England has a life to live as the greatest'. It is a basic moral proposition, around which there has to be moral choice. You either believe it or you do not, and with it the consequences for public policy and political action.

It informs and sustains the socialist vision of a classless society, just as it provides the basis for wanting to remove both injustice and unfairness which prevent its realisation. What it does not mean is literal or arithmetical equality, for that would be neither possible nor desirable. Treating people equally is not treating them the same. Diversity, choice and individuality will flourish to the extent that the structural impediments to a society of equals are removed. D.H. Lawrence remarked that equality did not mean A recognised B to be the same, but A recognised B to be different. The dull uniformities and suppression of opportunities that come from a society marked by class inequalities will be replaced by the human flourishing and release of talents that flow from their eradication.

All concepts are difficult and contested, but equality has also had to endure more than its share of wilful nonsense. Its moral axiom of equal worth has been misrepresented as a rigid imposition of equal treatments. An equality of opportunity has been opposed to an equality of outcome, as though it were possible to have genuine equality of opportunity without a buttress of practical equality to enable people to participate in the opportunities. A race may have no formal obstacles but it is nevertheless vitiated if the runners are so unequal that the prizes go only to the advantaged. These are elementary observations, obscured only by the deliberate obfuscation of those who want to evade the consequences of the moral choice they are being asked to make.

Of course people are not equal in talents, abilities, industry, righteousness or in countless other ways; and socialists have never been so foolish as to believe that they were. Nor have socialists (except eccentrically) embraced a vision in which equality of treatment has meant identity of treatment. As Bernard Crick has put it, these are other people's nightmares not democratic socialist dreams.

20

When such nonsense is put aside, the real character of the egalitarian project is clear. Rooted in that initial attachment to equal worth, as a fundamental moral axiom, it directs its attention to opening up access to the means of civilised life for all. This is a process much more than a product, a relentless engagement with the sources of power, wealth and opportunity to counter the social reproduction of inequality and to enhance the life chances of the many. The emphasis is always positive and inclusive, enabling the many to walk where only the few have walked before. Some will find this threatening and restricting; most will surely find it liberating and energising.

An egalitarian project of this kind is difficult and demanding, for the generation of inequality is a remorseless process and requires a no less persistent response. Public policy can and does make an impact, as it did in the contraction of inequality in the generation after the 1940s and in its shameful widening in the period since 1979. Behind the multitude of individual policy decisions there is a politics of moral choice at work. Nowhere is this seen more starkly than in the evidence showing a widening gap in life expectancy between rich and poor, a reminder that inequality can literally be a matter of life and death. This is offensive to socialists, and should be to others too. It provides a challenge and spur to public action.

Not all inequalities are unjustified, but those that structure basic life chances and divide society into classes certainly are. They are a standing affront to any notion of equal individual worth. It matters less to champion an idea of equality, though, than to make every inequality justify itself. This avoids the false pursuit of a literal equality of treatment and outcome, while subjecting every inequality to the test of fairness and justice. Some will pass the test but many (such as the outrageous payments that directors and executives have taken to awarding themselves) will not. A society of equals may sit as a distant vision, but it comes closer whenever an unjustified inequality is converted into an arena of fairness.

R.H. Tawney famously argued that equality was best seen as negating socially imposed inequalities. In other words, there could be no complete equality, but we could and should eliminate all unjustifiable inequalities. We need to show that clear public benefit follows from equality and that more equality will enhance and not destroy individuality. As the collection suggests, this means a strategy for equality that recognises:

First, equalising opportunity must be more than a once and for all event but a lifetime process.

Second, equalising opportunity means equality of power and therefore a redistribution of power from the strong to the weak, from institutions that enjoy privileges to people who are held back as a result. We must empower people to benefit from fresh opportunities.

Third, equalising opportunity means tackling not just the consequences of inequality – with policies for compensation through the social security system paid for through the tax system – but the causes of inequality, in education, the workplace, in the way the welfare system works, in fighting structural discrimination and in tackling entrenched interests. We must give people new power and fresh opportunities to develop their creativity and potential – and this means tackling the roots of inequality, not merely attending to its symptoms.

Finally and crucially, this commitment to equalising opportunity means the permanent creation and re-creation of economic, employment, and educational opportunities – not just a second chance but continuously available opportunities to work, to learn and upgrade skills, and to make the most of potential. Our fundamental aim must be to ensure that no one is permanently consigned on the basis of an accident of birth, or family life, or education in their teens to a permanent loss of potential. There is a responsibility on the part of government to ensure that this is achieved.

Freedom: a Practical Liberty

Democratic socialists have a passion for freedom. They want to extend it as widely as possible. It was Clement Attlee who announced simply that 'the aim of socialism is to give greater freedom to the individual' and it is a typically wise remark. Socialism is properly measured by the extent to which it enables individuals to live free lives. Indeed, the socialist tradition may be seen as a long crusade against the varieties of unfreedom that prevented people from living lives appropriate to free human beings. Voices from that crusade are heard throughout the extracts collected in this book. It is the language of emancipation.

Freedom suffers from its status as the rhetorical loose change of political debate in the west, yet British socialists have brought a distinctive understanding to it. In crucial respects the common ground that was established on this issue in the early part of this century between progressive liberals and democratic socialists in Britain came to define the terms of political debate and provided the basis for the politics of the post-war social democratic settlement. On one side, this involved a fierce attachment to the civil and political liberties that had been won against State tyrannies and needed continuing defence; while, on the other side, a recognition that the achievement of social and economic liberties through the actions of the State was also a necessary constituent of a freedom worthy of the name. There was complementarity, not rivalry, in these positions. This prompted the liberal philosopher, L.T. Hobhouse, to declare at the beginning of the century that the basis existed for a 'Liberal Socialism' which recognised that the nineteenth-century conception of liberty was 'too thin' and needed to be 'enlarged' through positive public action.

What he would not have anticipated was that nineteenth-century economic liberalism, in all its thinness and inadequacy, was to find itself resurrected in the late twentieth century as the doctrine of a 'new' conservatism. We are told once again that employers must have the 'freedom' to erode the securities of workers, that all taxation is a confiscatory infringement of 'freedom' and that poor people must be 'freed' from their dependency upon the State. In the fact of such sophistry, the good sense of British socialists on the matter of freedom has a refreshing sanity.

It does not shirk the difficulties. Liberties have to co-exist, one person's freedom has to respect the freedom of others, and there are always trade-offs and balances. The price of freedom is eternal messiness. The tradition of freedom has produced a politics of rights, but this has to be matched by a politics of duties and obligations. Self-maximising individuals remain social beings and are framed by a conception of the common good. There may be tensions here, but there are no inherent contradictions. It is possible to understand all this while still insisting that freedom involves treating people as ends and not as means and enabling people to define their own kind of freedom and to pursue it in their own way. If pushed too far, values may collide, which is why British socialists have been careful to espouse a vision of equality that enriches rather than damages its conception of freedom.

That conception has a number of elements. It combines an understanding that the State can be an enemy of freedom, requiring an armoury of protections and rights, with a recognition that the State can also enlarge freedom by diminishing the impediments to its achievement. The removal of want, fear and insecurity from people's lives is a huge gain for freedom (just as their growth is an equivalent loss for freedom). There is a real sense in which the National Health Service is also a national freedom service. Freedom is plural and it is practical, not a philosophical abstraction but a series of concrete capacities. The old gibe about everyone being free to dine at the Ritz still carries its ironic punch. Freedoms have to be exercisable if they are to deliver on their promise.

Too often freedom is the legitimising name given to privilege. The assertion of this kind of freedom for some frequently involves the denial of practical freedom to others. The freedom not to pay fair taxes is bought at the expense of those who need collective provision to extend their own freedom. The freedom to exploit is the denial of freedom to those who are exploited. In R.H. Tawney's memorable metaphor, freedom for the pike is death for the minnow. Yet it is too precious to be usurped by the few and denied to the many. That would not be acceptable in the case of civil and political liberty, nor should it be different with other kinds of liberties.

Socialists therefore reject a false dichotomy between freedom *from* and freedom *to,* negative and positive, and want to explore the conditions for practical freedoms for all. They also reject the false antithesis between equality and freedom, believing these to be partners and not antagonists (unless either is pushed beyond its proper limits). Liberties require equalities if they are to be extended to more than a few. Again Tawney goes to the heart of the matter: 'In so far as the opportunity to lead a life worthy of human beings is needlessly confined to a minority, not a few of the conditions applauded as freedom would more properly be denounced as privilege. Action which causes such opportunities to be more widely shared is, therefore, twice blessed. It not only subtracts from inequality, but adds to freedom.' Just so.

Community: All Together Now . . .

We have to be careful with community. In the wrong hands, it can be dangerous and oppressive, excluding and aggressive. In other hands, it can be simply nostalgic, or used to manufacture a warm rhetorical glow. Not all communities are pleasant places and not all apostles of community (or of communitarianism) issue invitations of the kind that ought to be accepted. Yet the fact remains that the idea of community, properly understood, is a defining idea of socialism and underpins the socialist vision of fraternity, cohesion and solidarity.

At its centre is the belief that society is a collective moral enterprise in which we are all engaged. It stands in polar contrast to market individualism, with its denial of common social purposes and dissolution of the bonds of citizenship into a contract culture. In simple terms, the socialist belief is that we are all in it together, that human beings are irredeemably social in character and that society is a network of mutual rights, duties, responsibilities and obligations. This contrast between social-ism and individual-ism as ways of understanding the world remains as sharp and pivotal as ever. We should not be surprised that the recent ascendancy in Britain of a politics that repudiated the existence of society has now produced a renewed concern with community as the consequences of that repudiation have made themselves felt in a painful process of fragmentation and loss of social cohesion.

Socialists affirm social solidarity. From the experiences and struggles of the past, also recorded in many of the extracts here, they have developed an enduring sense of the importance of working together for common ends. Not only does this lead to an understanding that through co-operative endeavour it is possible to achieve together what it is not possible to achieve separately (the basis for collective provision), but also to a vision of the quality of social relationships that should properly characterise such a society. Words such as fraternity and fellowship may perhaps have a rather old-fashioned ring to them, but their importance is undiminished in evoking the way of living appropriate to a society of common purposes, mutual obligations and shared responsibilities. They also serve as a reminder that principles have to be practised.

For the socialist, then, community expresses a view of social solidarity, the translation to society of the ancient cry of 'all for one and one for all'. It carries with it an aspiration towards social unity (even, in utopian moods, a flirtation with social harmony) and wants to remove those barriers and divisions that enforce social separation. This has meant grappling with the crippling effects of the British class structure, with its separate schools, intricate hierarchies and ruptured life experiences. Class stands as the crushing barrier to community and its force has been felt in Britain with a particular severity. It drove George Orwell to rail against this 'accursed itch of class difference, like the pea under the princess's mattress' that put a chasm across British society and enforced social distance. It prompted Raymond Williams to declare, in affirming that 'culture is ordinary', that 'the central problem of our society . . . is the use of our new resources to make a good common culture'. The contemporary discovery of a new 'underclass' mocks this aspiration to community and shames us all.

With solidarity at its core, the democratic socialist version of community has further features which give it a distinctive quality (and distinguish it from other versions). It is not a product to be imposed but a process in which free citizens voluntarily engage to shape a common life. Far from being inconsistent with diversity and individuality, it offers a collective individualism through which these may flourish. It recognises that a community is always a collection of communities and this means that it has to be tolerant and inclusive enough to enable all to share in it. This carries with it a commitment to equity, in which conscious and deliberate effort is made to include those who are at the receiving end of social exclusion. It is also an argument about power and its control, enabling people to participate in the decision processes that affect their lives, with an attention to the scale and sites where this can be cultivated.

Far from being amorphous and promiscuous, this version of community is tightly drawn and hard-edged. It affirms that what we share in common is more important than what separates us and that society is a purposive project rooted in shared responsibilities. It does not seek vainly to recover lost solidarities and old identities, but it does emphatically seek to retrieve the idea of social solidarity and to forge a new community for new times. We badly need to rediscover a sense of public purpose, along with the spaces and institutions where it can be exercised, in the wake of the depredations of market individualism. The collective response to insecurity that formed the basis of early socialism finds a new relevance in the face of the multiple insecurities now unleashed. The fractured and fragmented coalition of social life will undoubtedly evoke a response of some kind. It is in all our interests that this response should be to renew community rather than to destroy it.

We must retrieve the broad idea of community from the narrow focus on State action. Indeed the way in which communities act to empower the individual must change from decade to decade. For many – as the State became itself a vested interest – the fear of the evils of government became even greater than the awareness of the possibilities of acting together. This makes it essential that we should retrieve the wide and expansive notion of community from the narrow and restricted idea of the centralised State. This means ensuring, first, that individual rights are protected from any improper encroachment from the State and, secondly, examining very clearly how the community can organise its affairs in a much more decentralised way, more sensitively and flexibly, breaking out of the one-dimensional view of government that too easily assumes that where there is a public interest there must be a centralised public bureaucracy always directly involved in ownership of industry or services.

Sometimes the community will work through central government, sometimes local, sometimes voluntary organisations, sometimes through collective organisations such as trades unions. At the same time as we recognise the responsibilities of a world of new aspirations, diverse needs, changing ambitions, new demands for individual fulfilment, and fresh opportunities for people to realise their potential, we must equally recognise the implications for the changed way in which the community of the 1990s, and into the next millennium, must organise its affairs in these new circumstances where every individual in some sense has become a decision-maker in her or his own right. This means, for example, guaranteeing rights to independent information, training in the skills necessary to make choices, rights to resources essential for independence and an assurance that others will not illegitimately circumscribe their actions.

This notion of social responsibility goes far beyond traditional notions of devolution and decentralisation. It is more than just an encouragement to participation and involvement, important though these are. It is ambitious to redistribute power from State to individual, just as for a century we loosened private power with greater public responsibility. For a hundred years the socialist message has inevitably had to be that the State should assume power on behalf of the people. Now it is time that the people take power from the State. Instead of government for and on behalf of the people, now we want government by and through the people, not the government controlling people but people taking control of the government. In short, while as a government we take power, we do so not to entrench it but to give it away.

Where the Right's view is that individuals are held back by the community and do best when left to their own devices, requiring them to remove government or at least promote its withering away, socialists believe that an active community is a vehicle for the advancement of opportunity. However, this means a new settlement between individual, community and government, based on the principle that individuals must have safeguards against entrenched interests (including the State itself) and that the community should be able to organise its own affairs in its own ways.

Democracy: Politics for Citizens

This brings us to democracy. When we describe our tradition as democratic socialism, the coupling is more than a matter of habit. It is a genuine fusion, in which democracy lies at the dynamic centre of socialist belief. For much of this century it was necessary to distinguish democratic from undemocratic socialism, as a dark shadow was cast by those who used the name of socialism to practise their tyranny and who peddled the dangerous myth that the command economy was synonymous with human freedom. That shadow has now been lifted. Socialism without democracy is a contradiction, while democracy without socialism remains undeveloped. It may soon be possible for democratic socialism to remove its prefix again.

As many of the extracts here remind us, socialism has its roots in the historic struggle for democratic representation, equal rights and political freedom. Democracy is an argument about power and its organisation; and it had to be advanced and won against those who wanted to keep power for the few instead of being enjoyed by the many. Socialists hoped (and anti-democrats feared) that the achievement of political democracy would find its natural extension in social democracy, as the majority of people used the resources of a democratic State to create a more equal society. Yet this link between political and social democracy is not merely an historic aspiration; it is rooted in the idea of democracy itself. For democracy has a belief in equal rights at its centre and its inherent egalitarianism makes it not merely a kind of political system but a kind of society. There is real unity and comple-mentarity here. Socialism without political democracy is a negation of free and equal citizenship; political democracy without social democracy is an incomplete expression of the wider egalitarian impulse behind the democratic idea.

This same point may be made in a rather different way. If democracy entails that power should be held to public account, and puts in place a range of mechanisms to secure this, then this properly applies not merely to the State itself but to other concentrations of unaccountable power. For example, the fact that the public utilities have been moved from the public to the private sector does not dissolve questions about their accountability in the public interest: indeed, it intensifies them and demands a democratic response. Where power goes, there democracy follows. Against those who like to maintain that 'the economy' and 'the market' are arenas governed by their own mysterious laws and properly free from wider social obligations, the democratic socialist insists that their operation is emphatically a matter of public interest.

We also want to unpack, extend and enrich the democratic idea. It should not live merely as the complacent self-description of our kind of political system, but should have an active presence in our society. Its constituent elements of representation, accountability, participation and openness are all capable of substantial development. The British political system is notoriously centralised and concentrated, giving too much power to those who govern and too little to those who should hold them to account. It has a democratic deficit that has to be remedied through a radical programme of political reform. Since 1979 our democracy has been shamefully abused; it now has to be renewed.

The socialist tradition to which we belong wants to diffuse and pluralise power, enabling people to develop the art of self-government and the practice of citizenship. The role of the State is to enable and empower, nourishing active citizenship, not substituting for it. There are different levels at which decisions have to be taken, corresponding to the tasks to be done, but the presumption should always be that decisions will be taken as close as possible to citizens themselves. Nor should this democratic presumption be confined only to the operation of the formal political system. As G.D.H. Cole argued, the democratic principle applies 'not only or mainly to some special sphere of social action known as "politics", but to any and every form of social action'. That is why socialists have wanted to involve workers in their firms, neighbourhoods in planning, tenants in their housing, parents in schools and users in services. The classical ideal of citizenship, of governing and being governed in turn, is still searching for its modern expression. The world is big and citizens are small. If this is not to issue in apathy and despair, the task of developing new civic tools and techniques is inescapably urgent.

This is also why we see government's role as an enabler, catalyst, financier, sponsor, innovator, rule-maker rather than simply a one-dimensional State owning companies and industries. This view of government as catalyst, steering rather than rowing, setting the rules and standards, charting the course rather than driving the train, setting social priorities, comes with it a whole range of organisational possibilities. The idea of a withering away of the State is absurd. But it is good government we need rather than big government. What we must do, of course, is to strengthen the power of community in tackling vested interests. No one should exercise power without responsibility or accountability. No polluter should escape social responsibility; no vested interest should operate in an unaccountable manner; no private or public monopoly should be able to operate unchecked and against the public interest.

Nor should any entrenched interest be able to deny opportunity or hold people back. We believe that the historic role of the Labour Party has been to stand up for the individual citizen against any vested interests of power and privilege, or cartels and cliques in either public or private sector, wherever the abuse of power arises. It's purpose has always been about helping each other to help ourselves in situations where people are unfairly treated, their lives diminished, their aspirations frustrated, their horizons and ambitions narrowed by the abuses of power. If we were looking for a popular (and populist) way to express this, we might say that Labour's essential purpose is to stop people being ripped off or pushed around and to enable everyone to get the chance of a decent life.

For socialists democracy is also a cultural vision. The spirit of equality at the centre of the democratic idea offers the prospect of a society in which people are within reach of each other, engaging in a common life and sharing in a common culture, freed from distancing divisions and disabling distinctions. That vision remains; it includes the familiar apparatus of democracy but also goes beyond it. Yet it requires for its success that it will come to be widely shared and supported through the procedural requirements of democratic politics. Democratic socialists are ferocious in their attachment to these procedures, which they struggled with others to win. What this means is that democratic socialism will advance its vision only to the extent that it can persuade people to support it, not merely with their votes (the indispensable bottom line of democracy) but also with their hearts and minds. This is a formidable democratic discipline; but so it should be. It is also a formidable and continuing challenge for democratic socialists.

We have tried here to sketch some of the basic values and beliefs of British democratic socialism. The rest of the book is designed to put some flesh on these bones. No doubt the arguments could have been made differently, even using an alternative vocabulary in places, but we hope and believe that we have said some of the most important things that need to be said about our socialist tradition. Although we have separated out some of the core values, we emphasise again that what distinguishes the socialist project is the way in which these values connect with each other. It is a process of fusion, not merely of addition. This should be kept in mind in reading the extracts that follow.

We have been concerned with underlying values, not with particular policy applications. The latter will change, in the light of new problems, knowledge and circumstances, but the former will have an enduring quality. They will not provide an instant answer to policy questions, available to be read off on demand, but they should provide the framework of basic beliefs within which issues are discussed and responses developed. They also define the kind of political project that democratic socialism is. It does not expect human beings to be other than they are, although it does want to develop their potential and release their capacities. It does not offer an apocalyptic politics of total social transformation, although it does have a stubborn vision of improvement to be secured by persuasion, effort and thought. The essential character of democratic socialism is well described by the philosopher Leszek Kolakowski as 'an obstinate will to erode by inches the conditions which produce avoidable suffering, oppression, hunger, wars, racial and national hatred, insatiable greed and vindictive envy'. It is also expressed in Aneurin Bevan's declaration that democratic socialism is 'based on the conviction that free men can use free institutions to solve the social and economic problems of the day, if they are given the chance to do so'.

But it involves moral choice; and that is another of our themes here. There is nothing inevitable about democratic socialism. It requires people to share its values and the prospectus based upon them. We hope that by illuminating these values, through the voices assembled here, people will want to share them. It is not claimed that they offer an instant solution for the daunting problems facing our country and the world; but it is claimed that they provide a decent moral and intellectual basis upon which to face them. As we write this, the Labour Party is in the process of preparing a new statement of its basic values. We confidently expect that this will express and celebrate the tradition to be found here.

HUMAN EQUALITY

'Socialism is an imaginative belief that all men, however unequal they may be in powers of mind and body or in capacity for service, are in a really significant sense equal, not merely before the law but one with another'

G.D.H. Cole
EQUAL WORTH (1935)

I ask no one to call himself a socialist unless he wants society to recognise other men's claims as no less valid than his own. Socialism is an imaginative belief that all men, however unequal they may be in powers of mind and body or in capacity for service, are in a really significant sense *equal*, not merely before the law but one with another. They are equal as brothers and sisters are equal, the strong with the weak, the foolish with the wise – and the bad with the good, so far as men are good or bad in any final sense. Luck no social system can ever eliminate: there will be lucky ones and unlucky ones under socialism as there are today. Differences of quality and attainment, too, will exist, however society is organised. There will be a waste of genius, square pegs in round holes, backslidings and misfortunes due to passion and evil impulses under any social system. But we can at least greatly improve the chances of well-being and bring them nearer to equality between man and man. We can give everyone a much fairer start, a far more even chance of making the best of body and mind, and therewith a far better hope of escaping the doom of body or mind twisted awry by forces of nurture and environment. There is immense scope for increasing the sum of human happiness, even though, whatever we do, much unhappiness is bound to remain. The reason – the only valid reason – for being a socialist is the desire, the impassioned will, to seek the greatest happiness of the greatest number.

From *The Simple Case for Socialism* by G.D.H. Cole (Gollancz, 1935)

Robert Burns
A MAN'S A MAN FOR A' THAT (1795)

Is there, for honest poverty,
    That hangs his head, an' a' that?
The coward slave, we pass him by,
    We dare be poor for a' that!
        For a' that, an' a' that,
           Our toils obscure, an' a' that;
        The rank is but the guinea's stamp;
           The man's the gowd for a' that.

What though on hamely fare we dine,
     Wear hodden-gray, an' a' that;
Gie fools their silks, and knaves their wine,
     A man's a man for a' that.
        For a' that, an' a' that,
           Their tinsel show, an' a' that;
        The honest man, though e'er sae poor,
           Is king o' men for a' that.

Ye see yon birkie, ca'd a lord,
     Wha struts, an' stares, an' a' that;
Though hundreds worship at his word,
     He's but a coof for a' that.
        For a' that, an' a' that,
           His riband, star, an' a' that,
        The man o' independent mind,
           He looks and laughs at a' that.

A prince can mak a belted knight,
     A marquis, duke, an' a' that;
But honest man's aboon his might,
     Guid faith he mauna fa' that!
        For a' that, an' a' that,
           Their dignities, an' a' that,
        The pith o' sense, an' pride o' worth,
           Are higher rank than a' that.

Then let us pray that come it may,
     As come it will for a' that,
That sense and worth, o'er a' the earth,
     May bear the gree, an' a' that.
        For a' that, an' a' that,
           It's coming yet, for a' that,
        That man to man, the warld o'er,
           Shall brothers be for a' that.

From *Complete Poetical Works*, edited by J.L. Robertson (Oxford, 1931)

Percy Bysshe Shelley
MAN BEHIND THE MASK (1820)

I wandering went
Among the haunts and dwellings of mankind,
And first was disappointed not to see
Such mighty changes as I had felt within
Expressed in outward things; but soon I looked,
And behold, thrones were kingless, and men walked
One with the other even as spirits do,
None fawned, none trampled; hate, disdain or fear,
Self-love or self-contempt, on human brows
No more inscribed, as o'er the gate of hell,
'All hope abandon ye who enter here';
None frowned, none trembled, none with eager fear
Gazed on another's eye of cold command,
Until the subject of a tyrant's will
Became, worse fate, the abject of his own,
Which spurred him, like an outspent horse, to death . . .

The loathsome mask has fallen, the man remains
Sceptreless, free, uncircumscribed, but man
Equal, unclassed, tribeless and nationless,
Exempt from awe, worship, degree, the king
Over himself; just, gentle, wise: but man
Passionless? – no, yet free from guilt or pain.

From 'Prometheus Unbound' in *The Complete Poetical Works,*
edited by T. Hutchinson, revised by B.P. Kurtz (Oxford, 1934)

D.H. Lawrence
EACH MAN SHALL BE HIMSELF (c.1917)

Not people melted into oneness: that is not the new democracy. But people released into their single, starry identity, each one distinct and incommutable. This will never be an ideal; for of the living self you cannot make an idea, just as you have not been able to turn the individual 'soul' into an idea. Both are impossible to idealise. An idea is an abstraction from reality, a generalisation. And you can't generalise the incommutable . . .

Since every individual is, in his first reality, a single, incommutable soul, not to be calculated or defined in terms of any other soul, there can be no estab-

34

lishing of a mathematical ratio. We cannot say that all men are equal. We cannot say A = B. Nor can we say that men are unequal. We may not declare that A = B + C.

Where each thing is unique in itself, there can be no comparison made. One man is neither equal nor unequal to another man. When I stand in the presence of another man, and I am my own pure self, am I aware of the presence of an equal, or of an inferior, or of a superior? I am not. When I stand with another man, who is himself, and when I am truly myself, then I am only aware of a Presence, and of the strange reality of Otherness. There is me, and there is *another being*. That is the first part of the reality. There is no comparing or estimating. There is only this strange recognition of *present otherness*. I may be glad, angry, or sad, because of the presence of the other. But still no comparison enters in. Comparison enters only when one of us departs from his own integral being and enters the material-mechanical world. Then equality and inequality starts at once.

So, we know the first great purpose of democracy: that each man shall be spontaneously himself – each man himself, each woman herself, without any question of equality or inequality entering in at all; and that no man shall try to determine the being of any other man, or of any other woman.

From 'Democracy'(1963), reprinted in *Phoenix: The Posthumous Papers of D.H. Lawrence*, edited by E. Macdonald (Heinemann, 1961)

William Thompson and Anna Wheeler
AN APPEAL FOR EQUAL RESPECT (1825)

Whatever system of labour, that by slaves or that by freemen; whatever system of government, that by one, by a few, or by many, have hitherto prevailed in human society; under every vicissitude of MAN'S condition, he has always retained woman his slave. The republican has exercised over you that hateful spirit of domination which his fellow man and citizen disdained to submit to. Of all the sins and vices of your masters, you have been made the scapegoats: they have enjoyed, and you have suffered for their enjoyments; suffered for the very enjoyments of which they compel you to be the instruments! What wonder that your sex is indifferent to what man calls the progress of society, of freedom of action, of social institutions? Where amongst them all, amongst all their past schemes of liberty or despotism, is the freedom of action *for you*?

To obtain equal rights, the basis of equal happiness with men, you must be *respected* by them; not merely desired, like rare meats, to pamper their selfish appetites. To be respected by them, you must be respectable in your own eyes; you must exert more power, you must be more useful. You must regard yourselves as having equal capabilities of contributing to the general happiness with men, and as therefore equally entitled with them to every enjoyment. You must exercise these capabilities, nor cease to remonstrate till no more than equal duties are exacted from you, till no more than equal punishments are inflicted upon you, till equal enjoyments and equal means of seeking happiness are permitted to you as to men.

From *Appeal to One Half of the Human Race*

Matthew Arnold
THE INSTINCT FOR EQUALITY (1861)

Now, can it be denied, that a certain approach to equality, at any rate a certain reduction of signal inequalities, is a natural, instinctive demand of that impulse which drives society as a whole – no longer individuals and limited classes only, but the mass of a community – to develop itself with the utmost possible fullness and freedom? Can it be denied, that to live in a society of equals tends in general to make a man's spirits expand, and his faculties work easily and actively; while, to live in a society of superiors, although it may occasionally be a very good discipline, yet in general tends to tame the spirits and to make the play of the faculties less secure and active? Can it be denied, that to be heavily overshadowed, to be profoundly insignificant, has, on the whole, a depressing and benumbing effect of the character? I know that some individuals react against the strongest impediments, and owe success and greatness to the efforts which they are thus forced to make. But the question is not about individuals. The question is about the common bulk of mankind, persons without extraordinary gifts or exceptional energy, and who will ever require, in order to make the best of themselves, encouragement and directly favouring circumstances. Can any one deny, that for these the spectacle, when they would rise, of a condition of splendour, grandeur and culture, which they cannot possibly reach, has the effect of making them flag in spirit, and of disposing them to sink despondingly back into their own condition? Can any one deny, that the knowledge how poor and insignificant the best condition of improvement and culture attainable by them must be esteemed by a class incomparably richer-endowed, tends to cheapen this modest possible amelioration in the account of those classes also for whom it would be relatively a real progress, and to disenchant their imaginations with it? It seems to me impossible to deny this.

From *The Portable Matthew Arnold*, edited by Lionel Trilling (Viking, 1949)

Raymond Williams
EQUALITY OF BEING (1958)

Active reception, and living response, depend in their turn on an effective community of experience, and their quality, as certainly, depends on a recognition of practical equality. The inequalities of many kinds which still divide our community make effective communication difficult or impossible. We lack a genuinely common experience, save in certain rare and dangerous moments of crisis. What we are paying for this lack, in every kind of currency, is now sufficiently evident. We need a common culture, not for the sake of an abstraction, but because we shall not survive without it.

I have referred to equality, but with some hesitation, for the word is now commonly confusing. The theoretical emphasis on equality, in modern society, is in general an opponent response; it is less a positive goal than an attack on inequality, which has been practically emphasised in exact proportion to equalitarian ideas. The only equality that is important, or indeed conceivable, is equality of being. Inequality in the various aspects of man is inevitable and even welcome; it is the basis of any rich and complex life. The inequality that is evil is inequality which denies the essential equality of being. Such inequality, in any of its forms, in practice rejects, depersonalises, degrades in grading, other human beings. On such practice a structure of cruelty, exploitation and the crippling of human energy is easily raised. The masses, the dominative mood, the rejection of culture, are its local testaments in human theory.

A common culture is not, at any level, an equal culture. Yet equality of being is always necessary to it, or common experience will not be valued. A common culture can place no absolute restrictions on entry to any of its activities: this is the reality of the claim to equality of opportunity. The claim to such opportunity is of course based on the desire to become unequal, but this can mean any of a number of things. A desired inequality which will in practice deny the essential equality of being, is not compatible with a culture in common. Such inequalities, which cannot be afforded, have continually to be defined, out of the common experience. But there are many inequalities which do not harm this essential equality, and certain of these are necessary, and need to be encouraged. The point becomes practical in examples, and I would suggest these. An inequality in other than personal property – that is to say an inequality in ownership of the means of life and production – may be found intolerable because in practice it may deny the basic processes of equality of being. Inequality in a particular faculty, however, or unequal developments of knowledge, skill and effort, may not deny essential equality: a physicist will be glad to learn from a better physicist, and will not, because he is a good physicist, think himself a better man than a good composer, a good chess-player, a good carpenter, a good runner. Nor, in a common culture, will he think himself a better human being than a child, an old woman, or a cripple, who may lack the criterion (in itself inadequate) of useful service. The kind of respect for oneself and one's work, which is necessary to continue at all, is a different matter from a claim to inequality of being, such as would entitle one to deny or dominate the being of another. The inequalities which are intolerable are those which lead to such denial or domination.

From *Culture and Society 1780-1950* by Raymond Williams
(Chatto & Windus, 1958)

Bernard Crick
THE CHARACTER OF A MODERATE SOCIALIST (1976)

To appeal for more fraternity and less fratricide within the Labour movement needs a thick skin as well as a clear head. The Labour movement used to be proud of exhibiting within itself the very fraternity it wished to create in society as a whole, but of late brother seems more eager to revile brother, and sister sister, than to argue with opponents and to seek to persuade the vast majority of the unconvinced.

Any advance towards a socialist Britain needs, first, more democracy: a greater opening up to popular influence and knowledge of all the institutions that shape our lives. This is real liberty. Secondly, it requires a constant public demand for justification (if any) of each particular inequality or reward, together with gradual but systematic and determined action to reduce those inequalities. This is not equality but 'egalitarianism'. But, thirdly, it requires an attitude of mind, a morality, a psychology, which gives equal respect and care to everyone, irrespective of class, kin, race, religion, office, talent or learning – 'fraternity'. Our preachers should say: 'And now abideth liberty, equality, fraternity, these three: but the greatest of these is fraternity . . .'

Equality of respect does not, however, imply either – as Runciman puts it – 'equality of praise' or the confusion of sincerity with truth. Is it rational to treat all opinions as equal? And is it brotherly to treat all people as one would ideally have them rather than as they themselves are? Big brotherly, perhaps. But fraternity is treating all men as ends and not means, not just all societies. It does not mean treating everybody the same but according to their different personalities and needs; and it means reconciling conflicts by mutually acceptable, public political institutions.

An enforced equality is the destruction of brotherhood – the dark warning of Orwell's *Nineteen Eighty-Four*. Fraternity can, indeed, exist amid great inequality, but only in times of emergency: the comradeship of the trenches, the Dunkirk spirit, and 'the years of struggle' of both left-wing and right-wing political movements. But a fraternity for everyday wear in all seasons is hardly imaginable amid great inequalities which limit common purposes. Doing things together for ourselves in common enhances fraternity – unlike having equal welfare given to us which, if personal involvement is lacking, too often creates jealousies rather than comradeship. Economic controls by themselves can never guarantee a more fraternal society. Simple arithmetical equality could create even fiercer competition. We must not over-sociologise. Social conditions can help or hinder but they can neither guarantee the consummation of fraternity – nor even ensure its destruction. Fraternity is an ethic that can and should be chosen and pursued freely. It goes with simplicity, lack of ostentation, friendliness, helpfulness, kindliness, and decent restraint between individuals, not just with the fierce memories of the great occasions, the times of struggle or the Sunday 'socialism' of Saturday afternoon demos.

Fraternity does not mean no leadership: it only means no permanent class of leaders tomorrow and no *noblesse oblige* today – no condescension, no giving favours but rather receiving trust on account of peculiar skills of both empathy and action in helping common and commonly defined purposes. In Beethoven's *Fidelio* the king hails all men as brothers. But the power and arrogance of a king or a modern leader who thinks that he had such a gift to bestow will of itself negate the brotherhood. Even Edmund Burke said it was hard to argue on one's knees. Some still try. The boss in a small firm or office who drinks with the men and chats with the girls is only being matey, perhaps even condescending or politic, but not genuinely fraternal unless he seeks for their opinions and takes them seriously about how things should be run.

Nor does fraternity imply the necessity of pseudo-proletarian behaviour. Society is not altered as quickly as a change of costume on a bare stage. The oldest blue jeans will now attempt to hide the newest wealth. But that leaders of working-class parties are commonly bourgeois is neither surprising nor reprehensible. For bourgeois culture stresses individualistic skills of initiative, while working-class culture, in response to exploitation and oppression, stresses solidarity. The culture of the classless society is, indeed, more likely to be bourgeois in the best sense than proletarian. It will encourage and respect individual skills, talents, personality, character; not a new iron mould of conformity, however better than the one that went before. The virtue of class solidarity was an adaptation to class injustice and would become regressive if ever class differentiation vanishes to the point of irrelevance. So the cultural ideals of a democratic socialist movement must be more than the revival of a few folk songs and dialects: amid the new we should sift, refine, adapt, but offer the best of the old to all. And that best includes the moral seriousness of the puritan tradition of individualism as found in Lawrence and in Orwell, neither the purely acquisitive, competitive individualism of capitalism nor the indulgent, permissive, irresponsible individualism of anarchic socialism. Seriousness tempers personality into sociability.

From *The Political Quarterly,* January 1976

Sir Thomas More
THE UNJUST PUBLIC WEAL (1515)

Is not this an unjust and an unkind public weal, which giveth great fees and rewards to gentlemen, as they call them, and to goldsmiths, and to such other, which be either idle persons or else only flatterers and devisers of vain pleasures: And of the contrary part maketh no gentle provision for poor ploughmen, colliers, labourers, carters, ironsmiths, and carpenters: without whom no commonwealth can continue. But after it hath abused the labours of their lusty and flowering age, at the last when they be oppressed with old age and sickness, being needy, poor, and indigent of all things, then forgetting their so many painful watchings, not remembering their so many and so great benefits, recompenseth and aquiteth them most unkindly with miserable death.

And yet besides this the rich men not only by private fraud but also by common laws do every day pluck and snatch away from the poor some part of their daily living. So whereas it seemed before unjust to recompense with unkindness their pains that have been beneficial to the public weal, now they have to this their wrong and unjust dealing (which is yet a much worse point) given the name of justice, yea and that by force of a law. Therefore when I consider and weigh on my mind all these commonwealths, which nowadays anywhere do flourish, so God help me, I can perceive nothing but a certain conspiracy of rich men procuring their own commodities under the name and title of the commonwealth.

From *Utopia* by Sir Thomas More (Clarendon Press, 1895)

John Ball
SERMON TO THE PEOPLE (1381)

My good people, things cannot go well in England, nor ever shall, till everything be made common, and there are neither villeins nor gentlemen, but we shall all be united together, and the lords shall be no greater masters than ourselves. What have we deserved that we should be kept thus enslaved? We are all descended from one father and mother, Adam and Eve. What reasons can they give to show that they are greater lords than we, save by making us toil and labour, so that they can spend? They are clothed in velvet and soft leather furred with ermine, while we wear coarse cloth; they have their wines, spices and good bread, while we have the drawings of the chaff, and drink water. They have handsome houses and manors, and we the pain and travail, the rain and wind, in the fields. And it is from our labour that they get the means to maintain their estates. We are called their slaves, and if we do not serve them readily, we are beaten. And we have no sovereign to whom we may complain, or who will bear us, or do us justice. Let us go to the King, he is young, and tell him of our slavery; and tell him we shall have it otherwise, or else we will provide a remedy ourselves. And if we go together, all manner of people that are now in bondage will follow us, with the intent to be made free. And when the King sees us, we shall have some remedy either by justice or otherwise.

From 'Sermon to the People' by John Ball in *The Chronicles* by Jean Froissart, translated by John Bourchier (London, 1812)

Jonathan Swift
THE USE OF MONEY (1726)

Whereupon I was at much Pains to describe to him the Use of *Money*, the Materials it was made of, and the Value of the Metals: That when a *Yahoo* had got a great Store of this precious Substance, he was able to purchase whatever he had a mind to; the finest Clothing, the noblest Houses, great Tracts of Land, the most costly Meats and Drinks; and have his Choice of the most beautiful Females. Therefore since *Money* alone, was able to perform all these Feats, our *Yahoos* thought, they could never have enough of it to spend or to save, as they found themselves inclined from their natural Bent either to Profusion or Avarice. That, the rich Man enjoyed the Fruit of the poor Man's Labour, and the latter were a Thousand to One in Proportion to the former. That the Bulk of our People were forced to live miserably, by labouring every Day for small Wages to make a few live plentifully. I enlarged myself much on these and many other Particulars to the same Purpose: But his Honour was still to seek: For he went upon a Supposition that all Animals had a Title to their Share in the Productions of the Earth.

From *Gulliver's Travels* by Jonathan Swift, edited by J. Hayward (London, 1934)

Sir Francis Bacon
MONEY IS LIKE MUCK (1597)

Above all things good policy is to be used, that the treasure and money in a state be not gathered into few hands. For otherwise a state may have a great stock, and yet starve. *And money is like muck, not good except it be spread.*

This is done chiefly by suppressing, or at least keeping a strait hand upon, the devouring trades of usury, ingrossing, great pasturages, and the like.

From 'Essays Civil and Moral' in *Works* by Sir Francis Bacon, edited by J. Spedding, R.L. Ellis and D.D. Heath (London, 1857-72)

Gerrard Winstanley
THE EARTH IS OURS (1649)

All the men and women in England, are all children of this Land, and the earth is the Lord's, not particular men's that claims a proper interest in it above others, which is the devil's power.

But be it so, that some will say, This is my Land, and call such and such a parcel of Land his own interest; Then saith the Lord, let such a one labour that parcel of Land by his own hands, none helping him: for whosoever shall help that man to labour his proper earth, as he calls it for wages, the hand of the Lord shall be upon such labourers; for they lift up flesh above the spirit, by their labours, and so hold the Creation still under bondage.

Therefore if the rich will still hold fast this propriety of Mine and Thine, let them labour their own land with their own hands. And let the common-people, that are the gatherings together of Israel from under that bondage, and that say the earth is ours, not mine, let them labour together, and eat bread together upon the Commons, Mountains, and Hills.

For as the enclosures are called such a man's Land, and such a man's Land; so the Commons and Heath, are called the common-people's, and let the world see who labours the earth in righteousness, and . . . let them be the people that shall inherit the earth. Whether they that hold a civil propriety, saying, *This is mine*, which is selfish, devilish and destructive to the Creation, or those that hold a common right, saying, *The earth is ours*, which lifts up the Creation from bondage.

Was the earth made for to preserve a few covetous, proud men, to live at ease, and for them to bag and barn up the treasures of the earth from others, that they might beg or starve in a fruitful Land, or was it made to preserve all her children? Let Reason, and the Prophets' and Apostles' writings be judge, the earth is the Lord's, it is not to be confined to particular interest.

From 'The New Law of Righteousness', in *The Works*, edited by G.H. Sabine (Ithica, 1941)

Robert Tressell
THE OWNERSHIP OF AIR (1914)

Poverty is not caused by men and women getting married; it's not caused by machinery; it's not caused by 'over-production'; it's not caused by drink or laziness; and it's not caused by 'over-population'. It's caused by Private Monopoly. That is the present system. They have monopolised everything that it is possible to monopolise; they have got the whole earth, the minerals in the earth and the streams that water the earth. The only reason they have not monopolised the daylight and the air is that it is not possible to do it. If it were possible to construct huge gasometers and to draw together and compress within them the whole of the atmosphere, it would have been done long ago, and we should have been compelled to work for them in order to get money to buy air to breathe. And if that seemingly impossible thing were accomplished tomorrow, you would see thousands of people dying for want of air or of the money to buy it – even as now thousands are dying for want of the other necessaries of life. You would see people going about gasping for breath, and telling each other that the likes of them could not expect to have air to breathe unless they had the money to pay for it. Most of you here, for instance, would think so and say so. Even as you think at present that it's right for a few people to own the Earth, the Minerals and the Water, which are all just as necessary as is the air. In exactly the same spirit you now say: 'It's Their Land', 'It's Their Water', 'It's Their Coal', 'It's Their Iron', so you would say 'It's Their Air', 'These are Their gasometers, and what right have the likes of us to expect them to allow us to breathe for nothing?'. And even while he is doing this the air monopolist will be preaching sermons on the Brotherhood of Man; he will be dispensing advice on 'Christian Duty' in the Sunday magazines; he will give utterances to numerous more or less moral maxims for the guidance of the young. And meantime, all around, people will be dying for want of some of the air that he will have bottled up in his gasometers . . .

From *The Ragged-Trousered Philanthropist* by Robert Tressell (Paladin, 1991)

Anonymous
WARNING TO MASTERS AND OWNERS (1831)

I was at yor hoose last neet and meyd mysel very comfortable. Ye hay nee family and yor just won man on the colliery, I see ye hev a greet lot of rooms and big cellars and plenty wine and beer in them which I got ma share on. Noo I naw some at wor colliery that has three or fower lads and lasses and they live in won room not half as gude as yor cellar. I dont pretend to naw very much but I naw there shudnt be that much difference. The only place we can gan to o the week ends is the yel hoose and hev a pint. I dinna pretend to be a profit, but I naw this, and lots of ma marrers na's te, that were not tret as we owt to be, and a great filosopher says, to get noledge is to naw yer ignerent. But weve just begun to find that oot, and ye maisters and owners may luk oot, for yor not gan to get se much o yor way, wer gan to heve some o wors now . . .

A pitman's letter left in a colliery manager's house, from *The Miners of Northumberland and Durham* by Fynes, quoted in *Long March of Everyman*, edited by T. Barker (London, 1975)

Anonymous
STEALING THE COMMON

The law locks up the man or woman
Who steals a goose from off the common;
But leaves the greater villain loose
Who steals the common from the goose.

Traditional rhyme

Idris Davies
THE ANGRY SUMMER (1943)

Tonight the moon is bright and round
Above the little burial ground
Where father of Dai and father of John
After the sweat and blood sleep on.

They do not hear your voice tonight,
O singer on the slaggy height,
They do not know the song you sing
Of battle on this night of spring.

But in their blood in Maytimes past
The armies of the future massed,
And in their dream your dreams were born,
Out of their night shall break your morn.

Shine softly, moon, upon their sleep,
And, poet, in your music keep
Their memory alive and fair,
Echoing through the electric air.

What will you do with your shovel, Dai,
And your pick and your sledge and your spike,
And what will you do with your leisure, man,
Now that you're out on strike?

What will you do for your butter, Dai,
And your bread and your cheese and your fags,
And how will you pay for a dress for the wife,
And shall your children go in rags?

You have been, in your time, a hero, Dai,
And they wrote of your pluck in the press,
And now you have fallen on evil days,
And who will be there to bless?

And how will you stand with your honesty, Dai,
When the land is full of lies,
And how will you curb your anger, man,
When your natural patience dies?

O what will you dream on the mountains, Dai,
When you walk in the summer day,
And gaze on the derelict valleys below,
And the mountains farther away?

And how will the heart within you, Dai,
Respond to the distant sea,
And the dream that is born in the blaze of the sun,
And the vision of victory?

Stand up, and tell the robbers
'Tis time to drop the swag,
Avenge our cheated fathers,
Who bled for Viscount Bag.

'Tis time to scale the ramparts
That guard the bloody swag,
And speak appropriate language
To dropsical Viscount Bag.

From *The Collected Poems of Idris Davies*, edited by I. Jenkins (Gomer Press, 1972)

Frank Betts
THE PAWNS (1911)

Purple robed, with crowned hair,
Caesar sits in a golden chair,
And a proud cold Queen beside him there.
Knights in armour, many and tall,
And the holy Bishops throng the hall;
Why trouble your head with the pawns at all,
      Iscariot?

He sits at the chess and he plays with skill
On a board far flung over river and hill,
And many a pawn works out his will.
At the chess of war to be bold is wise,
And little he recks of sacrifice:-
For what are a pawn or two in our eyes,
      Iscariot?

Years agone, and a world away
Lived One who did not praise the play,
And He loved the pawns the best, men say.
And He damned the pieces for their pride:
So you sold Him to be crucified,
And bared unto the spear his side,
      Iscariot?

You sold Him and you thought Him slain,
And the old proud game begins again,
And Caesar plays with might and main.
But a hidden Player has the Black,
And the craft is foiled and the White attack,
Move by move is beaten back,
      Iscariot.

Knight or Bishop can resist
The pawns of his Antagonist
Whose countenance is dark with mist.
The game goes on and will not wait,
Caesar is gripped in a deadly strait -
What if the pawns should give checkmate,
      Iscariot?

Note from Barbara Castle:
I am daring to send you one of the poems of Frank Betts, my father, called 'The Pawns'. It always exhilarated me. As a civil servant (an inspector of taxes!) my father was forbidden to engage in politics publicly, but he was an uncompromising socialist and, as I describe in my *Memoirs,* used to gather round him in our home a group of young Bradford workers he introduced to the great literature and art he loved. He also encouraged them to write for the ILP weekly, the *Bradford Pioneer*, which he secretly edited: Vic Feather was one of his protégés. He also produced plays like the Kapek brothers' *The Insect Play* for the ILP Arts Guild. It was all very private, but by his writings and plays he helped to make Bradford with its lively ILP the Mecca of socialist politics in the 1920s.

Charles Dickens
THE DIVIDED SOCIETY (1854)

[Stephen Blackpool (the factory-worker) answering Mr Bounderby (the self-made man)]

Sir, I canna, wi' my little learning an' my common way, tell the genelman what will better aw this – though some working men o' this town could, above my powers – but I can tell him what I know will never do't. The strong hand will never do't. Agreeing fur to mak one side unnat'rally awlus and for ever right, and toother side unnat'rally awlus and for ever wrong, will never, never do't. Nor yet lettin alone will never do't. Let thousands upon thousands alone, aw leading the like lives and aw faw'en into the like muddle, and they will be as one, and yo will be as anoother, wi' a black impassable world betwixt yo, just as long or short a time as sitch-like misery can last. Not drawin nigh to fok, wi' kindness and patience and cheery ways, that so draws nigh to one another in the monny troubles, and so cherishes one another in their distresses wi' what they need themseln – like, I humbly believe, as no people the genelman has seen in aw his travels can beat – will never do't till th' Sun turns to ice. Most o' aw, rating 'em as so much Power, and reg'latin 'em as if they was figures in a soom, or machines, wi'out souls to weary and souls to hope – when aw goes quiet, draggin on wi' 'em as if they'd nowt o' th' kind, and when aw goes onquiet, reproachin 'em for their want o' sitch humanly feelins in their dealins wi' yo – this will never do't, Sir, till God's work is onmade.

From *Hard Times* by Charles Dickens (1854)

William Blake
HOLY THURSDAY

Is this a holy thing to see
In a rich and fruitful land,
Babes reduc'd to misery,
Fed with cold and usurous hand?

Is that trembling cry a song?
Can it be a song of joy?
And so many children poor?
It is a land of poverty!

And their sun does never shine,
And their fields are bleak & bare,
And their ways are fill'd with thorns:
It is eternal winter there.

For where-e'er the sun does shine,
And where-e'er the rain does fall,
Babe can never hunger there,
Nor poverty the mind appall.

From *The Complete Writings of William Blake*,
edited by Sir Geoffrey Keynes (London, 1966)

H.G. Wells
THIS MISERY OF BOOTS (1905)

Everybody does not suffer misery from boots.

One person I know, another friend of mine, who can testify to that; who has tasted all the miseries of boots, and who now goes about the world free of them, but not altogether forgetful of them. A stroke of luck, aided perhaps by a certain alacrity on his own part, lifted him out of the class in which one buys one's boots and clothes out of what is left over from a pound a week, into the class in which one spends seventy or eighty pounds a year on clothing. Sometimes he buys boots and shoes at very good shops; sometimes he has them made for him; he has them stored in a proper cupboard, and great care is taken of them; and so his boots and slippers never chafe, never pinch, never squeak, never hurt or worry him, never bother him; and when he sticks out his toes before the fire, they do not remind him that he is a shabby and contemptible wretch, living meanly on the dust heaps of the world. You might think from this that he had every reason to congratulate himself and be happy seeing that he has had good follow after evil; but, such is the oddness of the human heart, he isn't contented at all. The thought of the multitudes so much worse off than himself in this matter of footwear, gives him no sort of satisfaction. Their boots pinch him vicariously. The black rage with the scheme of things that once he felt through suffering in his own person in the days when he limped shabbily through gaily busy, fashionable London streets, in split boots that chafed, he feels now just as badly as he goes about the world very comfortably himself, but among people whom he knows with a pitiless clearness to illusion that things are all right with them. Stupid people who have always been well off, who have always had boots that fit, may think that; but not so, he. In one respect the thought of boots makes him even more viciously angry now, than it used to do. In the old days he was savage with his luck, but hopelessly savage; he thought that bad boots, ugly uncomfortable clothes, rotten houses, were in the very nature of things. Now, when he sees a child sniffing and blubbering and halting upon the pavement, or an old countrywoman going painfully along a lane, he no longer recognises the Pinch of Destiny. His rage is lit by thought, that there are fools in this world who ought to have foreseen and prevented this. He no longer curses fate, but the dullness of statesmen and powerful responsible people who have neither the heart, nor courage, nor capacity, to change the state of mismanagement that gives us these things.

Now do not think I am dwelling unduly upon my second friend's good fortune, when I tell you that once he was constantly getting pain and miserable states of mind, colds for example, from the badness of his clothing, shame from being shabby, pain from the neglected state of his teeth, from the indigestion of unsuitable food eaten at unsuitable hours, from the unsanitary ugly house in which he lived and the bad air of that part of London, from things indeed quite beyond the unaided power of a poor overworked man to remedy. And now all these disagreeable things have gone out of his life; he has consulted dentists and physicians, he has hardly any dull days from colds, no pain from toothache at all, no gloom of indigestion . . .

I will not go on with the tale of good fortune of this lucky person. My purpose is served if I have shown that this misery of boots is not an unavoidable curse upon mankind. If one man can evade it, others can. By good management it may be altogether escaped. If you, or what is more important to most human beings, if any people dear to you, suffer from painful or disfiguring boots or shoes, and you can do no better for them, it is simply because you are getting the worst side of an ill-managed world. It is not the universal lot.

And what I say of boots is true of all the other minor things of life. If your wife catches a bad cold because her boots are too thin for the time of the year, or dislikes going out because she cuts a shabby ugly figure, if your children look painfully nasty because their faces are swollen with toothache, or because their clothes are dirty, old, and ill-fitting, if you are all dull and disposed to be cross with one another for want of decent amusement and change of air – don't submit, don't be humbugged for a moment into believing that this is the dingy lot of all mankind. These people you love are living in a badly managed world and on the wrong side of it, and such wretchednesses are the daily demonstration of that.

Don't say for a moment: 'Such is life.' Don't think their miseries are part of some primordial curse there is no escaping. The disproof of that is for any one to see. There are people, people no more deserving than others, who suffer from none of these things. You may feel you merit no better than to live so poorly and badly that your boots are always hurting you; but do the little children, the girls, the mass of decent hard-up people, deserve no better fate?

From 'This Misery of Boots' by H.G. Wells in the *Independent Review*, December 1905

George Bernard Shaw
INEQUALITY FOSTERS DESPAIR (1890)

If you are rich, you perhaps think that inequality is a good thing – that it fosters a spirit of emulation, and prevents things from stagnating at a dead level. But if you are poor, you must know well that when inequality is so outrageous, it fosters nothing but despair, recklessness and drunkenness among the very poor, arrogance and wastefulness among the very rich; meanness, envy and snobbery among the middle classes. Poverty means disease and crime, ugliness and brutality, drink and violence, stunted bodies and unenlightened minds. Riches heaped up in idle hands mean flunkeyism and folly, insolence and servility, bad example, false standards of worth, and the destruction of all incentive to useful work in those who are best able to educate themselves for it. Poverty and riches together mean the misuse of our capital and industry for the production of frippery and luxury whilst the nation is rotting for want of good food, thorough instruction, and wholesome clothes and dwellings for the masses. What we want in order to make true progress is more bakers, more schoolmasters, more wool-weavers and tailors, and more builders: what we get instead is more footmen, more gamekeepers, more jockeys, and more prostitutes. That is what our newspapers call 'sound political economy'. What do you think of it? Do you intend to do anything to get it remedied?

From *What Socialism Is* (Fabian Tract no. 13) by George Bernard Shaw

George Orwell
REVOLT AGAINST PRIVILEGE (1941)

It is only by revolution that the native genius of the English people can be set free. Revolution does not mean red flags and street fighting, it means a fundamental shift of power. Whether it happens with or without bloodshed is largely an accident of time and place. Nor does it mean the dictatorship of a single class. The people in England who grasp what changes are needed and are capable of carrying them through are not confined to any one class, though it is true that very few people with over £2,000 a year are among them. What is wanted is a conscious open revolt by ordinary people against inefficiency, class privilege and the rule of the old. It is not primarily a question of change of government. British governments do, broadly speaking, represent the will of the people, and if we alter our structure from below we shall get the government we need. Ambassadors, generals, officials and colonial administrators who are senile or pro-fascist are more dangerous than Cabinet ministers whose follies have to be committed in public. Right through our national life we have got to fight against privilege, against the notion that a half-witted public-schoolboy is better for command than an intelligent mechanic. Although there are gifted and honest individuals among them, we have got to break the grip of the moneyed class as a whole. England has got to assume its real shape. The England that is only just beneath the surface, in the factories and the newspaper offices, in the aeroplanes and the submarines, has got to take charge of its own destiny.

From *The Lion and the Unicorn: Socialism and the English Genius* by George Orwell (Secker & Warburg, 1941)

George Orwell
CLASS DISTINCTIONS (1947)

Once civilisation has reached a fairly high technical level, class distinctions are an obvious evil. They not only lead great numbers of people to waste their lives in the pursuit of social prestige, but they also cause an immense wastage of talent. In England it is not merely the ownership of property that is concentrated in a few hands. It is also the case that all power, administrative as well as financial, belongs to a single class. Except for a handful of 'self-made men' and Labour politicians, those who control our destinies are the product of about a dozen public schools and two universities. A nation is using its capacities to the full when any man can get any job that he is fit for. One has only to think of some of the people who have held vitally important jobs during the past twenty years, and to wonder what would have happened to them if they had been born into the working class, to see that this is not the case in England.

Moreover, class distinctions are a constant drain on morale, in peace as well as in war. And the more conscious, the better educated the mass of the people become, the more this is so. The word 'They', the universal feeling that 'They' hold all the power and make all the decisions, and that 'They' can only be influenced in indirect and uncertain ways, is a great handicap in England. In 1940 'They' showed a marked tendency to give place to 'We', and it is time that it did so permanently.

From 'The English People' in *The Collected Essays, Journalism and Letters of George Orwell* (Secker & Warburg, 1968)

D.H. Lawrence
THE OXFORD VOICE

When you hear it languishing
and hooing and cooing and sidling through the front teeth,
  the Oxford voice
  or worse still
  the would-be-Oxford voice
you don't even laugh any more, you can't.

For every blooming bird is an Oxford cuckoo nowadays,
you can't sit on a bus nor in the tube
but it breathes gently and languishingly in the back of your neck.

And oh, so seductively superior, so seductively
  self-effacingly
  deprecatingly
  superior.

We wouldn't insist on it for a moment
  but we are
  we are
  you admit we are
  superior.

From *Selected Poems Chosen by W.E. Williams*
(Penguin Books in association with Heinemann, 1950)

Raymond Williams
CULTURE IS ORDINARY (1958)

Culture is ordinary: that is where we must start. To grow up in that country was to see the shape of a culture, and its modes of change. I could stand on the mountains and look north to the farms and the cathedral, or south to the smoke and the flare of the blast furnace making a second sunset. To grow up in that family was to see the shaping of minds: the learning of new skills, the shifting of relationships, the emergence of different language and ideas. My grandfather, a big hard labourer, wept while he spoke, finely and excitedly, at the parish meeting, of being turned out of his cottage. My father, not long before he died, spoke quietly and happily of when he had started a trade union branch and a Labour Party group in the village, and, without bitterness, of the 'kept men' of the new politics. I speak a different idiom, but I think of these same things.

Culture is ordinary: that is the first fact. Every human society has its own shape, its purposes, its own meanings. Every human society expresses these, in institutions, and in arts and learning. The making of a society is the finding of common meanings and directions, and its growth is an active debate and amendment, under the pressures of experience, contact, and discovery, writing themselves into the land. The growing society is there, yet it is also made and remade in every individual mind. The making of a mind is, first, the slow learning of shapes, purposes, and meanings, so that work, observation and communication are possible. Then, second, but equal in importance, is the testing of these in experience, the making of new observations, comparisons, and meanings. A culture has two aspects: the known meanings and directions, which its members are trained to; the new observations and meanings, which are offered and tested. These are the ordinary processes of human societies and human minds, and we see through them the nature of a culture: that it is always both traditional and creative; that it is both the most ordinary common meanings and the finest individual meanings. We use the word culture in these two senses: to mean a whole way of life – the common meanings; to mean the arts and learning – the special processes of discovery and creative effort. Some writers reserve the word for one or other of these senses; I insist on both, and on the significance of their conjunction. The questions I ask about our culture are questions about our general and common purposes, yet also questions about deep personal meanings. Culture is ordinary, in every society and in every mind.

From 'Culture is Ordinary' by Raymond Williams in *Conviction*, edited by Norman Mackenzie (MacGibbon & Kee; 1958)

Peter Townsend
A CLASSLESS SOCIETY (1958)

If there is any lesson in the experience of the last ten years it is that no social aim can be achieved merely by planning, and passing, the necessary legislation. The various services do not exist as self-perpetuating systems untouched by worldly sin. They need money and they need good staff. They therefore depend on political decisions about priorities and on all the subtle twists and turns of social, and human, change. Almost imperceptibly since 1945 the needs of the submerged fifth have grown and the differences between the rich and the poor in their living standards have widened. Powerful arguments can be advanced, as I have tried to show, for a new and ambitious policy, geared to the principle that the best possible standards of service should be available to all on the basis of equal sacrifice. This could be followed with imagination, hope and enthusiasm. There is just one condition. It is useless paying lip-service to equality. Better nothing than that.

You cannot live like a lord and preach as a socialist. Equality of sacrifice is not an ideal which applies to others but not yourself. It is essentially personal and is not just a matter of avoiding ostentatious displays of wealth. To be scornful about cigars, extravagant receptions, hunt balls, or a Rolls or Bentley with its superior number plate (like the elegant Bentley – UUU100 – which I recently saw parked outside the House of Commons) would be easy. The real test comes in all the trivial details of life – in choosing whether to dodge some taxes, use the firm's stamps for personal letters, add a pound or two to the bill for expenses, or jump the queue at the hospital; in asking repeatedly whether certain of our privileges look as reasonable to others as they so often do to ourselves. How many business lunches cost more than the National Assistance Board is paying a man to keep himself for a whole week? How many professional people, and how many workers, have four, six, or eight weeks holiday, a working week of less than thirty hours, and a centrally heated and carpeted workroom? The more privileges you have the fewer there are for others.

Everything turns on the way people behave to each other . . .

It is more difficult for those who have to make a conscious effort of will to achieve as much. The sort of socialism advocated by William Morris, or any simple expression of faith in the goodness of man, frightens and embarrasses the intellectual. He does not want to be taken for a sucker in public and you rarely find him saying anything so straightforward and naive. He is much too cynical and self-conscious. Yet if he is not prepared to live his socialism it stands little chance of attainment. He wants to stand apart from the crowd, to be original, to wear an outrageous shirt, condemn the mass media and talk of commitment, positivism and free cinema. He wants to reject many of the values of society. He may be right but continually he runs the risk, in his thoughts and actions, of alienating himself from ordinary people. There are few harder conflicts to resolve. Somehow he must preserve his independence and his right to criticise and yet keep in touch with people of every age and class, and laugh and cry with them, in his private life as well as in his public utterances. This is his one hope of becoming a constructive and not simply a destructive critic of society. For to believe in people is to subscribe to their strengths, their pride, their capacity to recognise humbug or to shrug off propaganda, their fair dealing, their unselfishness and their willingness to bear pain without fuss, but above all the strengths given them by their lives within their families . . .

If that overdone phrase 'a classless society' means anything it is a society where differences in reward are much narrower than in Britain today and where people of different background and accomplishment can mix easily and without guilt; but also a society where a respect for people is valued most of all, for that brings a real equality.

From 'A Society for People' by Peter Townsend, in *Conviction* ,
edited by Norman Mackenzie (MacGibbon & Kee, 1958)

FAIRNESS IN
ECONOMIC DISTRIBUTION

*'I do not want the earth. I only ask that
portion of its plenty which is mine'*

George Bernard Shaw
HOW MUCH IS ENOUGH? (1928)

We seem now to have disposed of all the plans except the socialist one. Before grappling with that, may I call your attention to something that happened in our examination of most of the others. We were trying to find out a sound plan of distributing money; and every time we proposed to distribute it according to personal merit or achievement or dignity or individual quality of any sort the plan reduced itself to absurdity. When we tried to establish a relation between money and work we were beaten: it could not be done. When we tried to establish a relation between money and character we were beaten. When we tried to establish a relation between money and the dignity that gives authority we were beaten. And when we gave it up as a bad job and thought of leaving things as they are we found that they would not stay as they are.

Let us then consider for a moment what any plan must do to be acceptable. And first, as everybody except the Franciscan Friars and the Poor Clares will say that no plan will be acceptable unless it abolishes poverty (and even Franciscan poverty must be voluntary and not compelled) let us study poverty for a moment.

It is generally agreed that poverty is a very uncomfortable misfortune for the individual who happens to be poor . . . Such poverty as we have today in all our great cities degrades the poor, and infects with its degradation the whole neighbourhood in which they live. And whatever can degrade a neighbourhood can degrade a country and a continent and finally the whole civilised world, which is only a large neighbourhood. Its bad effects cannot be escaped by the rich. When poverty produces outbreaks of virulent infectious disease, as it always does sooner or later, the rich catch the disease and see their children die of it. When it produces crime and violence the rich go in fear of both, and are put to a good deal of expense to protect their persons and property. When it produces bad manners and bad langauge the children of the rich pick them up no matter how carefully they are secluded; and such seclusion as they get does them more harm than good. If poor and pretty young women find, as they do, that they can make more money by vice than by honest work, they will poison the blood of rich young men who, when they marry, will infect their wives and children, and cause them all sorts of bodily troubles, sometimes ending in disfigurement and blindness and death, and always doing them more or less mischief. The old notion that people can 'keep themselves to themselves' and not be touched by what is happening to their neighbours, or even to the people who live a hundred miles off, is a most dangerous mistake. The saying that we are members one of another is not a mere pious formula to be repeated in church without any meaning: it is a literal truth; for though the rich end of the town can avoid living with the poor end, it cannot avoid dying with it when the plague comes. People will be able to keep themselves to themselves as much as they please when they have made an end of poverty; but until then they will not be able to shut out the sights and sounds and smells of poverty from their daily walks, nor to feel sure from day to day that its most violent and fatal evils will not reach them through their strongest police guards.

Besides, as long as poverty remains possible we shall never be sure that it will not overtake ourselves. If we dig a pit for others we may fall into it: if we leave a precipice unfenced our children may fall over it when they are playing. We see the most innocent and respectable families falling into the unfenced pit of poverty every day; and how do we know that it will not be our turn next?

It is perhaps the greatest folly of which a nation can be guilty to attempt to use poverty as a sort of punishment for offences that it does not send people to prison for. It is easy to say of a lazy man 'Oh, let him be poor: it serves him right for being lazy: it will teach him a lesson'. In saying so, we are ourselves too lazy to think a little before we lay down the law. We cannot afford to have poor people anyhow, whether they be lazy or busy, drunken or sober, virtuous or vicious, thrifty or careless, wise or foolish. If they deserve to suffer let them be made to suffer in some other way; for mere poverty will not hurt them half as much as it will hurt their innocent neighbours. It is a public nuisance as well as a private misfortune. Its toleration is a national crime.

We must therefore take it as an indispensable condition of a sound distribution of wealth that everyone must have a share sufficient to keep him or her from poverty . . .

We, after the terrible experience we have had of the effects of poverty on the whole nation, rich or poor, must go further and say that nobody must be poor. As we divide up our wealth day by day the first charge on it must be enough for everybody to be fairly respectable and well-to-do . . .

What we should have would be, not poor people and rich people, but simply people with enough and people with more than enough. And that brings up at last the knotty question, what is enough?

In Shakespeare's famous play, King Lear and his daughters have an argument about this. His idea of enough is having a hundred knights to wait on him. His eldest daughter thinks that fifty would be enough. Her sister does not see what he wants with any knights at all when her servants can do all he needs for him. Lear retorts that if she cuts life down to what cannot be done without, she had better throw away her fine clothes, as she would be warmer in a blanket. And to this she has no answer. Nobody can say what is enough. What is enough for a gipsy is not enough for a lady; and what is enough for one lady leaves another very discontented. When once you get above the poverty line there is no reason why you should stop there. With modern machinery we can produce much more than enough to feed, clothe, and house us decently. There is no end to the number of new things we can get into the habit of using, or to the improvement we can make in the things we already use. Our grandmothers managed to get on without gas cookers, electric light, motor cars, and telephones; but today these things are no longer curiosities and luxuries: they are matter-of-course necessities; and nobody who cannot afford them is considered well-off . . .

What is enough in one case is not enough in another. Therefore to ask baldly how much is enough to live on is to ask an unanswerable question. It all depends on what sort of life you propose to live. What is enough for the life of a tramp is not enough for a highly civilised life, with its personal refinements and its atmosphere of music, art, literature, religion, science, and philosophy. Of these things we can never have enough: there is always something new to be discovered and something old to be bettered. In short, there is no such thing as enough civilisation, though there may be enough of any particular thing like bread or boots at any particular moment. If being poor means wanting something more and something better than we have – and it is hard to say what else feeling poor means – then we shall always feel poor no matter how much money we have, because, though we may have enough of this thing or of that thing, we shall never have enough of everything. Consequently if it be proposed to give some people enough, and others more than enough, the scheme will break down; for all the money will be used up before anybody will be content. Nobody will stop asking for more for the sake of setting up and maintaining a fancy class of pampered persons who, after all, will be even more discontented than their poorer neighbours.

The only way out of this difficulty is to give everybody the same, which is the socialist solution of the distribution problem. But you may tell me that you are prepared to swallow this difficulty rather than swallow socialism. Most of us begin like that. What converts us is the discovery of the terrible array of evils around us and dangers in front of us which we dare not ignore. You may be unable to see any beauty in equality of income. But the least idealistic woman can see the disasters of inequality when the evils with which she is herself in daily conflict are traced to it.

From *The Intelligent Woman's Guide to Socialism* by George Bernard Shaw
(Pelican, 1937)

Robert Tressell
WHAT IS POVERTY? (1914)

'What do *you* mean by poverty, then?' asked Easton.

'What I call poverty is when people are not able to secure for themselves all the benefits of civilisation; the necessaries, comforts, pleasures and refinements of life, leisure, books, theatres, pictures, music, holidays, travel, good and beautiful homes, good clothes, good and pleasant food.'

Everybody laughed. It was so ridiculous. The idea of the likes of *them* wanting or having such things! Any doubts that any of them had entertained as to Owen's sanity disappeared. The man was as mad as a March hare.

'If a man is only able to provide himself and his family with the bare necessaries of existence, that man's family is living in poverty. Since he cannot enjoy the advantages of civilisation he might just as well be a savage: better, in fact, for a savage knows nothing of what he is deprived. What we call civilisation – the accumulation of knowledge which has come down to us from our forefathers – is the fruit of thousands of years of human thought and toil. It is not the result of the labour of the ancestors of any separate class of people who exist today, and therefore it is by right the common heritage of all. Every little child that is born into the world, no matter whether he is clever or dull, whether he is physically perfect or lame, or blind; no matter how much he may excel or fall short of his fellows in other respects, in one thing at least he is their equal – he is one of the heirs of all the ages that have gone before.'

Some of them began to wonder whether Owen was not sane after all. He certainly must be a clever sort of chap to be able to talk like this. It sounded almost like something out of a book, and most of them could not understand one half of it.

'Why is it,' continued Owen, 'that we are not only deprived of our inheritance – we are not only deprived of nearly all the benefits of civilisation, but we and our children are also often unable to obtain even the bare necessaries of existence?'

No one answered.

'All these things,' Owen proceeded, 'are produced by those who work. We do our full share of the work, therefore we should have a full share of the things that are made by work.'

From *The Rugged-Trousered Philanthropist* by Robert Tressell (Paladin, 1991)

George Lansbury
ATTACKING POVERTY (1916)

Even amongst most of those who earnestly desire better times there appears to be no thought, so far as I understand them, of securing equality of opportunity for all men and all women, no sort of demand that riches and poverty shall be swept away and equal conditions of life and service established. I do not mean 'equality' in the sense of everybody having to do the same kind of work, but I do mean that men and women who toil shall receive the full fruits of their toil; that for themselves there shall be secured good food, good clothes, good houses, and for their children the best education it is possible to give; and that nobody who is willing to serve the nation shall be obliged to live, as so many millions live today, with no certainty as to whence tomorrow's daily bread will come. There is always the horror of sickness and the dread of physical breakdown, which almost always means semi-starvation for the whole family. The lot of the average working-class family is one of respectable, precarious poverty. Cloak it, gloss it over as we may, we cannot get away from this fact, and all people who want conditions to be changed must first of all understand how people live, and what the conditions of life are which it is desired to change. They must also understand that it is impossible to have the best of two worlds at one and the same time. The rich cannot hope to see the poor living in comfortable surroundings until these conditions are swept away. To improve conditions a thorough and radical change must take place. Poverty cannot be destroyed unless the causes which produce poverty are destroyed. These causes are so apparent to any thoughtful person that it is always a mystery to me why those who are so anxious for a change do not attack the root causes of poverty, rather than pour out so much money and effort in an attempt to palliate the ruin and disaster which come from evil social conditions.

From *Your Part in Poverty* by George Lansbury (*The Herald*, 1916)

William Morris
EQUALITY OF CONDITION (1888)

Dear Sir,
Socialism is a theory of life, taking for its starting point the evolution of society; or, let us say, of man as a social being.

Since man has certain material *necessities* as an animal, society is founded on man's attempts to satisfy those necessities; and socialism, or social consciousness, points out to him the way of doing so which will interfere least with the development of his specially human capacities, and the satisfaction of what, for lack of better words, I will call his spiritual and mental necessities.

The foundation of socialism, therefore, is economical. Man as a social animal tends to the acquirement of power over nature, and to the beneficent use of that power, which again implies a condition of society in which everyone is able to satisfy his needs in return for the due exercise of his capacities for the benefit of the race. But this economical aim which, to put it another way, is the fairer apportionment of labour and the results of labour, must be accompanied by an ethical or religious sense of the responsibility of each man to each and all of his fellows.

Socialism aims, therefore, at realising equality of condition as its economic goal, and the habitual love of humanity as its rule of ethics.

Properly speaking, in a condition of equality, politics would no longer exist; but, to use the word as distinguishing the social habits that have not to do directly with production, the political position of socialism is to substitute the relation of persons to persons for the relation of things to persons. A man, I mean, would no longer take his position as the dweller in such and such a place, or the filler of such and such an office, or (as now) the owner of such and such property, but as being such and such a man. In such a state of society laws of repression would be minimised, and the whole body of law which now deals with things and their domination over persons would cease to exist. In a condition of personal equality, also, there could no longer be rivalry between those inhabiting different places. Nationality, except as a geographical or ethnological expression, would have no meaning.

Equality as to livelihood, mutual respect and responsibility, and complete freedom within those limits – which would, it must be remembered, be accepted voluntarily and indeed habitually – are what socialism looks forward to.

From *Letters on Socialism (1888)* by William Morris (London, 1894)

E.F.M. Durbin
A NEW AND BETTER SOCIETY (1942)

Economic equality will not only bring justice and social freedom but it will also release immense resources of ability now running to waste. No one can teach, as I have now done for ten years, both inside the walls of the universities and in the various types of extra-mural classes open to adult men and women (who have not taken a university degree), without knowing that we are failing to train a great number of first-class minds; while at the same moment we are allowing persons of third- and fourth-rate intelligence to crowd out our classes and waste our time merely because their parents possess enough money to pay the fees. This is social inefficiency of the worst type. And what is true of the particular natural talent that it is my professional business to train – academic or intellectual intelligence – must be true of all the other human gifts. We are neglecting immense, almost unimaginable, stores of vitality, imagination, executive ability, aesthetic and manual skill. All the ingenuity that we possess – all of which we should mobilise in our battle for happiness – could be brought to a rich harvest if we throw open the door of opportunity to our children.

The citadels of vandalism and the closed mind could then be forced. With knowledge would come power. Better educated men and women, freed from the bonds of social subservience, would see more clearly the society in which they wished to live and guide more firmly the conduct of democratic policy by which alone their hopes can slowly be established in the practice of the nation. Economic planning and social equality are the ideas upon whose slow growth the purification of our social order chiefly depends.

This is, then, what I mean by a new or a better society. I believe we could create in one generation an economic system that provided continuous employment for every able-bodied worker; that maintained a steady and substantial rise in real wages; that would enable us to set a minimum standard of living, well above the present 'poverty line', below which no single man, woman or child would be allowed to fall; in which all forms of education were open and free to the talented; in which property was equally distributed, thus becoming a growing source of personal freedom for us all. And upon the same foundation of this stable and progressive economy it would be possible to build a better society from which all educational inferiority had been removed; in which all men and women could live a richer life of friendship, free from the barriers of class distinction; that was able to protect the treasures of its ancient culture in town and country and could free the strong and merciful hand of science to cure physical and mental ill-health – holding back the dark waters of death to give us more life and lifting the burden of guilt and fear from the hearts of children in order that there may be more joy in the longer tale of our years.

This hope is *not* utopian. It is a moderate and practicable programme of improvement. There is nothing in this list of changes that is not easily within our physical and intellectual powers to bring about. We need only become united in a wish to possess this better order and in understanding that we can have it for the asking.

From *What Have We Done to Defend?* by E.M.F. Durbin (George Routledge & Sons, 1942)

Douglas Jay
MINIMUM PRACTICABLE INEQUALITY (1962)

What matters most, however, for the present and future, is to determine what are the right aims for society, and by what means they can be achieved. Let us, therefore, start by clearly distinguishing between ends and means. Socialists believe in equality as an end. This belief in equality rests not on dubious statements of fact such as 'men are born equal'. Plainly they are not. They are born with an endless variety of character, intelligence, energy and ability. It rests on a moral judgment. Any and every human being has as much right as anyone else to whatever gives value to human life. If anyone questions this judgment, one can only reply: on what ground should it not be so? Why should I have more right to happiness than you? Why should a white man have more right to a vote than a black? Or a Christian to freedom of speech than a Moslem? Or a man to equality before the law than a woman? Or a communist to higher living standards than a non-communist? Of course, any of these individuals may temporarily forfeit these rights by infringing the rights of others. But there cannot be any good reason for denying such rights, on any other ground, to any individual or group. To do this, whether on grounds of race, birth, religion, colour, politics, or any distinction other than the anti-social conduct of the individual, is the fundamental evil in society which socialists

64

condemn. Their belief in equality is not just limited to its economic form. It embraces all the political and personal rights which make happiness and civilised human life possible; and it is founded on the conviction that no man or woman has a naturally greater claim to these than any other.

Many secondary reasons for valuing equality can be, and often have been, advanced. Most of them are strictly arguments against inequality rather than in favour of equality. Matthew Arnold, who believed profoundly in equality as the essential foundation of any good society, thought excessive inequality incompatible with the spirit of humanity and sense of the dignity of man as man, and said that 'on the one hand, in fact, inequality harms by pampering; on the other by vulgarising and depressing'. Professor Tawney, thirty years later in a slightly less unequal society, wrote of the 'moral humiliation which gross contrasts of wealth and economic power necessarily produce'. Many since have deplored the resentment, envy or servility on the one hand, and snobbery and corruption on the other, which inequality brings. These arguments are all too obviously valid; have been often stated; and need not be repeated here. Yet, in the last resort, they are all secondary, and do not touch the basic case for equality. If we believe that all human beings have an equal right to happiness and civilised life, then it is for this reason that we should seek to establish a society in which these rights are embodied. The ultimate ground for condemning inequality is that it is unjust, not that it causes resentment or envy. It is the injustice which is the evil, not the resentment. Indeed, if the injustice were not evil, you could doubtless get rid of the resentment without getting rid of the inequality. But if the injustice is evil, the resentment is not evil but good; justifiable indignation against something which is wrong. The secondary consequences of a denial of equality, therefore, are highly important, but not fundamental. Many of them should be deplored and deflated. But they are not the root of evil. The solid rock at the core of the argument for equality, and so in the modern world for socialism, must remain the equal moral claim of all men to basic human rights . . .

But in the economic world, unfortunately, the issue of equality – even in principle – is rather more complex. Very few socialists have ever advocated literal economic equality; an identical income, or even equal property. Bernard Shaw did for a time nominally advocate equality of income, though he ended his life grumbling, like any stockbroker, about the surtax. At any rate, no articulate British socialist does today. The belief in 'differentials', higher earned incomes for skill, experience and merit, is extremely strongly held by industrial workers and throughout the organised trade union movement in Britain. There are at least three reasons why literal equality of incomes is not advocated as a serious aim. First, it would be unenforceable. Even if it were achieved, it could not in any sort of free society be maintained. Secondly – and most important by far – many of those whose skill, character, knowledge or experience were above the lowest would not use their ability fully if they earned no more than those who contributed less. Therefore, the whole output of goods and services would be less, and society as a whole would be poorer.

But there is surely also a third reason. Not merely would society not work very well if the more productive were paid no more than the less; but the great majority of mankind, including socialists, believe that the more skilful and the more diligent deserve some extra reward. It is certainly the general belief that the man or woman who works more conscientiously or diligently, or bears more responsibility, deserves – other things being equal – a rather greater reward.

From these arguments two fundamental conclusions follow; the first of which is usually much better understood than the second. It follows, first, that in the economic world 'equality' is not literally the aim, as in the case of basic human and political rights. The aim is the minimum practicable inequality. It follows, secondly, that inequality is not justified beyond the point necessary to ensure that the productive abilities of the community are reasonably fully used. There is no justification for going beyond this. For nothing more than this follows from the argument that some differentials are necessary to get abilities fully used. Nor does there appear to be any reason to think that most people regard ability or character as deserving a higher differential than this. The skilful or diligent or responsible worker is felt to deserve more; but this perfectly valid moral judgment does not tell us how much more. The only rational answer to the question 'how much more?' is, therefore, this: that amount more which will ensure that their talents are exercised and that society benefits from them.

This then emerges as the basic *economic* aim for socialists; not literally 'equality'; but the *minimum of inequality that is workable if human beings are actively to use their talents; not equal shares, but fair shares; not equality, but social justice.*

From *Socialism in the New Society* by Douglas Jay (Longmans, Green & Co, 1962)

R.H.S. Crossman
FAIR SHARES (1951)

Fair shares is one of the vital concepts of British socialism. But I do not believe you will get fair shares by studying the cost-of-living index, and proving to the housewives that it really has not gone up when they all think it has. That is not fair shares; fair shares is not a statistical concept. Fair shares means feeling as a community that things are fairly distributed. There may be communities which feel things are fair, even when there are economic inequalities. Do not assume that sheer statistical, economical equalitarianism feels fair. It does not feel fair to a butcher's wife when miners come up in the social scale and earn more than she does. I am not saying you should not raise miners' wages, but do not imagine that she will feel it is fair. Fair shares means that people are feeling, roughly speaking, that they are getting what they deserve. That may be very remote from strict statistical equalitarianism; you will find out what sort of fair shares you ought to have, not by studying economics, but by studying human beings, seeing what they really feel about it and about each other and about the people with whom they live.

From 'Socialist Values in a Changing Civilisation' (Fabian Tract no. 286)
by R.H.S. Crossman (1951)

Joe Batey
(a South Shields pitman)

THE PLEA OF LABOUR (1904)

I do not want the earth. I only ask
    That portion of its plenty which is mine;
    That I may live the life which God's design
Marked not for slothful ease or endless task.
I will not fawn at fortune's feet, nor bask
    Contented where reflected glories shine,
    Until the coming day when wrath divine
Shall tear away from Mammon's face the mask.
Give me fair recompense for dangers faced:
    Give me but fair reward for labour done;
    A chance to breathe of God's pure air a breath
And time for rest in all the hours of haste.
    That I may see the smiling of the sun
    Ere darkness cometh in the guise of death.

From *We Do Not Want the Earth: the History of the South Shields Labour Party*
by David Clark (Bewick Press, 1992)

Edward Carpenter

THE DIGNITY OF HUMAN LABOUR (1883)

At the bottom, and behind all the elaborations of economic science, theories of social progress, the changing forms of production, and class warfare, lies today the fact that the old ideals of society have become corrupt, and that this corruption has resulted in dishonesty of life. It is this dishonesty of personal life which is becoming the occasion of a new class-war, from whose fierce parturition-struggle will arise a new ideal – destined to sway human society for many a thousand years, and to give shape to the forms of its industrial, scientific, and artistic life . . .

The canker of effete gentility has eaten into the heart of this nation. Its noble men and women are turned into toy ladies and gentlemen; the eternal dignity of (voluntary) poverty and simplicity has been forgotten in an unworthy scramble for easy-chairs. Justice and honesty have got themselves melted away into a miowling and watery philanthropy; the rule of honour between master and servant, and servant and master, between debtor and creditor, and buyer and seller, has been turned into a rule of dishonour, concealment, insincere patronage, and sharp bargains; and England lies done to death by her children who should have loved her.

As for you, working men and working women – in whom now, if anywhere, the hope of England lies – I appeal to you at any rate to cease from this ideal, I appeal to you to cease your part in this gentility business - to cease respecting people because they wear fine clothes and ornaments, and because they live in grand houses. You know you do these things, or pretend to do them, and to do either is foolish. We have had ducking and forelock pulling enough. It is time for *you* to assert the dignity of human labour . . .

Be arrogant rather than humble, rash rather than stupidly contented; but, best of all, be firm, helpful towards each other, forgetful of differences, scrupulously honest in yourselves, and charitable even to your enemies, but determined that *nothing* shall move you from the purpose you have set before you – the righteous distribution in society of the fruits of your own and other men's labour, the return to honesty as the sole possible basis of national life and national safety, and the redemption of England from the curse which rests upon her.

From *Towards Democracy* by Edward Carpenter

Julian le Grand
EQUALITY AND FAIRNESS (1982)

The first, and perhaps most important, issue to tackle is whether the current distribution of economic resources is fair or just. A basic belief that it is indeed fair is an essential element of the ideology of inequality. It is widely held, implicitly or explicitly, that people have 'earned' their incomes, and that the State has no right to take their money or even to give them more. It is manifest, for example, in the common attitude that accepts as normal, or even praiseworthy, the avoidance or evasion of taxation – considered as protecting one's 'own' money – while condemning in the severest terms social security fraud – viewed as trying to obtain 'other people's'. It is part of the reason why the poor often refuse welfare benefits to which they are entitled, for they feel that they have not 'earned' them, a feeling that in turn led to many of the services designed to help the poor being set up in the form of being free to all, with the consequences for equality that have been seen in earlier chapters.

To tackle properly the ideology of inequality, therefore, it is necessary to question the belief that the present distribution of income is fair. To do so, it is necessary to see if there is a consensus on what is meant by fair. Elsewhere I have argued at some length that there is a consensus definition of fairness; what follows is an informal summary of the basic idea.

Suppose we observe three individuals, A, B and C. B and C have the same income, but A has a higher income than both. We are informed that the reason why B's income is depressed relative to A's is because there are imperfections in the market which prevent him or her from receiving the same wage as A. (An example could be if he or she were black and employers had a taste for discrimination.) C, on the other hand, faces the same wage rate as A, but has a lower income because he or she has decided to take more time off from work than A. They have the same job opportunities, they are equally aware of the advantages of working, including receiving a higher income, but C prefers to trade those advantages in return for a greater amount of leisure.

Now both B and C are equally deprived relative to A in income terms. But the degree of unfairness inherent in their deprivation seems to be different. C has voluntarily 'deprived' himself or herself of income, in return for increased leisure; hence it is difficult to regard the disparity between his or her income and A's as, *ipso facto*, unfair. B, on the other hand, has not chosen to be relatively deprived but has been prevented by factors beyond his or her control from raising his or her income. Here inequity does seem to be present. Although the differences between the incomes of the two individuals and that of A are the same, our judgments concerning the respective fairness of their situations are different, a difference which arises from our perception of the degrees of choice involved.

Now suppose we realised that some of the evidence about the situation with which we had been supplied was incorrect. Specifically, imagine we learned that the reason why B received a lower wage rate than A was not because of imperfections in the market, but because he or she is less highly skilled than A. Moreover, we were informed, both B and A had exactly the same opportunity to acquire those skills by undergoing training, and both were equally aware of the cost and benefits that would result if they trained. In that case our judgment as to the inequity of the situation might change. We may now feel that B chose to have a lower income than A, not because he or she has a higher rate of 'trading-off' income for leisure at the going wage rate (as does C) at least in the current period, but because he or she exercised his or her preferences at an earlier period. As a result, we may now feel that the difference between A's and B's income (as between A's and C's) is not inequitable.

Suppose we then received a further bit of information. We discovered that the reason why C has a higher rate of trade-off between leisure and income than

A is, because he or she has an invalid child and hence has to spend time at home in order to look after this child. We might then say, well, the disparity in incomes between A and C does now appear unfair. A has a higher income than C, but this is not really the result of choice on C's part.

Note what has happened. Our judgment about the fairness of the situation has undergone a number of changes and indeed has ended in a complete reversal of our initial judgment. This has occurred, not because the disparities in income have changed, nor because our basic values have changed, but because at each stage we acquired new information concerning the freedom of choice each individual had in determining his situation.

The element that is crucial to determining the fairness or otherwise of a situation thus seems to be the existence or otherwise of choice. For, as is apparent from the example considered, *our judgment as to the degree of unfairness inherent in a given income distribution is dependent on the degree to which we see that distribution as an outcome of individual choices.*

There are many other examples which can reinforce the point. This conception of fairness is implicit in the judgment that inequalities of cost are inequitable. But it is also implicit in the views of many of those who advocate equality of outcome, for the reason they do so is because they believe differences in allocations usually arise not through individual choices but because of factors beyond individual control. It is often regarded as unfair if one child receives less education than another because his parents had a lower socio-economic status, again an example of restricted choice. Under most social security systems those who resign from their job voluntarily are not eligible for unemployment pay. The judgment seems to be that it is not fair to pay social security to those who have voluntarily decided to reduce their income, a judgment that follows directly if fairness is related to choice.

If this argument is accepted, then the question as to whether incomes in our society are fair becomes essentially an empirical one. For it will depend on the extent to which the income distribution arises from factors within individual control; not always an easy question to answer in practice but one that has considerably more potential for eventual resolution than a clash of values . . .

So the incomes people receive are heavily influenced, if not completely dominated, by factors beyond individual control. In that case it is difficult to argue that the current distribution of income is fair – at least in the sense that the term is generally used. The ideology of inequality has lost one of its major supports.

From *The Strategy of Equality: Redistribution and the Social Services* by Julian le Grand (George Allen & Unwin, 1982)

Anthony Crosland
HOW FAR TOWARDS EQUALITY? (1956)

How far towards equality do we wish to go? I do not regard this as either a sensible or a pertinent question, to which one could possibly give, or should attempt to give, a precise reply. We need, I believe, more equality than we now have. We can therefore describe the direction of advance, and even discern the immediate landscape ahead; but the ultimate objective lies wrapped in complete uncertainty.

This must be the case unless one subscribes to the vulgar fallacy that some ideal society can be said to exist, of which blueprints can be drawn, and which will be ushered in as soon as certain specific reforms have been achieved. The apocalyptic view that we might one day wake up to find that something called 'socialism' had arrived was born of evolutionary theories of capitalist collapse. But in Western societies change is gradual and revolutionary, and not always either foreseeable or even under political control. It is therefore futile and dangerous to think in terms of an ideal society, the shape of which can already be descried, and which will be reached at some definite date in the future. Countries like Britain do not leap from one fully-fledged social system to another, but are, on the contrary, in a state of permanent transition.

Moreover, socialism is not an exact descriptive term, connoting a particular social structure, past, present or even imminent in some sage's mind, which can be empirically observed or analysed. It simply describes a set of values, or aspirations, which socialists wish to see embodied in the organisation of society. One must confine oneself to saying, therefore, that society at any given moment either does or does not sufficiently embody these values, and if it does not, then further changes are required. But exactly what degree of equality will create a society, which does sufficiently embody them, no one can possibly say. We must reassess the matter in the light of each new situation.

We can thus only venture very general statements of the objective. I feel clear that we need large egalitarian changes in our educational system, the distribution of property, the distribution of resources in periods of need, social manners and style of life, and the location of power within industry; and perhaps some, but certainly a smaller, change in respect of incomes from work. I think that these changes, taken together, will amount to a considerable social revolution.

On the other hand, I am sure that a definite limit exists to the degree of equality which is desirable. We do not want complete equality of incomes, since extra responsibility and exceptional talent require and deserve a differential reward. We are not hostile as our opponents sometimes foolishly suggest, to 'detached residences in Bournemouth where some elderly woman has obviously more than a thousand a year'. I do not myself want to see *all* private education disappear: nor the Prime Minister denied an official car, as in one Scandinavian country: nor the Queen riding a bicycle: nor the House of

Lords instantly abolished: nor the manufacture of Rolls-Royces banned: nor the Brigade of Guards, nor Oxford and Cambridge, nor Boodle's, nor (more doubtfully) the Royal Yacht Squadron, nor even, on a rather lower level, the Milroy Room, lose their present distinctive character: nor anything so dull and colourless as this.

But where en route, before we reach some drab extreme, we shall wish to stop, I have no idea. Our society will look quite different when we have carried through the changes mentioned earlier; and the whole argument will then need to be restated, and thought out afresh, by a younger generation than mine.

From *The Future of Socialism* by Anthony Crosland (Jonathan Cape, 1956)

Hugh Gaitskell
OPPORTUNITY FOR ALL TO DEVELOP (1955)

The central socialist ideal is equality. By this I do not mean identical incomes or uniform habits and tastes. But I do mean a classless society – one in which the relations between all people are similar to those hitherto existing within one social class; one in which though there are differences between individuals, there are no feelings or attitudes of superiority and inferiority between groups; one in which although some jobs are paid more than others, the differentials are based on generally acceptable criteria – skill, responsibility, effort, danger, dirt, etc; one in which though people develop differently, there is equal opportunity for all to develop.

Equality is not the only socialist ideal. We are not interested in an equality of misery. We expect living standards to be adequate and to rise. Our economic institutions must be capable of achieving this. Our society must also enjoy economic security – or what we nowadays call 'full employment' – since this is a basic condition of happiness.

Our industrial system too must be of such a character that the relations of people to one another in their work are satisfactory. The general atmosphere of equality must prevail here as in society generally – though this should not mean cheerful anarchy or a failure to pinpoint responsibilities. To describe this, industrial democracy is still the best phrase – though it does not imply that all the workers are expected to be continually inspired by a positive collective enthusiasm for running the factory, any more than the citizens who elect a government at a general election ought to spend their whole lives worrying over politics!

Nevertheless I must make it absolutely plain that the socialism in which I believe is impossible except in a political democracy. For at rock-bottom this socialism is based on a respect for the individual human personality which is derided and scorned in a fascist or communist dictatorship. But if this be accepted, then it is also essential to understand the implications of political democracy for socialist policy. I mention in passing that in my opinion the lack of such understanding lies at the root of much current confusion.

Finally our socialist ideals by their very nature cannot be limited to one country. We must desire to extend them throughout the world. We cannot believe in a classless society at home and a colour bar abroad. If we want equality and democracy for ourselves, we must want it for everybody. Unfortunately our power is much more limited outside than within our own territory; and we must face the sad fact that most people's imaginations are weak and that their generous impulses flourish more easily in relation to what is near than to what is distant.

From 'Public Ownership and Equality' by Hugh Gaitskell,
in *Socialist Commentary*, June 1955

Social Justice Commission
EQUALITY OF OPPORTUNITY (1994)

Equality of opportunity is often dismissed as a weak aspiration. But if every child and every adult is to fulfil his or her potential, we need a social and economic revolution. We have to create an economy that generates new jobs and businesses faster than old ones are destroyed. Instead of an inefficient and divided labour market, we need fairness and flexibility to allow men and women to combine employment, family, education and leisure in different ways at different stages of their lives. In place of the old conflict between better protection for working people and lower profits for employers, we need new social standards designed to raise the contribution which workers can make to the productivity of their organisations. Above all, we will have to transform our old education system, designed to serve an academic elite and to fail the rest, into a means for lifelong learning.

Deregulators argue that the less government does, the more opportunities there are for individuals. But opportunity does not depend only on individual effort. That is why investors argue for collective action and above all collective investment – whether it is public, private, voluntary or a partnership of all three – to promote individual opportunity. The first and most important task for government is to set in place the opportunities for children and adults to learn to their personal best. By investing in skills, we raise people's capacity to add value to the economy, to take charge of their own lives, and to contribute to their families and communities. 'Thinking for a living' is not a choice but an imperative.

Social Justice – Strategies for National Renewal, the Report of the Commission
on Social Justice (Vintage, 1994)

Bernard Williams
THE IDEA OF EQUALITY (1962)

This line of thought points to a connexion between the idea of equality of opportunity, and the idea of equality of persons, which is stronger than might at first be suspected. We have seen that one is not really offering equality of opportunity to Smith and Jones if one contents oneself with applying the same criteria to Smith and Jones at, say, the age of 11; what one is doing there is to apply the same criteria to Smith as affected by favourable conditions and to Jones as affected by unfavourable but curable conditions. Here there is a necessary pressure to equal up the conditions: to give Smith *and* Jones equality of opportunity involves regarding their conditions, where curable, as themselves part of what is done to Smith and Jones, and not part of Smith and Jones themselves. Their identity, for these purposes, does not include their curable environment, which is itself unequal and a contributor of inequality. This abstraction of persons in themselves from unequal environments is a way, if not of regarding them as equal, at least of moving recognisably in that direction; and is itself involved in equality of opportunity.

From 'The Idea of Equality' by Bernard Williams, in *Philosophy, Politics and Society*, edited by Peter Laslett and W.G. Runciman (Basil Blackwell, 1962)

T.H. Marshall
EQUALITY OF STATUS (1950)

The extension of the social services is not primarily a means of equalising incomes. In some cases it may, in others it may not. The question is relatively unimportant; it belongs to a different department of social policy. What matters is that there is a general enrichment of the concrete substance of civilised life, a general reduction of risk and insecurity, an equalisation between the more and the less fortunate at all levels – between the healthy and the sick, the employed and the unemployed, the old and the active, the bachelor and the father of a large family. Equalisation is not so much between classes as between individuals within a population which is now treated for this purpose as though it were one class. Equality of status is more important than equality of income.

From *Citizenship and Social Class* by T.H. Marshall and Tom Bottomore (Pluto Press, 1992)

Bernard Crick

CREATING AN EGALITARIAN SOCIETY (1984)

I actually prefer to speak of an egalitarian society rather than an equal society. Even so, without a sincere desire to achieve an egalitarian society, any democratic socialist movement loses its dynamic and lapses back into a directionless pragmatism and the paternalism of a benevolent hierarchy – in homely terms, the councillor and the social worker perpetually sad that their people are not grateful for their efforts on their behalf, and cannot be trusted to make collective decisions for themselves without untidy results.

The concept of equality, however, has notorious difficulties and is often parodied: a literal and exact, universal equality, whether of opportunity, treatment or result is almost as undesirable as it is impossible. Equality of opportunity, even if obtainable, could only be a once-off affair, a way of reshuffling or new-dealing the pack – unless everyone was childless and there was no inheritance of property, skills or even predispositions. Equality of result would either be, indeed, the death of liberty or a response to a very precise specification of particular areas, such as income, for instance, but not necessarily all work, trade or barter in leisure time. Nevertheless an egalitarian society is both conceivable and desirable. Certainly some societies are remarkably less unequal than others; but if by an egalitarian society is meant a classless society, one in which every man would see every other man as brother, sister as sister, brother and sister, of equal worth and potential, then one can readily imagine a genuinely fraternal society with no conceit or constraint of class. It would not be a society in which everyone was exactly equal in power, status, wealth and acquired abilities, still less in end-products of happiness; but it would be a society in which none of these marginal differences was unacceptable and regarded as unjust by public opinion – a public opinion which would itself become, as gross inequalities diminished, far more critical and active, far less inert and fatalistic than today. These margins would remain perpetually ambiguous, open, flexible, debatable, a moving horizon that is never quite reached, irreducible to either economic formula or legislative final solution; but less intense and less fraught with drastic consequences than today.

No difficulties about the concept are so great as to warrant abandoning it or treating it as pure ritual of the socialist church. One difficulty is that socialists want, rhetorically and politically, to make something sound positive which is philosophically best stated in negative terms. There is no 'complete equality' which can 'finally be realised', unless genetic engineering were to come to the aid of economic planning (with about equal accuracy and predictability, one would hope). But there are so many unjustifiable inequalities. Poverty, for instance, limits life and the exercise of freedom in nearly every possible way, and if riches or affluence give undoubted freedom to their possessors, it is usually at the cost of their humanity and fellow feeling. If we believe in the moral equality or the fraternity of all mankind, then *all* inequalities of power, status and wealth need justifying. The boot should be worn on that foot. Inequalities can be justified only if these inequalities can be shown to be of positive advantage to the less advantaged. Some inequalities can be justified, many not – particularly if one adds the vital condition of democratic citizenship: actually to ask the disadvantaged and to depend on their reply. No precise agreement is ever likely to be reached or, if so, only for a particular time and place. Nor can philosophy supply incontrovertible criteria for what is an unjustifiable inequality. Each case will stand on its merits and opinions will differ. But the important point is to see that inequalities of reward and power are unjustifiable in principle unless some clear public benefit follows from them that could not otherwise exist.

Here I am following the arguments of John Rawls in his monumental *A Theory of Justice* and of W.G. Runciman in his *Relative Deprivation and Social Justice*. Some socialists have misread their arguments as merely a radical form of liberalism. But even if that was their intent, if in fact all inequalities were called into question, constantly questioned, criticised and forced to justify themselves in the public interest, then one would at least be in a society with a dominant egalitarian spirit. The vast differences in power, status and wealth that are in fact acceptable to most people in a class-conscious society, will grow less tolerable as income differences diminish and as egalitarian spirit grows, by argument, agitation and example, as well as by legislation.

Equality does not mean sameness. Men, not robots, animate an egalitarian spirit. The idea that even a strict and absolute equality of condition would destroy human individuality and character is not so much a Tory nightmare as a science fiction fantasy. Are most of the things we most enjoy doing in life likely to be repetitive and 'the same' if they are always done between two people, walking and talking together, who would have, whoever they were, roughly equal income and be of the same, or no, social class? The fears of Tory and 'market liberal' authors that high taxation and State intervention will necessarily destroy individuality, these are literally absurd. Do they really think that man is so artificial and individuality so fragile? Can they really not imagine that everyone could have roughly the same standard of living, equal status and equal access to the processes of political power and yet still retain individuality? Or can they, more understandably, simply not imagine how their fancy selves could adjust to such a society? For some people genuinely believe that individuality, character and culture only exist among the prosperous and well educated, and that 'the masses', as the natives used to, 'all look the same'. Masses can be generalised about but not the educated and the gentry. It is the saddest fate of the poor to have even their individuality removed from them in principle as well as threatened in practice . . .

Now 'less unjustifiable inequality today!' and 'no unjustifiable inequality tomorrow!' may not be slogans that 'warm the blood like wine', but that may be fortunate. For 'Forward to Equality' is more likely to warm the hearts of party activists than those whom they need to persuade. In practice in modern societies not only trade unionists are highly interested in differentials. And philosophically no one value, be it liberty, equality, fraternity, love, truth, reason, even life itself (as Thomas Hobbes taught) can at all times override all the others or be sure never to contradict them. Equality could certainly be maximised in a totalitarian State, but only at the expense of liberty, so that genuine fraternity is destroyed. The political socialist, who knows that democracy must be the means as well as part of the end, having a theory of society, looks at values together, both in their social setting and in relation to each other. He no more postpones liberty until the classless society than he reserves egalitarian and fraternal behaviour and example until the classless society. If he does, he will not get there; and when he does, classlessness by itself will not have solved all problems and removed all possibilities of injustice.

The political socialist as egalitarian need not get drawn into the parody argument which assumes exact equality of income and wealth: that is somebody else's nightmare, not his dream.

From 'Socialist Values and Time' (Fabian Pamphlet no. 495) by Bernard Crick (1984)

Raymond Plant
WHY DO INEQUALITIES MATTER? (1993)

The point at issue is this: why do inequalities matter?

If one accepts that liberty does indeed involve ability and the associated resources and opportunities, then radically different resources and opportunities will have a close bearing on liberty. This is not so for the economic liberal for whom liberty is the absence of coercion not the possession of resources or opportunities. However, we have seen reason to doubt this. Historically, Western societies have held out the ideal of equal liberty and thus if there is a link between liberty and resources then a fairer distribution of resources and opportunities is necessary for a fairer value of liberty in society.

However, we have to be careful about how this argument is handled because this does not mean equality of outcome, as it has done for some socialists, nor does it mean procedural equality of opportunity – removing intentionally erected barriers to advancement – as it does for the liberal. The concern with fairness is with what Rawls and Crosland called 'democratic equality' – that social institutions should be concerned with a fair distribution of resources as a way of securing a fair value for liberty. We cannot equalise outcomes even if this were desirable without the most extravagant acts of government intervention and likely mutual impoverishment. It would be irrational to prefer a more equal distribution of resources which left everyone, including the poor, worse off than they would be under a system in which there would be some inequalities but

77

which would also benefit the poor. We cannot get an equal value for liberty without threatening to destroy it but we can get a fairer distribution of resources and opportunities which bear most directly on the capacity for action. Our distributive concern is with the fair conditions for the exercise of liberty (not equalising outcomes) and because of the link between the rent of ability and wealth creation this must allow for sensitivity both to the concerns of the worst-off and what economic incentives are necessary to pay the rent of ability. This has to be a matter of political judgment and market realities.

The second reason why we should be concerned with the relative position of the poor in society has to do with the idea of citizenship. The economic liberal wants to define citizenship in purely civil and political terms, not in social and economic terms. However, as I have already suggested, free democratic citizenship goes beyond civil and political rights, vitally important though these are, to citizenship in the social and economic sphere and this involves trying to make sure that the terms of social and economic citizenship embody some idea of the fair value of liberty. If we are concerned only with the absolute position of the worst-off we will exclude the latter from the citizenship which those higher up the ladder take for granted.

Finally, there is a further central point. Since 1979 the Government has made a good deal of the idea that the market empowers people. The 'trickle down' effect of the market economy is held to improve the absolute position of those in work and this is a form of empowerment. This is, however, difficult to accept because it implies that the power of one group in society can increase while its relative position declines because of inequality. But this cannot be so. Power is a positional good in the sense that its value depends on some other people not having it; indeed, it might be regarded as a pure positional good in the sense that if power were to be distributed equally then it would disappear altogether. If this is so then power has to be connected to relativities and cannot simply be increased like the supply of washing machines which may be subject to the trickle down effect. An ideal of empowerment cannot therefore be secured by the market mechanism through the trickle down effect and the improvement of the absolute position of the worst-off. Empowerment has to be concerned with relativities and not just absolutes. If we believe in a fair distribution of power as well as liberties, then we cannot avoid distributive questions and have to move beyond the economic liberal's concern with absolute levels. The distribution of economic power in society must be a matter of central concern for the Left but for the Right, despite their trumpeting of choice, it is not on offer as a choice to be made in a market society.

From 'Social Justice, Labour and the New Right' (Fabian Pamphlet no. 556) by Raymond Plant (1993)

Neil Kinnock
SHOULD WE ABANDON EQUALITY? (1986)

Equality stands alongside freedom and democracy in the vocabulary and values of socialism. Yet it is not of the same order. Equality is possibly the most problematic of all values insofar as it is not an absolute objective, but, rather, an implication and a means towards achieving freedom and democracy. Equality is not built or secured, as some would believe, on envy. It is, indeed, the very opposite. It is implicit in fellowship and provides the basis for community. Yet it, too, has been distorted and associated with a tolerance – indeed a pursuit – of mediocrity and uniformity.

How absurd that it should be. Socialism *celebrates* diversity. It believes in the flowering of all talents, the elevation of all individuals. This does not mean a romantic belief that everyone can be *made* equal. It does not mean uniformity of human beings or anything so socially repulsive; it does not mean accepting that all human beings are equal in ability or anything so biologically preposterous, and it does not mean believing that there can be mathematical parity of incomes or anything so economically impractical. But it does mean that those institutions and influences which protect, reward and perpetuate those inequalities which are *not* natural and *not* earned must be removed. And it does mean that as a conscious purpose of policy every means should be exploited to establish an equal right for individuals to realise and fulfil their capabilities, regardless of background, sex or race. But – despite the welfare state – the key pillars of social and economic inequality remain intact. While the very rich have lost some of their riches to the less rich, over time, the poor have hardly profited proportionately. That has been true through the history of the welfare state.

Inequalities of income are reflected in inequalities of power and status. We have at the moment a society which wilfully wastes its material and human resources; where 'equality' is derided and yet where children in different regions, different towns, different families, different schools, stand different chances of health, education, employment and even life and death. To those who sneer at equality as a useful or relevant objective, I have to say 'Look around you!'. Look at the million young people under 25 on the dole; at the evidence of increased mortality and morbidity rates for those at the bottom end of the social scale; at the difficulties faced by women and people from ethnic minority groups in finding and keeping well-paid jobs. I would also say to those who complacently see equality as something automatically consequent upon our institutions – our schools or the health service – listen to the evidence that disproves the idea that left to themselves without the stimulus of constant policies of equality our present institutions and past policies can serve the interests of all the people more effectively. I would also say – look at the vulnerability of children born in our inner cities, to families on the dole, in ill-health, in multiple disadvantage, and listen to those who know tell us that these disadvantages are transferred across generations. And then ask the question – have we achieved equality? Should we abandon it – or apologise for it as an objective? Should we succumb to the argument that the constructive efforts for equality are 'social engineering' when we know that deprivation, poverty, the ignoring of talent, the failure to treat disease are themselves the very worst forms of social engineering that have constructed a society which is under-educated, depressed and divided?

The problem is not with our objectives, but with the institutions and patterns of provision, produced by past policies. Policies for positive discrimination in education, policies designed to achieve equal access, have been insufficient, inconsistent and unco-ordinated. The problems of our inner cities grow worse because our strategies have been incomplete, ill-thought out, and – usually – externally imposed by people who will not have to live with the consequences. Equally seriously, we have failed to tackle the roots of real inequality – the bastions of privilege built into our social and economic institutions and perpetuated in our education system. Unless we tackle these problems at source we will continue to accept a system based on fundamental inequality, hoping that the occasional escape will prove that the system is not without some virtue.

We do understand now that we must act across a broad front. Better schools alone cannot spring children out of poverty; better housing will not solve all social problems; a free health service does not guarantee an equal chance that all children will thrive; more police will not eradicate crime or by themselves reduce the insecurity which pervades whole districts. Indeed, we understand better than ever the inadequacies of our institutions. Equality of opportunity must inform all policies, and must be asserted, not simply through statutes and limited financial gestures, but directed through a range of policies which all have the explicit aim of helping people to lift themselves out of poverty of resources and poverty of aspirations whether they endure multiple disadvantage because they are black or among those – the majority – who because they are women and girls are still not afforded access or encouragement on the same basis as boys and men.

Freedom, democracy and equality are values which, separately, can belong to other philosophies and applied for other ends. What cannot be borrowed, however, is that economic and social analysis which democratic socialism brings to the structural economic and social problems of capitalism, and the commitment to radical but realistic methods and objectives which are not only part of our historical tradition and our philosophical apparatus, but which inform our view of what democratic society is, and could be.

From 'The Future of Socialism' (Fabian Pamphlet no. 509) by Neil Kinnock (1986)

R.H.Tawney
EQUALITY (1931)

What a community requires, as the word itself suggests, is a common culture, because, without it, it is not a community at all. And evidently it requires it in a special degree at a moment like the present, when circumstances confront it with the necessity of giving a new orientation to its economic life, because it is in such circumstances that the need for co-operation, and for the mutual confidence and tolerance upon which co-operation depends, is particularly pressing. But a common culture cannot be created merely by desiring it. It must rest upon practical foundations of social organisation. It is incompatible with the existence of sharp contrasts between the economic standards and educational opportunities of different classes, for such contrasts have as their result, not a common culture, but servility or resentment, on the one hand, and patronage or arrogance, on the other. It involves, in short, a large measure of economic equality – not necessarily in the sense of an identical level of pecuniary incomes, but of equality of environment, of access to education and the means of civilisation, of security and independence, and of the social consideration which equality in these matters usually carries with it . . .

It is obvious, indeed, that, as things are today, no redistribution of wealth would bring general affluence, and that statisticians are within their rights in making merry with the idea that the equalisation of incomes would make everyone rich. But, though riches are a good, they are not, nevertheless, the only good; and because greater production, which is concerned with the commodities to be consumed, is clearly important, it does not follow that greater equality, which is concerned with the relations between the human beings who consume them, is not important also. It is obvious, again, that the word 'equality' possesses more than one meaning, and that the controversies surrounding it arise partly, at least, because the same term is employed with different connotations. Thus it may either purport to state a fact, or convey the expression of an ethical judgment. On the one hand, it may affirm that men are, on the whole, very similar in their natural endowments of character and intelligence. On the other hand, it may assert that, while they differ profoundly as individuals in capacity and character, they are equally entitled as human beings to consideration and respect, and that the well-being of a society is likely to be increased if it so plans its organisation that, whether their powers are great or small, all its members may be equally enabled to make the best of such powers as they possess . . .

The equality which . . . these thinkers emphasise as desirable is not equality of capacity of attainment, but of circumstances, institutions, and manner of life. The inequality which they deplore is not inequality of personal gifts, but of the social and economic environment. They are concerned, not with a biological phenomenon, but with a spiritual relation and the conduct to be based on it. Their view, in short, is that, because men are men, social institutions – property

81

rights, and the organisation of industry, and the system of public health and education – should be planned, as far as is possible, to emphasise and strengthen, not the class differences which divide, but the common humanity which unites, them . . .

It is true that human beings have, except as regards certain elementary, though still sadly neglected, matters of health and development, different requirements, and that these different requirements can be met satisfactorily only by varying forms of provision. But equality of provision is not identity of provision. It is to be achieved, not by treating different needs in the same way, but by devoting equal care to ensuring that they are met in the different ways most appropriate to them, as is done by a doctor who prescribes different regimens for different constitutions, or a teacher who develops different types of intelligence by different curricula. The more anxiously, indeed, a society endeavours to secure equality of consideration for all its members, the greater will be the differentiation of treatment which, when once their common human needs have been met, it accords to the special needs of different groups and individuals among them.

It is true, finally, that some men are inferior to others in respect of their intellectual endowments, and it is possible – though the truth of the possibility has not yet been satisfactorily established – that the same is true of certain classes. It does not, however, follow from this fact that such individuals or classes should receive less consideration than others, or should be treated as inferior in respect of such matters as legal status, or health, or economic arrangements, which are within the control of the community . . .

Everyone recognises the absurdity of such an argument when it is applied to matters within his personal knowledge and professional competence. Everyone realises that, in order to justify inequalities of circumstance or opportunity by reference to differences of personal quality, it is necessary . . . to show that the differences in question are relevant to the inequalities. Everyone now sees, for example, that it is not a valid argument against women's suffrage to urge, as used to be urged not so long ago, that women are physically weaker than men, since physical strength is not relevant to the question of the ability to exercise the franchise, or a valid argument in favour of slavery that some men are less intelligent than others, since it is not certain that slavery is the most suitable penalty for lack of intelligence.

Not everyone, however, is so quick to detect the fallacy when it is expressed in general terms. It is still possible, for example, for one eminent statesman to ridicule the demand for a diminution of economic inequalities on the ground that every mother knows that her children are not equal, without reflecting whether it is the habit of mothers to lavish care on the strong and neglect the delicate; and for another to dismiss the suggestion that greater economic equality is desirable, for the reason apparently, that men are naturally unequal. It is probable, however, that the first does not think that the fact that some children are born with good digestions, and others with bad, is a reason for supplying good food to the former and bad food to the latter, rather than for giving to both food which is equal in quality but different in kind, and that the second does not suppose that the natural inequality of men makes legal equality a contemptible principle . . .

Many services are supplied by collective effort today which in the recent past were supplied by individual effort or not supplied at all, and many more, it may be suspected, will be so supplied in the future. At any moment there are some needs which almost everyone is agreed should be satisfied on equalitarian principles, and others which are agreed should be met by individuals who purchase what their incomes enable them to pay for, and others, again, about the most suitable provision for which opinions differ. Society has not been prevented from seeking to establish equality in respect of the first by the fear that in so doing it may be perpetrating a scientific impossibility. Nor ought it to be prevented from moving towards equality in respect of the second and third, if experience suggests that greater equality in these matters also would contribute to greater efficiency and to more general happiness

Perhaps, therefore, the remote Victorian thinkers, like Arnold and Mill, who dealt lightly with mumbo-jumbo, and who commended equality to their fellow-countrymen as one source of peace and happiness, were not speaking so unadvisedly as at first sight might appear. It is the fact that, in spite of their varying characters and capacities, men possess in their common humanity a quality which is worth cultivating, and that a community is most likely to make the most of that quality if it takes it into account in planning its economic organisation and social institutions – if it stresses lightly differences of wealth and birth and social position, and establishes on firm foundations institutions which meet common needs, and are a source of common enlightment and common enjoyment. The individual differences of which so much is made, they would have said, will always survive, and they are to be welcomed, not regretted. But their existence is no reason for not seeking to establish the largest possible measure of equality of environment, and circumstance, and opportunity. On the contrary, it is a reason for redoubling our efforts to establish it, in order to ensure that these diversities of gifts may come to fruition . . .

So to criticise inequality and to desire equality is not, as is sometimes suggested, to cherish the romantic illusion that men are equal in character and intelligence. It is to hold that, while their natural endowments differ profoundly, it is the mark of a civilised society to aim at eliminating such inequalities as have their source, not in individual differences, but in its own organisation, and that individual differences, which are a source of social energy, are more likely to ripen and find expression if social inequalities are, as far as practicable, diminished. And the obstacle to the progress of equality is something simpler and more potent than finds expression in the familiar truism that men vary in their mental and moral, as well as in their physical characteristics, important and valuable though that truism is as a reminder that different individuals require different types of provision. It is the habit of mind which thinks it, not regrettable, but natural and desirable, that different sections of a community should be distinguished from each other by sharp differences of economic status, of environment, of education and culture and habit of life. It is the temper which regards with approval the social institutions and economic arrangements by which such differences are emphasised and enhanced, and feels distrust and apprehension at all attempts to diminish them . . .

Most social systems need a lightning-conductor. The formula which supplies it to our own is equality of opportunity. The conception is one to which homage is paid today by all, including those who resist most strenuously attempts to apply it. But the rhetorical tribute which it receives appears sometimes to be paid on the understanding that it shall be content with ceremonial honours. It retains its throne, on condition that it refrains from meddling with the profitable business of the factory and marketplace. Its credit is good, as long as it does not venture to cash its cheques. Like other respectable principles, it is encouraged to reign, provided that it does not attempt to rule . . .

It is possible that intelligent tadpoles reconcile themselves to the inconveniences of their position, by reflecting that, though most of them will live and die as tadpoles and nothing more, the more fortunate of the species will one day shed their tails, distend their mouths and stomachs, hop nimbly on to dry land, and croak addresses to their former friends on the virtues by means of which tadpoles of character and capacity can rise to be frogs. This conception of society may be described, perhaps, as the Tadpole Philosophy, since the consolation which it offers for social evils consists in the statement that exceptional individuals can succeed in evading them. Who has not heard it suggested that the presence of opportunities, by means of which individuals can ascend and get on, relieves economic contrasts of their social poison and their personal sting? Who has not encountered the argument that there is an educational 'ladder' up which talent can climb, and that its existence makes the scamped quality of our primary education – the overcrowded classes, and mean surroundings, and absence of amenities – a matter of secondary importance? And what a view of human life such an attitude implies! As though opportunities for talent to rise could be equalised in a society where the circumstances surrounding it from birth are themselves unequal! As though, if they could, it were natural and proper that the position of the mass of mankind should permanently be such that they can attain civilisation only by escaping from it! As though the noblest use of exceptional powers were to scramble to shore, undeterred by the thought of drowning companions!

It is true, of course, that a community must draw on a stream of fresh talent, in order to avoid stagnation, and that, unless individuals of ability can turn their powers to account, they are embittered by a sense of defeat and frustration. The existence of opportunities to move from point to point on an economic scale, and to mount from humble origins to success and affluence, is a condition, therefore, both of social well-being and of individual happiness, and impediments which deny them to some, while lavishing them on others, are injurious to both. But opportunities to 'rise' are not a substitute for a large measure of practical equality, nor do they make immaterial the existence of sharp disparities of income and social condition. On the contrary, it is only the presence of a high degree of practical equality which can diffuse and generalise opportunities to rise. The existence of such opportunities in fact, and not merely in form, depends, not only upon an open road, but upon an equal start. It is precisely, of course, when capacity is aided by a high level of general well-being in the *milieu* surrounding it, that its ascent is most likely to be regular and rapid, rather than fitful and intermittent . . .

If a high degree of practical equality is necessary to social well-being, because without it ability cannot find its way to its true vocation, it is necessary also for another and more fundamental reason. It is necessary because a community requires unity as well as diversity, and because, important as it is to discriminate between different powers, it is even more important to provide for common needs. Clever people, who possess exceptional gifts themselves, are naturally impressed by exceptional gifts in others, and desire, when they consider the matter at all, that society should be organised to offer a career to exceptional talent, though they rarely understand the full scope and implications of the revolution they are preaching. But, in the conditions characteristic of large-scale economic organisation, in which ninety per cent of the population are wage-earners, and not more than ten per cent employers, farmers, independent workers or engaged in professions, it is obviously, whatever the level of individual intelligence and the degree of social fluidity, a statistical impossibility for more than a small fraction of the former to enter the ranks of the latter; and a community cannot be built upon exceptional talent alone, though it would be a poor thing without it. Social well-being does not only depend upon intelligent leadership; it also depends upon cohesion and solidarity. It implies the existence, not merely of opportunities to ascend, but of a high level of general culture, and a strong sense of common interests, and the diffusion throughout society of a conviction that civilisation is not the business of an elite alone, but a common enterprise which is the concern of all. And individual happiness does not only require that men should be free to rise to new positions of comfort and distinction; it also requires that they should be able to lead a life of dignity and culture, whether they rise or not, and that, whatever their position on the economic scale may be, it shall be such as if fit to be occupied by men.

From *Equality* by R.H. Tawney (George Allen & Unwin Ltd, 1931)

FREEDOM: A PRACTICAL LIBERTY

*'Freedom is the goal of politics. To establish and secure
true freedom is the primary object of all right political
action. For it is in and through this freedom that a man
makes fully real his personality'*

Percy Bysshe Shelley
WHAT ART THOU FREEDOM? (1819)

What art thou Freedom? O! could slaves
Answer from their living graves
This demand – tyrants would flee
Like a dream's dim imagery:

Thou art not, as imposters say,
A shadow soon to pass away,
A superstition and a name
Echoing from the cave of Fame.

For the labourer thou art bread,
And a comely table spread
From his daily labour come
In a neat and happy home.

Thou art clothes, and fire, and food
For the trampled multitude –
No – in countries that are free
Such starvation cannot be
As in England now we see.

To the rich thou art a check,
When his foot is on the neck
Of his victim, thou dost make
That he treads upon a snake.

Thou art Justice – ne'er for gold
May thy righteous laws be sold
As laws are in England – thou
Shield'st alike the high and low.

Thou art Wisdom – Freemen never
Dream that God will damn for ever
All who think those things untrue
Of which Priests make such ado.

Thou art Peace – never by thee
Would blood and treasure wasted be
As tyrants wasted them, when all
Leagued to quench thy flame in Gaul.

What if English toil and blood
Was poured forth, even as a flood?
It availed, Oh, Liberty,
To dim, but not extinguish thee.

Thou art Love – the rich have kissed
Thy feet, and like him following Christ,
Give their substance to the free
And through the rough world follow thee.

Or turn their wealth to arms, and make
War for thy beloved sake
On wealth, and war, and fraud – whence they
Drew the power which is their prey.

Science, Poetry, and Thought
Are thy lamps; they make the lot
Of the dwellers in a cot
So serene, they curse it not.

Spirit, Patience, Gentleness,
All that can adorn and bless
Art thou – let deeds, not words, express
Thine exceeding loveliness.

Let a great Assembly be
Of the fearless and the free
On some spot of English ground
Where the plains stretch wide around.

Let the blue sky overhead,
The green earth on which ye tread,
All that must eternal be
Witness the solemnity.

From the corners uttermost
Of the bounds of English coast;
From every hut, village, and town
Where those who live and suffer moan
For others' misery or their own,

From the workhouse and the prison
Where pale as corpses newly risen,
Women, children, young and old
Groan for pain, and weep for cold –

From the haunts of daily life
Where is waged the daily strife
With common wants and common cares
Which sows the human heart with tares –

Lastly from the palaces
Where the murmur of distress
Echoes, like the distant sound
Of a wind alive around

Those prison halls of wealth and fashion,
Where some few feel such compassion
For those who groan, and toil, and wail
As must make their brethren pale –

Ye who suffer woes untold,
Or to feel, or to behold
You lost country bought and sold
With a price of blood and gold –

Let a vast assembly be,
And with great solemnity
Declare with measured words that ye
Are, as God has made ye, free –

* * * * *

And those words shall then become
Like Oppression's thundered doom
Ringing through each heart and brain,
Heard again – again – again –

Rise like Lions after slumber
In unvanquishable number –
Shake your chains to earth like dew
Which in sleep had fallen on you –
Ye are many – they are few.

From 'The Mask of Anarchy' in*The Complete Poetical Works of Percy Bysshe Shelley*,
edited by T. Hutchinson (revised by B.P. Kurtz), (Oxford, 1934)

William Blake
LONDON (1791–93)

I wander thro' each charter'd street,
Near where the charter'd Thames does flow,
And mark in every face I meet
Marks of weakness, marks of woe.

In every cry of every Man,
In every Infant's cry of fear,
In every voice, in ever ban,
The mind-forg'd manacles I hear.

How the Chimney-sweeper's cry
Every black'ning Church appalls;
And the hapless Soldier's sigh
Runs in blood down Palace walls.

But most thro' midnight streets I hear
How the youthful Harlot's curse
Blasts the new born Infant's tear,
And blights with plagues the Marriage hearse.

From *The Complete Writings of William Blake*,
edited by Sir Geoffrey Keynes (London, 1966)

J.B. Priestley
A GREAT COUNTRY? (1934)

Women have always worked in these textile trades, which could not exist – on their present economic basis – without them. One unmarried elderly woman of my acquaintance, up there, had just retired, after working fifty years as a weaver in one mill. Fifty years. During that time, she and her relatives and most of her friends had not only worked in that enormous mill but had lived all their lives in its shadow. Time for them had been marked by the sound of its hooter – locally known as a 'whew'. Fifty years, only broken by an occasional four or five days at Morecambe or Blackpool. Fifty years, living in the same back-to-back houses, just behind the mill. Millions of yards of fine fabrics had gone streaming out, from their hands, to almost every part of the world, to be cut into the fashions of the '80s, the '90s, the Edwardians, the Georgians. Fifty years of quick skilled work, with hours, in winter, lasting from dark to dark. If a world that once went bare is now partly clothed and decorated with fabrics, then these folk may be said to have lent a hand in the great processes of civilisation; they have not been passengers in the ship; a brief childhood at one end and a few sinking weary years at the other end, and between them these five solid decades of work: that is their record. Such services do not go unrewarded, of course. A weaver fit to be kept on working for fifty years has proved herself a valuable old servant of the firm. Therefore she receives a pension of five shillings a week from the mill, five shillings to do what she likes with; and when to that is added the ten shillings that the rashly generous State is flinging her way, it will be seen that she has a whole fifteen shillings a week for herself, which, if she had only herself to consider – and unfortunately, in this instance, she has to help an invalid sister – would undoubtedly leave her splendidly idle and luxurious at the end of her fifty years. It is a pity that she has somebody else to support, because otherwise, no doubt, in this pensioned ease, she could see something of the world for which she has been weaving so long, could be waited on for once in her life, could look at the big shops and buy pretty little presents for her grand-nieces and nephews, could, in short, have a wonderful time with her fifteen shillings. But perhaps it is as well that she cannot go splashing her fifteen shillings about, because if she could, although she is old and heavy and tired, she might arouse the indignation of those honest fiery Tory patriots who write articles for and letters to the newspapers, protesting against the treatment afforded this pampered class, talking like the noblest Romans of us all in this later age of bread and circuses. Perhaps she is better as she is, wishing she had strength enough to work more than those fifty years, wondering how to get through the coming week, and never asking herself, as she stirs in the dark mornings when she hears the hooter blowing and the clatter of feet outside, whether mills were created for men and women or men and women for mills. She does not complain much, perhaps because she realises, like all the protesting gentlemen who lounge before large club fireplaces, that if, during and after her fifty years of toil, she had been treated with any more consideration it would have meant the ruin of a great country. And, not being a literary sentimentalist, she does not say that a country in these years has no title to greatness, had better face and risk ruin, if it still allows its people to suffer such damnable injustice.

From *English Journey* by J.B. Priestley (William Heinemann Ltd, in association with Victor Gollancz Ltd, 1934)

Charles Kingsley
FREEDOM TO RISE? (1848)

'Did you ever do a good day's farm work in your life? If you had, man or boy, you wouldn't have been game for much reading when you got home; you'd do just what these poor fellows do – tumble into bed at eight o'clock, hardly waiting to take your clothes off, knowing that you must turn up again at five o'clock the next morning, to get a breakfast of bread, and perhaps a dab of the squire's dripping, and then back to work again; and so on, day after day, sir, week after week, year after year, without a hope or a chance of being anything but what you are, and only too thankful if you can get work to break your back, and catch the rheumatism over.'

'But do you mean to say that their labour is so severe and incessant?'

'It's only God's blessing if it is incessant, sir, for if it stops, they starve, or go to the house to be worse fed than the thieves in gaol. And as for its being severe, there's many a boy as their mothers will tell you, comes home night after night, too tired to eat their suppers, and tumble, fasting, to bed in the same foul shirt which they've been working in all the day, never changing their rag of calico from week's end to week's end, or washing the skin that's under it once in seven years.'

'No wonder,' said Lancelot, 'that such a life of drudgery makes them brutal and reckless.'

'No wonder, indeed, sir: they've no time to think; they're born to be machines, and machines they must be; and I think, sir,' he added bitterly, 'it's God's mercy that they daren't think. It's God's mercy that they don't feel. Men that write books and talk at elections call this a free country, and say that the poorest and meanest has a free opening to rise and become prime minister, if he can. But you see, sir, the misfortune is, that in practice he can't; for one who gets into a gentleman's family, or into a little shop, and so saves a few pounds, fifty know that they've no chance before them, but day-labourer born, day-labourer live, from hand to mouth, scraping and pinching to get not meat and beer even, but bread and potatoes; and then, at the end of it all, for a worthy reward, half a crown a week of parish pay – or the workhouses. That's a lively hopeful prospect for a Christian man!'

From 'Yeast' by Charles Kingsley in *Fraser's Magazine*, 1848

Charles Dickens
THE POOR WILL ALWAYS BE WITH US (1865)

'There is not,' said Mr Podsnap, flushing angrily, 'there is not a country in the world, sir, where so noble a provision is made for the poor as in this country.'

The meek man was quite willing to concede that, but perhaps it rendered the matter even worse, as showing that there must be something appallingly wrong somewhere.

'Where?' said Mr Podsnap.

The meek man hinted, wouldn't it be well to try, very seriously, to find out where?

'Ah!' said Mr Podsnap. 'Easy to say somewhere; not so easy to say where!

But I see what you are driving at. I knew it from the first. Centralisation. No. Never with my consent. Not English.'

An approving murmur arose from the heads of tribes; as saying, 'There you have him! Hold him!'

He was not aware (the meek man submitted of himself) that he was driving at any isation. He had no favourite isation that he knew of. But he certainly was more staggered by these terrible occurrences than he was by names, of howsoever so many syllables. Might he ask, was dying of destitution and neglect necessarily English?

'You know what the population of London is, I suppose,' said Mr Podsnap.

The meek man supposed he did, but supposed that had absolutely nothing to do with it, if its laws were well administered.

'And you know; at least I hope you know,' said Mr Podsnap, with severity, 'that Providence had declared that you shall have the poor always with you?'

The meek man also hoped he knew that.

'I am glad to hear it,' said Mr Podsnap, with a portentous air. 'I am glad to hear it. It will render you cautious how you fly in the face of Providence.'

In reference to that absurd and irreverent conventional phrase, the meek man said, for which Mr Podsnap was not responsible, he the meek man had no fear of doing anything so impossible; but –

But Mr Podsnap felt that the time had come for flushing and flourishing this meek man down for good. So he said:

'I must decline to pursue this painful discussion. It is not pleasant to my feelings. It is repugnant to my feelings. I have said that I do not admit these things. I have also said that if they do occur (not that I admit it), the fault lies with the sufferers themselves. It is not for *me*' – Mr Podsnap pointed 'me' forcibly, as adding by implication, though it may be all very well for *you* – 'it is not for me to impugn the workings of Providence. I know better than that, I trust, and I have mentioned what the intentions of Providence are. Besides,' said Mr Podsnap, flushing high up among his hair-brushes, with a strong consciousness of personal affront, 'the subject is a very disagreeable one. I will go so far as to say it is an odious one. It is not one to be introduced among our wives and young persons, and I –' He finished with the flourish of his arm which added more expressively than any words, And I remove it from the face of the earth.

From *Our Mutual Friend* by Charles Dickens (London, 1865)

Walter Greenwood
HANKY PARK (1933)

Larry's presence, somehow, seemed to demand your best behaviour. You became so very conscious of the loose way of your speech when you heard him speaking. She suddenly discovered a thousand faults in herself, and, for a moment, felt dispirited at their enormity.

The moment passed: she listened to what he was saying.

'. . . And to find the cost of this present system you have only to look at our own lives and the lives of our parents and their parents. Labour never ending, constant struggles to pay the rent and to buy sufficient food and clothing; no time for anything that is bright and beautiful. We never see such things. All we see are these grey depressing streets; mile after mile of them; never ending . . . And the houses in which we are compelled to live are as though they have been designed by fiends in hell for our especial punishment. When work is regular we are just able to live from week to week: there is no surplus. But for ever, there hangs over us that dread threat of unemployment. Unemployment that can and does reduce most honest working folk to pauperdom, that saddles them with a debt that takes years to repay. Even at its best I say that this is not life. And it is not the lot of one or two individual families. Look around you here in Hanky Park; not a part but the whole of it is so affected. This existence is what is fobbed off on to us as Life. And Hanky Park is not the whole of England. In every industrial city of the land you will find such places as this, where such people as us who do the work of the world are forced to spend their days. *That* is the price we will continue to pay until you people awaken to the fact that Society has the means, the skill, and the knowledge to afford us the opportunity to become Men and Women in the fullest sense of those terms.' He stepped down; another man took his place.

From *Love on the Dole* by Walter Greenwood (1933; Vintage, 1993)

J.B. Priestley
RUSTY LANE (1934)

I have never seen such a picture of grimy desolation as that street offered me. If you put it, brick for brick, into a novel, people would not accept it, would condemn you as a caricaturist and talk about Dickens. The whole neighbourhood is mean and squalid, but this particular street seemed the worst of all. It would not matter very much – though it would matter – if only metal were kept there; but it happens that people live there, children are born there and grow up there. I saw some of them. I was being shown one of the warehouses, where

95

steel plates were stacked in the chill gloom, and we heard a bang and rattle on the roof. The boys, it seems, were throwing stones again. They were always throwing stones on the roof. We went out to find them, but only found three frightened little girls, who looked at us with round eyes in wet smudgy faces. No, they hadn't done it, the boys had done it, and the boys had just run away. Where they could run to, I cannot imagine. They need not have run away for me, because I could not blame them if they threw stones and stones and smashed every pane of glass for miles. Nobody can blame them if they grow up to smash everything that can be smashed. There ought to be no more of those lunches and dinners, at which political and financial and industrial gentlemen congratulate one another, until something is done about Rusty Lane and West Bromwich. While they still exist in their present foul shape, it is idle to congratulate ourselves about anything. They make the whole pomp of government here a miserable farce. The Crown, Lords and Commons are the Crown, Lords and Commons of Rusty Lane, West Bromwich. In the heart of the great empire on which the sun never sets, in the land of hope and glory, Mother of the Free, is Rusty Lane, West Bromwich. What do they know of England who only England know? The answer must be Rusty Lane, West Bromwich. And if there is another economic conference, let it meet there, in one of the warehouses, and be fed with bread and margarine and slabs of brawn. The delegates have seen one England, Mayfair in the season. Let them see another England next time, West Bromwich out of the season. Out of all seasons except the winter of our discontent.

From *English Journey* by J.B. Priestley (William Heinemann Ltd, in association with Victor Gollancz Ltd, 1934)

Ronald Murphy
SLAGTIPS (1994)

Like sentinels sombre and grey, grim reminders of bygone days, of pits whose shiny seams of coal first gave men work and then the dole. Of men and boys, slag and stone, early graves and broken bones.

Sweat and toil in headings, stalls, feared of gas and dread of falls,
Working hidden out of sight in another world where it's always night.

No moon nor stars are seen down there just total darkness everywhere.
No city lights to show the way, no sign to tell if it's night or day.

No birds there sing or fly on wing, no crocus grow to welcome spring.
No scented rose on summer breeze, no autumn leaves to fall from trees.

No winter snow or sun or sky, the changing seasons pass them by.

Their world of darkness underground where nothing changes all year round.
Where nature's beauty never treads, they spend their lives in fear and dread.

Oil lamps dim with tiny flame, lifeline, numbered, miner's name.
Spikes and chalk, moleskins, yorks, bread and cheese, tea-jack, corks.

Mandrills, shovels, clamps and nedge, hatchet, bar and heavy sledge.
Pairs of timber, props and flats, hornets, black-bats, hungry rats.

Horses with impressive names like Royal, Roman, Easter Flame.
Windroads, airways, double doors, brattice sheets draped to the floor.

Big vein, black vein, drams raced high, journey ropes that kick and fly.
Rippings, slag and drams of muck go up the pit to waiting trucks.

Engines, hooters, whistles blow, trucks are full and off they go.
Down the line for slag tip bound, carrying muck from underground.

Bloodstained stones and slag and shale, broken timber, bent up nails,
Brattice sheets all torn and ripped all went hurtling down the tips.

Waiting there in bitter cold, men and women, young and old,
Fingers, bodies numb to bone, picking coal from slag and stone.

But now the tips are grassed and green, its slag and stone by them unseen.
No sign of blood, of pain, or grief, that lies there buried underneath.

Nothing. Nothing to show unless you know of those sad days so long ago.

*(Ronald Murphy, the father of Paul Murphy MP, was a miner for 25 years
and then a TGWU shop steward)*

Bill Douglas
WE WILL BE FREE (1987)

This piece is taken from the film *Comrades* which was based on the Tolpuddle
Martyrs, a group of Dorchester labourers who were sentenced in 1834 to seven
years' transportation for forming a union.

He [George Loveless] hobbles across the street, continuing to look at the
ground as though he hopes to find something more. He hands the paper to a
gentleman bystander, pointing down to where he made his find.

The possessor of the paper is Mr Pitt. He looks up, turns.

We can see George now some distance away going up the street.

Mr Pitt reads from the paper:

PITT: 'God is our guide! From field, from wave,
        From plough, from anvil and from loom,
        We come, our country's rights to save,
        And speak the tyrant's faction's doom;
        We raise the watchword "Liberty",
        We will, we will, we will be free!'

George has reached the end of the road where there is an exchange of papers and a carriage waiting. He is helped on to the carriage.

PITT: 'God is our guide! No swords we draw,
        We kindle not war's battle fires,
        By reason, union, justice, law,
        We claim the birthright of our sires;
        We raise the watchword "Liberty",
        We will, we will, we will be free!'

The vehicle has turned amid the clatter of hoofs, comes towards us for a bit. Among the sightseers children run alongside. The carriage turns a corner disappearing from sight.

Mr Pitt is still looking after it has gone.

PITT: He meant this for you and others like you, not for me.

He hands the paper back to the Tramp, who looks moved as if he had never been given anything before.

PITT: When you have done with it, don't throw it away. Let it go from hand to hand. My task will be to teach the members of my class, injustice cannot be allowed to go unchallenged.

With that he hurries away, a sense of determination in his stride. The town is alive with a clatter of hoofs and wheels.

From *Comrades* by Bill Douglas (Faber & Faber)

John Stuart Mill
WHOSE RESPONSIBILITY? (1869)

First among existing social evils may be mentioned the evil of Poverty. The institution of Property is upheld and commended principally as being the means by which labour and frugality are insured their reward, and mankind enabled to emerge from indigence. It may be so; most Socialists allow that it has been so in earlier periods of history. But if the institution can do nothing more or better in this respect than it has hitherto done, its capabilities, they affirm, are very insignificant. What proportion of the population, in the most civilised countries of Europe, enjoy in their own persons anything worth naming of the benefits of property?

It may be said, that but for property in the hands of their employers they would be without daily bread; but, though this be conceded, at least their daily bread is all that they have; and that often in insufficient quantity; almost always of inferior quality; and with no assurance of continuing to have it at all; an immense proportion of the industrious classes being at some period or other of their lives (and all being liable to become) dependent, at least temporarily, on legal or voluntary charity. Any attempt to depict the miseries of indigence, or to estimate the proportion of mankind who in the most advanced countries are habitually given up during their whole existence to its physical and moral sufferings, would be superfluous here. This may be left to philanthropists, who have painted these miseries in colours sufficiently strong. Suffice it to say that the condition of numbers in civilised Europe, and even in England and France, is more wretched than that of most tribes of savages who are known to us.

It may be said that of this hard lot no one has any reason to complain, because it befalls those only who are outstripped by others, from inferiority of energy or of prudence. This, even were it true, would be a very small alleviation of the evil. If some Nero or Domitian were to require a hundred persons to run a race of their lives, on condition that the fifty or twenty who came in hindmost should be put to death, it would not be any diminution of the injustice that the strongest or nimblest would, except through some untoward accident, be certain to escape. The misery and the crime would be that any were put to death at all. So in the economy of society; if there be any who suffer physical privation or moral degradation, whose bodily necessities are either not satisfied or satisfied in a manner which only brutish creatures can be content with, this, though not necessarily the crime of society, is *pro tanto* a failure of the social arrangements. And to assert as a mitigation of the evil that those who thus suffer are the weaker members of the community, morally or physically, is to add insult to misfortune. Is weakness a justification of suffering?

Is it not, on the contrary, an irresistible claim upon every human being for protection against suffering? If the minds and feelings of the prosperous were in a right state, would they accept their prosperity if for the sake of it even one person near them was, for any other cause than voluntary fault, excluded from obtaining a desirable existence?

From 'Chapters on Socialism' in *John Stuart Mill: On Liberty and Other Writings*, edited by Stefan Collini (Cambridge University Press, 1989)

Robert Blatchford
MERRIE ENGLAND (1892-93)

You have very likely heard, Mr Smith, of the thing called Individualism. You may have read articles or heard speeches in which socialism has been assailed as an interference with the rights of the individual. You may have wondered why, among the rights of the individual, no place was given to the right to live; or that the apostles of Individualism should be so strangely blind to the danger of leaving private enterprise *un*curbed. But you need not wonder about these things, for Individualism is a relic of savagery, and its apologists would be agitating for the return of the good old individual right of carrying a stone club and living by promiscuous robbery and murder, were they not convinced that the law of supply and demand, although a more cowardly and brutal weapon than the cannibal's club, is infinitely more deadly and effective.

Society consists of individuals – so Herbert Spencer says. And that dogma, if it means anything, means that society is a concourse of independent atoms, and not a united whole. But you know that statement is not in accord with fact or reason – not to speak of morality. You know that society consists of a number of more or less antagonistic parties, united amongst themselves for purposes of social warfare, and that where an independent individual is found he is always either a good man, trying to persuade the combatants to reason and righteousness; or a bad man, trying to fleece them that his own nest may be warm.

How, indeed, can society be a multitude of unconnected units? I look in my dictionary, and I find the word 'society' defined as 'a union of persons in one interest; fellowship'. And clearly a society means a number of men joined by interest or affection. For how can that be a society which has no social connections? A mob of antagonistic individuals is a chaos, not a society.

And with regard to that claim that men should be left free to fight each for his own hand – is that civilisation or anarchy? And will it result in peace or in war, in prosperity or in disaster? Not civilisation, John, but savagery; not Christianity, but cannibalism is the spirit of this doctrine of selfishness and folly. And I ask you again in this case, as I did in the case of the gospel of 'avarice': is not love stronger than hate? And will not a society founded on love and justice certainly flourish, as the society founded on hate and strife will certainly perish?

Before you answer look around you at the state of England today, and cast back in your mind for the lessons of the nations that are gone. What is the apex of the gospel of avarice and of the law of supply and demand? Sweating! What is the result of the liberty of the individual to cozen the strong and destroy the weak for the sake of useless gain or worthless power? Does not one man wax rich by making many poor – one man dwell in a palace by keeping many in hovels? And are not the people crushed with taxation, which the impotent and lazy squander and misuse? . . .

Society, according to my philosophy, is a union of people for mutual advantage. Every member of a society must give up some small fraction of his own will and advantage in return for the advantages he gains by association with his fellows. One of the advantages he derives from association with his fellows is protection from injury. The chief function of government – which is the executive power of the society's will – is to protect the subject. Against whom is the subject to be protected? I should say against foreign enemies, against injury by fellow-subjects, and against calamities caused by his own ignorance. We will lay by the first and third propositions, and consider the second.

The subject is to be protected by the Government from injury by his fellow-subjects. Here I traverse the position of the individualists. They will restrain the assassin and the passer of base coin, but they will not suffer any interference with the sacred liberty of the slum landlord or the sweater. And I fail to see their reason.

There is no reason visible to my mind for empowering the Government, or society, to hang the man who steals a watch and murders the owner, except the reason I have given – that it is for the general advantage that society should be allowed to protect one of its members from injury by another. If that is the real reason why government may hang a Charles Peace or send an 'Artful Dodger' to gaol, then it is also a sufficient reason why government protection should be extended beyond the limits laid down in Mr Herbert's tracts. Because the sweater, and the rack-renter, and the respectable dealer in adulterated goods are not only morally worse than the footpad and the area-sneak, but they are also guilty of greater and more deadly injury to their fellow-subjects.

True, sweating and land-grabbing and other forms of the basest villainy are not illegal; and I would not have them legally meddled with. But I would alter the law so that they should be illegal. This, I presume, Mr Herbert would not do. He will only defend us from the garrotter and the confidence-trick man. But I think it is as bad for a railway company to work a man a hundred and eight hours for seventeen shillings, or for a landlord to charge rent for a death trap, or for a tailor to grind his hands down to a slavery that takes up all their waking hours and gives them in return a diet of bread and coffee, as for a thief to come and steal your false teeth. Nay, the sweater is altogether a more hateful, dangerous, deadly, and cowardly scoundrel than the pickpocket.

Of course, the sweater's slave and the railway porter are the 'free' parties to the bargain. They need not accept the bloodsucker's terms unless they choose. They have an alternative – they can starve. But I presume that even the most confirmed individualist would stop a man from jumping down a precipice, or throwing himself under a train. That would be physical injury, against which it is right to protect each other. But the poor girl who takes her suicide in the form of shirt-making is not to be interfered with. You must respect free contract and the liberty of the individual.

Individual liberty is what we all desire – so far as it is possible to have it. But it is *not* possible to have it in its complete form, whilst we live in communities. By living in communities, men get many advantages. It is not good for man to be alone. For the advantages that society gives us, we must make some sacrifice. We might well have much more individual liberty than we now have. We might easily have too much. We *have* too much – and too little – as things stand. A state of socialism would give us all as much liberty as we need. A state of Individualism – of anarchy – would give *some* of us more liberty than it is wise and beneficial we should have . . .

If it had not been for interference with the liberty of the individual and the freedom of contract in the past the lot of the workers would have been unbearable.

Do you know anything about the Truck Act, which abolished the nefarious custom of paying wages in bad food? Did you ever consider the effect of forbidding the payment of wages in public houses, or the employment of climbing-boys by sweeps? Have you ever read the history of the Factory Acts? . . .

You will find further particulars of these horrors, Mr Smith, in the Blue Books of the period. Read them; read also the Blue Books on the sweating system, and the reports of the Labour Commission; read the facts relating to the Truck Acts and the chain and nail trades, and then read Mrs Browning's pathetic poem of 'The Cry of the Children', and I think you will be cured of any lingering affection for the 'Freedom of Contract' and the 'Rights of the Individual'.

I quite understand Mr Herbert's desire for 'Liberty'. But we cannot have liberty while we have rascals. Liberty is another of the things we have to pay for the pleasure of the rascal's company. Now I think Individualism strengthens the hands of the rogue in his fight with the true man; and I think socialism would fortify the true men against the rascals. I grant you that State socialism would imply some interference with the liberty of the individual. But *which* individual? The scoundrel. Imagine a dozen men at sea in a boat with only two days' provisions. Would it be wise to consider the liberty of the individual? If the strongest man took all the food and left the others to starve would it be right or wrong for the eleven men to combine to bind him and divide all fairly? To let the strong or the cunning rob the weak or honest is Individualism. To prevent the rascal from taking what is not his own is socialism.

From *Merrie England* by Robert Blatchford (Clarion Office, 1893)

William Cobbett
LANCASHIRE GIRLS (1833)

We have, Sir, this night made one of the greatest discoveries ever made by a House of Commons, a discovery which will be hailed by the constituents of the Hon. Gentlemen behind me with singular pleasure. Hitherto, we have been told that our navy was the glory of the country, and that our maritime commerce and extensive manufactures were the mainstays of the realm. We have also been told that the land has its share in our greatness, and should justly be considered as the pride and glory of England. The Bank, also, has put in its claim to share in this praise, and has stated that public credit is due to it; but now, a most startling discovery has been made, namely, that all our greatness and prosperity, that our superiority over other nations, is owing to 300,000 little girls in Lancashire. We have made the notable discovery that, if these little girls work two hours less in a day than they do now, it would occasion the ruin of the country; that it would enable other nations to compete with us; and thus make an end to our boasted wealth, and bring us to beggary!

Speech in the House of Commons quoted in *Class and Conflict in Nineteenth-Century England* by Patricia Hollis (London, 1973)

John Elliott McCutcheon
THE HARTLEY COLLIERY DISASTER (1862)
(204 men and boys paid with their lives for the hard lesson that a coalmine needs two shafts.)

They had been right into the Yard Seam and had found all the men and boys. They were all dead. They were lying not far from the shaft, waiting for the help which never came. They were lying side by side, tiny pit boys clinging to their fathers. The pit ponies' corn bins were empty, but corn was found in the pockets of some of the men. Near where they lay a pit pony was found dead but untouched.

It now became necessary to break this sad news, officially, to the waiting crowd. The difficult task was undertaken by Mr John Taylor, the colliery viewer from Backworth. A great hush descended on the crowd as he cleared his throat to speak. Quietly and sympathetically he told of the tragic discoveries. There were lots of corpses but not a living soul had been found.

'Have the sinkers been as far as the Low Main Staple?' cried one man.

They hadn't as yet, Mr Taylor replied. He appealed for them to be patient a little longer. The sinkers had gone as far as they could with safety. It's no use, he said forcefully, throwing away good lives to obtain dead bodies. Finally, he

103

requested those present to communicate this intelligence to any of the relatives and friends who were not present.

Despite all the dark forebodings of this tragic end, Mr Taylor's announcement fell like a thunderbolt. There was a crushing finality about it. And it told many of those present that they were now widows, orphans or childless.

From *The Hartley Colliery Disaster, 1862*
by John Elliott McCutcheon (E. McCutcheon, 1963)

Neil Kinnock
THE NEED FOR A PLATFORM (1987)

Why am I the first Kinnock in a thousand generations to be able to get to university? Was it because *all* our predecessors were 'thick'? Did they lack talent – those people who could sing, and play, and recite poetry; those people who could make wonderful, beautiful things with their hands; those people who could dream dreams, see visions; those people who had such a sense of perception as to know in times so brutal, so oppressive, that they could win their way out of that by coming together?

Were those people not university material? Couldn't they have knocked off their A-levels in an afternoon? But why didn't they get it? Was it because they were weak – those people who could work eight hours a day underground and then come up and play football? Weak? Those women who could survive eleven child-bearings, were they weak? Those people who could stand with their backs and legs straight and face the great – the people who had control over their lives, the ones that owned their workplaces and tried to own them – and tell them 'No, I won't take your orders'. Were they weak? Does anybody really think that they didn't get what we had because they didn't have the talent, or the strength, or the endurance, or the commitment? Of course not. It was because there was no platform on which they could stand.

From a speech to the Welsh Labour Party Annual Conference,
in *Thorns and Roses: Speeches 1983-91* by Neil Kinnock (Hutchinson, 1992)

James Maxton
THE WILL TO SOCIALISM (1927)

Why should people live lives of poverty and toil? Why should people rise in the morning fearing to face life because of the evils, the cares and the sorrows it brings. Should life not rather be a carefree joyous adventure that all should meet with confidence and hope? This great world we live in is full of interest, beauty and variety and is peopled by men and women with infinite capacity for happiness. Through the centuries men and women have struggled to extract the secrets of nature and of mother earth and today we have amassed a great store of knowledge and of skill that give mankind the control of the earth and its forces so that these may be pressed into the service of humanity. From tropical zone to frigid pole the fruits of the soil are garnered and conveyed to all parts of the globe and men of all races work in the service of all races.

Invention and discovery from day to day bring men closer together, pile up the quantities of wealth produced at ever increasing rate and ever with increasing speed transport it thousands of miles across the earth's surface, over the sea or even through the air, yet men and women starve and children cry for bread because a very few men claim the earth as their own and make the millions toil for them.

The task of the socialist movement in every country in the world is to lighten the workers' toil and increase the supply of material things of life in every home, to remove the horrible insecurity that kills the joy of life and to sweep the owning classes from the shoulders of the disowned.

The scientist has played his part, the writer has played his part, the traveller and explorer have played their parts and now the worker, the common people, must play their part. The wealthy and powerful, blinded by their material wealth, do not see the real wealth of humanity itself and to the worker is left the task of freeing mankind from the fetters of servitude. The will to liberty, the will to security, the will to happiness are what is necessary. Then comes the need for an organisation to give expression to that will and after that a clear idea of the social structure which can enable mankind freely and easily to give his quota of service and receive his full reward.

The socialist movement fulfils these two functions – it tries to create the will, it builds up the organisation to express it and it has devised a social structure that can produce the world's needs and supply them in secure and certain fashion. It calls aloud for the willing help of good and true men and women who are not afraid to fight for a just cause.

Quoted in *James Maxton: Beloved Rebel* by John McNair
(George Allen & Unwin, 1955)

J.B. Priestley
WHY? (1934)

It was all very puzzling. Was Jarrow still in England or not? Had we exiled Lancashire and the North-east coast? Were we no longer on speaking terms with cotton weavers and minders and platers and riveters? Why had nothing been done about these decaying towns and their workless people? Was everybody waiting for a miracle to happen? I knew that doles had been given out, Means Tests applied, training places opened, socks and shirts and old books distributed by the Personal Service League and the like; but I was not thinking of feeble gestures of that kind, of the sort of charity you might extend to a drunken old ruffian begging at the back door. I meant something constructive and creative. If Germans had been threatening these towns instead of Want, Disease, Hopelessness, Misery, something would have been done quickly enough. Yet Jarrow and Hebburn looked much worse to me than some of the French towns I saw at the end of the war, towns that had been occupied by the enemy for four years. Why has there been no plan for these areas, these people? The dole is part of no plan; it is a mere declaration of intellectual bankruptcy. You have only to spend a morning in the dole country to see that it is all wrong. Nobody is getting any substantial benefit, any reasonable satisfaction out of it. Nothing is encouraged by it except a shambling dull-eyed poor imitation of life. The Labour Exchanges stink of defeated humanity. The whole thing is unworthy of a great country that in its time has given the world some nobly creative ideas. We ought to be ashamed of ourselves. Anybody who imagines that this is a time for self-congratulation has never poked his nose outside Westminster, the City and Fleet Street. And, I concluded, he has not used his eyes and ears much even in Westminster and Fleet Street.

From *English Journey* by J.B. Priestley (William Heinemann Ltd, in association with Victor Gollancz Ltd, 1934)

L.T. Hobhouse
THE STATE AS ENABLER (1911)

That system holds out no hope of an improvement which shall bring the means of such a healthy and independent existence as should be the birthright of every citizen of a free state within the grasp of the mass of the people of the United Kingdom. It is this belief slowly penetrating the public mind which has turned it to new thoughts of social regeneration. The sum and substance of the changes that I have mentioned may be expressed in the principle that the individual cannot stand alone, but that between him and the State there is a reciprocal obligation. He owes the State the duty of industriously working for himself and his family. He is not to exploit the labour of his young children, but to submit to the public requirements for their education, health, cleanliness and general well-being. On the other side society owes to him the means of maintaining a civilised standard of life, and this debt is not adequately discharged by leaving him to secure such wages as he can in the higgling of the market.

This view of social obligation lays increased stress on public but by no means ignores private responsibility. It is a simple principle of applied ethics that responsibility should be commensurate with power. Now, given the opportunity of adequately remunerated work, a man has the power to earn his living. It is his right and his duty to make the best use of his opportunity, and if he fails he may fairly suffer the penalty of being treated as a pauper or even, in an extreme case, as a criminal. But the opportunity itself he cannot command with the same freedom. It is only within narrow limits that it comes within the sphere of his control. The opportunities of work and the remuneration for work are determined by a complex mass of social forces which no individual, certainly no individual workman, can shape. They can be controlled, if at all, by the organised action of the community, and therefore, by a just apportionment of responsibility, it is for the community to deal with them.

But this, it will be said, is not liberalism but socialism. Pursuing the economic rights of the individual we have been led to contemplate a socialistic organisation of industry. But a word like socialism has many meanings, and it is possible that there should be a liberal socialism, as well as a socialism that is illiberal.

There emerges a distinction between unsocial and social freedom. Unsocial freedom is the right of man to use his powers without regard to the wishes or interests of anyone but himself. Such freedom is theoretically possible for an individual. It is antithetic to all public control. It is theoretically impossible for a plurality of individuals living in mutual contact. Socially it is a contradiction, unless the desires of all men were automatically attuned to social ends. Social freedom, then, for any epoch short of the millennium rests on restraint. It is a freedom that can be enjoyed by all the members of a community, and it is the freedom to choose among those lines of activity which do not involve injury to others. As experience of the social effects of action ripens, and as the social conscience is awakened, the conception of injury is widened and insight into its causes is deepened. The area of restraint is therefore increased. But, inasmuch as injury inflicted is itself crippling to the sufferer, as it lowers his health, confines his life, cramps his powers, so the prevention of such injury sets him free. The restraint of the aggressor is the freedom of the sufferer, and only by restraint on the actions by which men injure one another do they as a whole community gain freedom in all course of conduct that can be pursued without ultimate social disharmony . . .

Thus individualism, when it grapples with the facts, is driven no small distance along socialist lines. Once again we have found that to maintain individual freedom and equality we have to extend the sphere of social control. But to carry through the real principles of liberalism, to achieve social liberty and living equality of rights, we shall have to probe still deeper. We must not assume any of the rights of property as axiomatic. We must look at their actual working and consider how they affect the life of society . . .

We said above that it was the function of the State to secure the conditions upon which mind and character may develop themselves. Similarly we may say now that the function of the State is to secure conditions upon which its citizens are able to win by their own efforts all that is necessary to a full civic efficiency. It is not for the State to feed, house, or clothe them. It is for the State to take care that the economic conditions are such that the normal man who is not defective in mind or body or will can by useful labour feed, house, and clothe himself and his family. The 'right to work' and the right to a 'living wage' are just as valid as the rights of a person or property. That is to say, they are integral conditions of a good social order. A society in which a single honest man of normal capacity is definitely unable to find the means of maintaining himself by useful work is to that extent suffering from malorganisation. There is somewhere a defect in the social system, a hitch in the economic machine. Now, the individual workman cannot put the machine straight. He is the last person to have any say in the control of the market. It is not his fault if there is over-production in his industry, or if a new and cheaper process has been introduced which makes his particular skill, perhaps the product of years of application, a drug in the market. He does not direct or regulate industry. He is not responsible for its ups and downs, but he has to pay for them. That is why it is not charity but justice for which he is asking. Now, it may be infinitely difficult to meet his demand. To do so may involve a far-reaching economic reconstruction. The industrial questions involved may be so little understood that we may easily make matters worse in the attempt to make them better. All this shows the difficulty in finding means of meeting this particular claim of justice, but it does not shake its position as a claim of justice. A right is a right none the less though the means of securing it be imperfectly known; and the workman who is unemployed or underpaid through economic malorganisation will remain a reproach not to the charity but to the justice of society as long as he is to be seen in the land.

From *Liberalism* by L.T. Hobhouse (Williams & Norgate, 1911)

Fred Henderson
POSITIVE LIBERTY (1911)

If the absence of restraint upon the exercise of man's faculties is the merely negative aspect of liberty then surely the positive aspect of liberty is the presence of actual opportunity for the exercise of those faculties.

It is not enough that a man should have the right to use his earnings as he thinks best. To enjoy liberty in the full sense, he must first of all have the positive opportunities to get those earnings. He must have access to opportunity before he can exercise his power of initiative or his free play of intelligence upon it.

If a civilised community is to safeguard effectively the liberty of its members, it has, therefore, a twofold duty: the negative duty of refraining from coercion or restraint except so far as is necessary to prevent men from encroaching on the liberty of others or becoming a nuisance or a danger to the community; and the positive duty of providing and keeping open the widest possible range of opportunity, and guaranteeing to its citizens the right of access to that opportunity.

Thus liberty in its negative aspect means what the State is to refrain from doing; while liberty in its positive aspect means constructive civilisation, and finds its expression in the activities of the State.

The whole worth and meaning of civilisation is to make men secure in the possession and enjoyment of this opportunity, this ever widening range of opportunity. Our advance in civilisation depends upon the extent to which the individual is set free from the individual gamble against the chances and accidents of life. Progress consists in men ceasing to have to struggle for their old objects, and so being set free to work for new ideals; achieving security in lower things, and going on to higher things. The difference between civilisation and savagery is just in that. . . .

And how are they so set free? By co-operation and collective action. The old parable of the bundle of sticks holds good. It is the business of a civilised community to set its members free in this way; constantly to gather up the attainment of the race and embody it in secure collective provision – in other words in access to opportunity – so that individual gambling and uncertainty ceases in connection with that attainment; the struggle being constantly raised to the next higher level of human endeavour until that in time and turn becomes part of the secure and completely mastered human heritage. That is the inner process of all civilisation – constantly to widen the range of that provision for human needs within which struggle ends and uncertainty ceases, and men stand secure within the shelter and guarantee of the collective life.

That is constructive civilisation; the positive as distinguished from the negative aspect of liberty; the 'something more' than the mere absence of restraint . . .

From *The Case for Socialism* by Fred Henderson (Messrs Jarrolds Ltd, 1911)

John Maynard Keynes
A QUESTION OF DEVELOPMENT (1939)

The question is about whether we are prepared to move out of the nineteenth-century *laissez-faire* state into an era of liberal socialism, by which I mean a system where we can act as an organised community for common purposes and to promote social and economic justice, whilst respecting and protecting the individual – his freedom of choice, his faith, his mind and its expression, his enterprise and his prosperity.

From *The New Statesman*

Clement Attlee
LIBERTY FOR ALL (1937)

The first point which I desire to make is that the aim of socialism is to give greater freedom to the individual. British socialists have never made an idol of the State, demanding that individuals should be sacrificed to it. They have never accepted the beehive or the ants' nest as an ideal. They leave that to the advocates of the corporate state. They have never desired that men and women should be drilled and regimented physically and mentally so that they should be all of one pattern. On the contrary, they appreciate that the wealth of a society is in its variety, not its uniformity. Progress is not towards, but away from the herd. It is no part of the socialist idea that there should be in every human activity an orthodox pattern to which all must conform.

State action is advocated by socialists not for its own sake, but because it is necessary to prevent the oppression of an individual by others, and to secure that the liberty of the one does not restrict that of others, or conflict with the common good of society.

Those who attack socialism on the ground that it will mean the enslavement of the individual belong invariably to the class of people whose possession of property has given them liberty at the expense of the enslavement of others. The possession of property in a capitalist society has given liberty to a fortunate minority who hardly realise how much its absence means enslavement. The majority of the people of this country are under orders and discipline for the whole of their working day. Freedom is left behind when they 'clock in' and only resumed when they go out. Such liberty as they have got as workers has been the fruit of long and bitter struggles by the trade unions. But a far greater restriction on liberty than this is imposed on the vast majority of the people of this country by poverty. There is the narrowing of choice in everything. The poor man cannot choose his domicile. He must be prepared at the shortest notice to abandon all his social activities, to leave the niche which he had made for himself in the structure of society, and to remove himself elsewhere, if economic circumstances demand it. How little would those who so easily recommend this to the workers appreciate being transferred from their pleasant homes in Surrey or Buckingamshire to Whitechapel or the Black Country. Yet this is an ordinary incident of working-class life. The poor man is restricted in his food, his clothing, his amusements, and his occupation. The liberty which it is feared socialism may restrict is the liberty of the few . . .

The liberty which socialists desire is liberty for all. The restrictions which will be imposed will be those only which are essential to secure it. The current misconception of a socialist society as one in which everyone will be subject to the constant interference of an army of officials is due to the fact that in order to avoid the worst abuses of capitalism society has had to institute a whole series of services of inspection to check the anti-social actions of those engaged in private enterprise. Factory inspectors are necessary because many employers lack social sense, just as 'speed cops' are needed because many motorists lack road sense and a feeling of responsibility to the community. Their presence is not due to the socialist but the anti-socialist spirit.

It is true that in the socialist State people will be deprived of the right of living in idleness at the expense of the community, but this right is in practice denied to the majority already by their economic circumstances. On the other hand, when the community is organised for service instead of profit there will be no such thing as the enforced deprivation of the right to work which is now imposed on nearly two million people in this country at the height of a trade boom, and on many more whenever there is a slump. The denial of the right to work is one of the great infringements of liberty imposed under capitalism, for it deprives the individual of the right of expressing his personality and exercising his functions as a citizen.

My conclusion is that men and women will be more free, not less free, under socialism. Freedom will be more widely disseminated. There will be no attempt made to impose rigid uniformity. There will be no forcible suppression of adverse opinion. The real change will be that a man will become a citizen, with the rights of a free man during his hours of labour just as in his leisure time. This does not mean that he will have the right to do just as he will. He will have freedom within the necessary restraints which life in a complex society imposes.

From *The Labour Party in Perspective* by Clement Attlee
(Victor Gollancz Ltd, 1937)

William Temple
EXTENDING CHOICE (1942)

The primary principle of Christian ethics and Christian politics must be respect for every person simply as a person. If each man and woman is a child of God, whom God loves and for whom Christ died, then there is in each a worth absolutely independent of all usefulness to society. The person is primary, not the society; the State exists for the citizen, not the citizen for the State. The first aim of social progress must be to give the fullest possible scope for the exercise of all powers and qualities which are distinctly personal; and of these the most fundamental is deliberate choice.

Consequently, society must be so arranged as to give to every citizen the maximum opportunity for making deliberate choices and the best possible training for the use of that opportunity. In other words, one of our first considerations will be the widest possible extension of personal responsibility; it is the responsible exercise of deliberate choice which most fully expresses personality and best deserves the great name of freedom.

Freedom is the goal of politics. To establish and secure true freedom is the primary object of all right political action. For it is in and through his freedom that a man makes fully real his personality – the quality of one made in the image of God.

Freedom is a great word, and like other great words is often superficially understood. It has been said that to those who have enough of this world's goods the claim to freedom means 'Leave us alone', while to those who have not enough it means 'Give us a chance'. This important difference of interpretation rests on a single understanding of freedom as absence of compulsion or restraint. But if that is all the word means, freedom and futility are likely to be so frequently combined as to seem inseparable. For nothing is so futile as the unhampered satisfaction of sporadic impulses; that is the sort of existence which leads through boredom to suicide. Freedom so far as it is a treasure must be freedom *for* something as well as freedom *from* something. It must be the actual ability to form and carry out a purpose. This implies discipline – at first external discipline to check the wayward impulses before there is a real purpose in life to control them, and afterwards a self-discipline directed to the fulfilment of the purpose of life when formed. Freedom, in short, is self-control, self-determination, self-direction. To train citizens in the capacity for freedom and to give them scope for free action is the supreme end of all true politics . . .

Liberty is actual in the various cultural and commercial and local associations that men form. In each of these a man can feel that he counts for something and that others depend on him as he on them. The State which would serve and guard liberty will foster all such groupings, giving them freedom to guide their own activities provided these fall within the general order of the communal life and do not injure the freedom of other similar

112

associations. Thus the State becomes the Community of communities – or rather the administrative organ of that Community – and there is much to be said for the contention that its representative institutions should be so designed as to represent the various groupings of men rather than (or as well as) individuals . . .

In any case the Christian conception of men as members in the family of God forbids the notion that freedom may be used for self-interest. It is justified only when it expresses itself through fellowship; and a free society must be so organised as to make this effectual; in other words it must be rich in sectional groupings or fellowships within the harmony of the whole.

From *Christianity and the Social Order* by William Temple
(Penguin 1942; reprinted Pelican 1958)

Harold J. Laski
JUSTICE IS THE TWIN-SISTER OF FREEDOM (1925)

No accusation against socialism is more common than the taunt that its exponents do not understand the worth of freedom. It is supposed to be a system under which men will lose all trace of individuality. They will, we are warned, be regimented and dragooned by a powerful bureaucracy which will prescribe each item of their daily lives. The socialist State is depicted as though it were a platonic Utopia in which the guardians were replaced by the grim henchmen of Lenin and Trotsky. The indictment varies in its emphasis. Sometimes it is against the family that the socialist appeal is said to be directed; and we are bidden to compare the proud freedom of Laburnum Villa with the relentless organisation of some nationalised phalanstery. Sometimes it is the artist and the thinker who are said to be in peril; for in a state like the socialist State the absence of a leisured class is held to involve the necessary disappearance of art and philosophy. Nor, we are told, will the adventurer's risk remain; the boy who is engaged as an apprentice in a motor factory can never dream of attaining to the eminence of Mr Ford. A world reduced to plan and system will lose the colour and variety that are the essence of freedom. We shall lose the marks of separate and identifiable personality. We shall become items in a vast card catalogue, marionettes responsible to the control of others. Socialism, so it is said, involves a world of robots living by the orders of officials. It is a system from which all chance and vividness have gone; in which no man remains, as now, eager and able to be master of the event . . .

The socialist approaches the problem of freedom from a different angle. The purpose of society, he argues, is to enable each man to be himself at his best. Freedom is the system of conditions which makes that purpose effectively possible. Those conditions define themselves out of the historic record. They are impossible in the presence of special privilege, whether political, or religious, or economic. They are impossible unless I can report fully to those who govern what my experience of life is doing to me. They are impossible, also, unless my education has been of such a kind as to enable me to make articulate the meaning of my experience. They are impossible, further, unless I am safeguarded against the pressure of material want. I must have a wage that gives me a reasonable standard of life. I must work each day only that number of hours which will leave opportunity for creative leisure. And, in the hours of work, I must live under conditions which I assist in making. I must have the sense that they are intelligible in the same way that the orders of a medical man or a sanitary engineer are intelligible; they must be referable, that is to say, to principles which can be established as rational by scientific investigation. I must feel that the State recognises my equal claim with others, in the things essential to the good life; and that no one is admitted to an equal claim save as he pays for it by personal service. There must be equality in these essential things for all before there is superfluity for any; and the differences that exist between the rewards of men must be differences that do not weight the scales unduly in favour of those above the minimum level.

It is the socialist case that without these things there cannot be freedom. Broadly, they imply equality; and their argument is that freedom and equality are inseparable. It is insisted, further, that in an individualist regime like the present anything in the nature of equality is unattainable. For those who own in any society the essential instruments of production are able, in the nature of things, to affect the emphasis of social good towards themselves. It is their view of what is right that prevails; and their view of what is right will, in general, coincide with a policy which makes their own interest the index to what ought to be done. It therefore becomes necessary to socialise the ownership of the essential means of production . . . The socialist does not dogmatise as to the forms such social ownership should take. All that he insists is that until they are effectively the possession of the community, they cannot be fully administered in the interest of the community. That means such administration as will realise the system of conditions we call freedom . . .

'I feel sure,' wrote William Morris, in perhaps the noblest of his lectures, 'I feel sure that the time will come when people will find it difficult to believe that a rich community such as ours, having such command over external nature, could have submitted to live such a mean, shabby, dirty life as we do.' But this, it is said, is all utopian; it forgets the ignobility of human nature. It makes abstraction of the ignorance of men, their laziness, their brutality. It is to expect from them an effort and a quality of effort that they have neither the endurance nor the capacity to undertake.

That is the kind of pessimism that has always been an essential part of the tactic of reaction. We have to build our philosophy on hopes and not on fears. We have to lay the foundations of our systems on what the courage of men has achieved, not on what their cowardice has failed in achieving. Almost every progressive change has met opposition on the ground of its impossibility; and every progressive change has been achieved because a handful of idealists have refused to admit it was impossible. The real sin in social philosophy is lowness of aim. We need not cry for the sun; but, at least equally, we need not deny the possibility of light. Men, whether they will or not, are members of a commonwealth which can be preserved only as they discover the reality of fellowship. They will discover it only as they seek to experiment with the best of themselves. But, so to experiment, we need to be members of a State to which the allegiance of men is given with a passion at once vivid and intelligent, and, to that end, it must be a State conceived in justice. For justice is the twin sister of freedom and each lives in the victory of the other.

From *Socialism and Freedom* (Fabian Tract no. 216) by Harold J. Laski (1925)

R.H.S. Crossman
ENLARGING FREEDOM OF CHOICE (1952)

This is the point of departure for a modern theory of socialism. Instead of regarding social change as tending towards the enlargement of freedom, we must assume that increased concentration of power, whether in the form of technological development or social organisation, will always produce exploitation, injustice and inequality in a society, unless the community possesses a social conscience strong enough to civilise them . . .

In the nineteenth century this challenge was the task of liberalism. Today it has fallen to socialism. But we cannot fulfil it so long as we base our policy on the materialist fallacy that material progress *makes* men either free or equal. One particularly vicious form of this fallacy is the belief that economics are the determinant factors in social change and that, if we achieve economic justice, we automatically secure human freedom . . .

The planned economy and the centralisation of power are no longer socialist objectives. They are developing all over the world as the result of the Political Revolution, and the process is accelerated by the prevalence of war economy. The main task of socialism today is to prevent the concentration of power in the hands of *either* industrial management *or* the State bureaucracy – in brief, to distribute responsibility and so to enlarge freedom of choice.

From 'Towards a Philosophy of Socialism' in *New Fabian Essays*,
edited by R.H.S. Crossman (Turnstile Press, 1952)

R.H.Tawney
WE MEAN FREEDOM (1953)

There is no such thing as freedom in the abstract, divorced from the realities of a specific time and place. Whatever else it may or may not imply, it involves a power of choice between alternatives – a choice which is real, not merely nominal, between alternatives which exist in fact, not only on paper. It means, in short, the ability to do – or refrain from doing – definite things, at a definite moment, in definite circumstances, or it means nothing at all. Because a man is most a man when he thinks, wills, and acts, freedom deserves the sublime things which poets have said about it; but, as part of the prose of everyday life, it is quite practical and realistic. Every individual possesses certain requirements – ranging from the material necessities of existence to the need to express himself in speech and writing, to share in the conduct of affairs of common interest, and to worship God in his own way or to refrain from worshipping Him – the satisfaction of which is necessary to his welfare. Reduced to its barest essentials, his freedom consists in the opportunity secured him, within the limits set by nature and the enjoyment of similar opportunities by his fellows, to take the action needed in order to ensure that these requirements are satisfied.

It is not my intention to add yet another catalogue of essential rights to the libraries of such lists which already exist; but two observations apply to all of them. In the first place, if the rights are to be an effective guarantee of freedom, they must not be merely formal, like the right of all who can afford to dine at the Ritz. They must be such that, whenever the occasion arises to exercise them, they can in fact be exercised. The rights to vote and to combine, if not wholly valueless, are obviously attenuated, when the use of the former means eviction and of the latter the sack; the right to education, if poverty arrests its use in mid-career; the right to the free choice of an occupation, if the expenses of entering a profession are prohibitive; the right to earn a living, if enforced unemployment is recurrent; the right to justice, if few men of small earnings can afford the cost of litigation; the right 'to life, liberty, and the pursuit of happiness', if the environment is such as to ensure that, as in a not distant past, a considerable proportion of those born will die within twelve months, and that the happiness-investments of the remainder are a gambling stock.

In the second place, the rights which are essential to freedom must be such as to secure the liberties of all, not merely of a minority. Some sage has remarked that marriage would not be regarded as a national institution if, while five per cent of the population were polygamous, the majority passed their lives unsolaced and unencumbered by husbands or wives. The same is true of freedom. A society in which some groups can do much what they please, while others can do little of what they ought, may have virtues of its own; but freedom is not one of them. It is free in so far, and only in so far, as all the elements composing it are able in fact, not merely in theory, to make the most

116

of their powers, to grow to their full stature, to do what they conceive to be their duty, and – since liberty should not be too austere – to have their fling when they feel like it. In so far as the opportunity to lead a life worthy of human beings is restricted to a minority, what is commonly described as freedom would more properly be called privilege . . .

The only sound test of a political doctrine is its practical effect on the lives of human beings. The results of this doctrine we know, and it need not, therefore, be discussed at length. It is perfectly true, of course, that there have been circumstances – those, for example, of a simple economic system combined with political absolutism – in which the chief enemy of freedom was the despotism of an autocrat, and in which, therefore, the obvious way of enlarging freedom was to insist that as many spheres of life as possible should be excluded from his field of action. It should be equally obvious that, in the different conditions of an industrial civilisation, the effect of that alluring formula is precisely the opposite.

It is constantly assumed by privileged classes that, when the State refrains from intervening in any department of economic or social affairs, what remains as the result of its inaction is liberty. In reality, as far as the mass of mankind are concerned, what commonly remains is, not liberty, but tyranny. In urban communities with dense populations, or in great productive undertakings employing armies of workers, someone must make rules and see that they are kept, or life becomes impossible and the wheels do not turn. If public power does not make them, the effect is not that every individual is free to make them for himself. It is that they are made by private power – by landlords interested in increasing rents or by capitalists interested in increasing profits. The result, in either case, is not freedom, but a dictatorship, which is not the less oppressive because largely unconscious, and because those whom it profits regard it, quite sincerely, as identical with liberty.

The classical example in the past, so far as the wage-earners were concerned, was the condition of British workers in the days when trade unions were still feeble, industrial codes crude, social services in their infancy, and measures either to prevent unemployment or to enable its victims to weather the storm not yet in existence. The classical example in the present generation was the condition of many American workers down almost to yesterday. When, just over thirty years ago, I first visited Washington, I was informed on good authority that the miners in West Virginia were in trenches behind barbed wire; that the owners had a corps of snipers and a captive military . . .

The war should have taught us one lesson, if it has taught us nothing else. It is that it is idle to blazon liberty, equality, and fraternity on the façades of public buildings, if to display the same motto in factories and mines would arouse only the cynical laughter that greets a reminder of idealisms turned sour and hopes unfulfilled. What men desire is, not paragraphs in constitutions, but results, in the form of arrangements which ensure them the essentials of a civilised existence and show a proper respect for their dignity as human beings. If they do not get them in one way, they will try to get them in another. If the interpretation given to freedom reduces it to a formal phrase, they will not fight for it against an alternative which pretends, at least, to offer them substance, not a shadow. We are not ignorant what that alternative is. Should some gentlemanly version of fascism – it will be called, of course, not fascism, but True Democracy – ever arrive in this country, it will be established, not by the tyranny of a ruthless minority, but as the result of the indifference of an apathetic majority, so sickened by shams as to yield to any regime which promises them the practical conditions of a tolerable life, without which freedom is a phantom.

If socialists are to restore to the idea of freedom the magic which once belonged to it, they must bring it down to earth. They must state its meaning in realistic and constructive terms, not as a possession to be defended, but as a goal to be achieved. They must prove that it is they, not the interests that use it as a stalking-horse, who are the true champions of the faith. They must make it evident that their policy is to end economic, as well as political, tyranny, by making economic, as well as political, power responsible to authorities acting for the nation.

From *The Attack and Other Papers* by R.H. Tawney (George Allen & Unwin, 1953)

Barbara Wootton
ARGUING FOR FREEDOMS (1945)

The freedoms that matter in ordinary life are definite and concrete; and they change with the changing ways of different ages and different civilisations. Freedom today might mean, for instance, freedom to ask for your cards and sweep out of an objectionable job; freedom to say what you think of the Government in language of your own choosing; freedom to join, or refuse to join, the Transport and General Workers' Union; freedom to start a rival union on your own; freedom to be a Freemason, a Catholic or a Plymouth Brother; freedom from concentration camps, official spying and detention without trial; freedom to stand for Parliament or the parish council on any programme that you like; freedom to strike or not to strike; freedom to wear a nightdress or pyjamas if you prefer. No one would suggest that all these freedoms are of equal importance; nor do these examples necessarily cover all the freedoms that we actually have, can have, or ought to have. The relative value of different freedoms, and the conditions under which they can in fact be realised are difficult and debatable matters, and are, in fact, debated in the pages that follow. But a random list of typical contemporary freedoms is useful as a reminder that free*dom* has to be perpetually reinterpreted into free*doms*. You can philosophise endlessly about freedom; but in daily life it is freedoms that you want . . .

It is, however, possible to use the word freedom in such a comprehensive way that it covers practically every conceivable social end. For instance, a full belly and an educated mind are commonly thought of today as good things in themselves; and the view is widely held that it is the business of the State to see that people are in fact in a position to enjoy these blessings. But the use of the terms 'freedom from want' and 'freedom from ignorance' to describe these desirable conditions is liable to confuse any serious discussion of freedom, and to obscure real problems. For in this way the term freedom is easily stretched so wide as to be emptied of distinctive meaning; and the very possibility of conflict, real enough in experience, between freedom and other praiseworthy social ends is disposed of by a verbal trick. The fact is, of course, that people's freedom – their ability to do what they want – is affected in many and complex ways by nearly every kind of organised social activity. Thus, one of the reasons for desiring a full stomach is that, if your stomach is empty, you will not be free to do anything else until you have filled it. But it is absurd to infer from this either that freedom consists in, and is identical with, a state of repletion, or that the limitation which the pangs of hunger impose on your freedom is the only reason for wishing to be rid of those pangs. A condition of well-fed, well-housed, well-clad, even well-entertained, slavery is not an imaginary impossibility. It is only too possible. But it is not freedom. Freedom should not be defined in terms which, even by implication, deny the possibility that a high degree of material well-being may be accompanied by deprivation of freedom. Prisoners would not become free men even if they were looked after as well as racehorses . . .

Nevertheless, I doubt if the difference between freedom 'from' and freedom 'to' amounts to much more than the habit of calling the freedoms that we already enjoy by one set of names, and those which we lack by another. If this country were to become subject to a Hitlerite gestapo, the vocal classes would sigh for freedom *from* spying and arbitrary arrest, just as the unemployed used to clamour for freedom *from* want. All freedoms are simultaneously freedom *to* do what you want, and freedom *from* whatever prevents you from doing this. The question whether emphasis is laid upon the obstacles, or upon the use to be made of the freedom, is a question which of the two, in the circumstances of the moment, happens to loom larger. It has nothing to do with the qualitative nature of different freedoms, or the purpose to which they are put.

From *Freedom Under Planning* by Barbara Wootton (George Allen & Unwin, 1945)

Richard Titmuss
ENTERING GIFT RELATIONSHIPS (1970)

In a positive sense we believe that policy and processes should enable men to be free to choose to give to unnamed strangers. They should not be coerced or constrained by the market. In the interests of the freedom of all men they should not, however, be free to sell their blood or decide on the specific destination of the gift. The choice between these claims – between different kinds of freedom – has to be a social policy decision; in other words, it is a moral and political decision for society as a whole.

There are other aspects of freedom raised in this study which are or can be the concern of social policy. Viewed negatively or positively they relate to the freedom of men not to be exploited in situations of ignorance, uncertainty, unpredictability and captivity; not to be excluded by market forces from society and from giving relationships, and not to be forced in all circumstances – and particularly the circumstances described in this study – to choose always their own freedom at the expense of other people's freedom.

There is more than one answer and there should be more than one choice in responding to the cry 'Why should I not live as I like?'. The private market in blood, in profit-making hospitals, operating theatres, laboratories and in other sectors of social life limits the answers and narrows the choices for all men – whatever freedoms it may bestow, for a time, on some men to live as they like. It is the responsibility of the State, acting sometimes through the processes we have called 'social policy' to reduce or eliminate or control the forces of market coercions which place men in situations in which they have less freedom or little freedom to make moral choices and to behave altruistically if they so will.

The notion of social rights – a product of the twentieth century – should thus embrace the 'Right to Give' in non-material as well as material ways. 'Gift relationships', as we have described them, have to be seen in their totality and not just as moral elements in blood distribution systems; in modern societies they signify the notion of 'fellowship' which Tawney, in much that he wrote, conceived of as a matter of right relationships which are institutionally based. Voluntary blood donor systems, analysed in this book, represent one practical and concrete demonstration of fellowship relationships institutionally based in Britain in the National Health Service and the National Blood Transfusion Service. It is one example of how such relationships between free and equal individuals may be facilitated and encouraged by certain instruments of social policy. If it is accepted that man has a social and a biological need to help then to deny him opportunities to express this need is to deny him the freedom to enter into gift relationships.

From *The Gift Relationship: From Human Blood to Social Policy* by Richard Titmuss
(George Allen & Unwin Ltd, 1970)

Raymond Plant
EMANCIPATING INDIVIDUALS (1988)

In the view of conservatives there is a categorical distinction between being free to do something and being able to do it . . . In the first sense someone is free to do X if no one is deliberately preventing him from doing it. The fact that someone lacks the capacity to do it – perhaps because of a lack of resources – does not in itself limit the freedom to do X.

Clearly if freedom is understood in this sense, then government has a rather limited role in the protection of free and equal citizenship. Its role is to provide equal freedom under the law and collective resources such as police forces and courts to secure this. It is *not* a legitimate function of government to secure for individuals specific resources to enable them to do what they are free to do. No one is able to do all that they are free to do, and this indicates that there is a distinction to be drawn between freedom on the one hand and capacities, resources and opportunities on the other. If this were not so then I am unfree whenever I am unable to fulfil my desires. If government had the role of securing resources for liberty in this positive sense, then its task would be endless.

But there is a stronger reason why conservatives wish to separate freedom and resources, identified by Hayek (one of the gurus of the neo-liberal right). If freedom and ability along with associated resources are seen as the same thing, then resources should be redistributed in the interests of more equal liberty. The sharp distinction which they draw between freedom and resources effectively blocks this argument and makes it impossible to argue for a collective redistribution of resources in the interests of individual freedom.

Excluding government as far as possible from the allocation of resources is reinforced by the New Right's belief that markets are the correct mechanism for allocation between individuals, because they cannot infringe freedom.

Markets are complex institutions within which millions of people buy and sell goods and services and no doubt do so deliberately and intentionally. These complex interactions produce a distribution of income and wealth and other resources, which is an unintended consequence of all this buying and selling. If the outcomes of free markets are unintended then markets cannot limit freedom because freedom under the neo-liberal definition can only be limited by intentional or deliberate coercion.

Hence, the New Right argues, there can again be no case for collective action to preserve the liberty of individuals in the face of markets . . .

The central argument against the neo-liberal's distinction between freedom and ability is to ask what is freedom in the sense of the absence of coercion valuable for? The most obvious answer to this question would be that if I am free from deliberate interference then I am free to do what I want, to live a life shaped by my own values and purposes. Freedom is valuable because it is a necessary condition of autonomy. But if this is why freedom is valuable, it cannot be separated from ability, resources and opportunities. I can do what I want, lead a life shaped by my own values, only if I have the capacity to fulfil my desires . . .

The neo-liberal will reject this account. If people who lack the resources to do what they desire to do are unfree, then equal liberty is an unattainable ideal. There are always going to be limits on people's abilities and they will differ from one another.

There are two answers to this charge. The first is to recognise that only some forms of inability or incapacity can be changed by collective action – natural inabilities will always remain and they lie beyond the scope of political remedy. So it is perfectly true that we cannot finally equalise abilities, but that should not rule out action towards achieving a fairer distribution of resources. Most conservatives regard perfect competition as utopian but it does not stop them regarding a more and more competitive economy as a goal.

Secondly, it is clearly absurd to believe that to be free one has to have all the resources to fulfil one's wants whatever they are, so that someone who wishes to live a life marked by a desire for expensive tastes will not be free unless he or she has the resources to pursue such tastes. Public provision is concerned to secure access to that range of resources which are necessary conditions of living an autonomous and purposive life – the necessary conditions of agency, not the necessary conditions of pursuing individual preferences. We are concerned with needs rather than wants. The satisfaction of the needs of agency are part of a feasible collective programme for active citizenship, because they are general within our society.

Without education, health care, income, self-respect and a framework of law within which one can live one's own life in one's own way, one cannot be an agent in the sense of having the resources to pursue goals which make freedom worth while in human life. But these resources must be provided in ways which do not threaten their overall purpose – the emancipation of individuals and communities.

From *Citizenship, Rights and Socialism* (Fabian Society pamphlet no. 531)
by Raymond Plant (1988)

Roy Hattersley
WHAT WE STAND FOR IS FREEDOM (1987)

A clear definition of our ideological position is now essential – particularly if that definition can give the Labour Party a new and broad appeal that trans-cends classes, races and regions. Democratic socialism, properly defined, is a philosophy with an immense natural appeal, for it is the gospel of personal emancipation, and much of our past unpopularity has been the product of the fear that we stand either for regulation rather than emancipation or for nothing at all.

What we stand for is freedom. That is the ultimate objective of socialism. The immediate intention of socialist policies is the creation of a more equal society within which power and wealth are more evenly distributed. But socialism's fundamental purpose – indeed, the purpose of the equality which we seek – is the extension of liberty. Socialists may, in the short term, be concerned with the problems of property, wealth, earnings and economic organisation – but they are concerned with them only as a means by which a more fundamental aim may be achieved. The true measure of socialism is not the extent of public ownership, the degree of central planning or the degree of government regulation. Indeed, in some cases, central planning and government regulation may limit freedom, and thus be the enemies of socialism. *A socialist society is judged by the extent to which it succeeds in providing, for the largest possible number of its citizens, the power to exercise rights which, under other forms of organisation, are either denied or made available only in theory. Socialism is the promise that the generality of men and women will be given the economic strength which makes the choices of a free society have meaning. It is a commitment to organise society in a way which ensures the greatest sum of freedom, the highest total amount of real choice and, in consequence, the most human happiness. It is the understanding that the collective power should be used to enhance individual liberties.*

To socialists, freedom is not the absence of restraint on the rich and the powerful, but the ability of the generality of men and women to exercise their inherent rights. A socialist society sees liberty 'not as a possession to be defended but as a goal to be achieved' and its achievements depend upon the creation of rights – social and economic, as well as political – 'which must be such that wherever the occasion for their exercise arises, they can in fact be exercised'. It is, to paraphrase Keynes, *effective* freedom which socialists seek.

Yet, despite socialism's traditional ideological dependence on a highly developed theory of liberty, Labour has increasingly allowed itself to be caricatured as the 'We Know Best Party' when we are (or ought to be) the 'We Will Make You Free Party'. We have failed to proclaim our purpose and describe our destiny largely because of intellectual reticence – the lack of self-confidence which prevented us from moving liberty out of our opponents' ground by insisting that their definition of that ideal condition is prejudiced, and perverse. We should not have been afraid to argue that extending choices as widely as possible makes inevitable the removal of those exclusive rights which have previously been the prerogative of privilege. Every public footpath is an infringement of the landlord's right to fence his property. We all know that and accept the limitation on landlords' liberties as a feature of a free society. Yet by espousing the landlords' cause, the Conservatives have represented themselves as the freedom party and successfully pretended that those who would protect the footpath are dictators, whilst those who proclaim the right of way are tyrants. It is in our failure to be visibly the party of liberty that our careless unconcern about a proper ideological framework for policies is most damagingly reflected. There have, of course, been other contributory reasons for our damagingly authoritarian reputation – reasons concerned with petty town hall tyrannies, Soviet friendship societies and trades union restrictive practices. But the prime cause has been our willingness to argue about liberty in the language of our opponents, to contend that freedom amounts to no more that the removal of restraints. Instead of arguing for a better definition of freedom, we have stayed silent as if we either had nothing better to put in its place or actually accepted the phoney notion and chosen to neglect what passes, within it, for liberty in the hope of creating greater equality. *As we evangelised for equality, we should have made clear that without it, for a majority of the population, the promise of liberty is a cruel hoax. Liberty is our aim. Equality is the way in which it can truly be achieved. It is time that we made our ideological purpose clear.*

From *Choose Freedom: the Future for Democratic Socialism* by Roy Hattersley
(Michael Joseph, 1987)

Independent Labour Party Declaration (1922)

The Labour Members of Parliament for the City of Glasgow and the West of Scotland, inspired by zeal for the welfare of humanity and the prosperity of all peoples and strengthened by the trust reposed in them by their fellow–citizens, have resolved to dedicate themselves to the reconciliation and unity of the nations of the world and the development and happiness of the people of these islands.

They record their infinite gratitude to the pioneer minds who have opened up the path for the freedom of the people.

They send to all peoples a message of goodwill, and to the sister nations of the British Commonwealth fraternal greetings.

They will not forget those who suffered in the war, and will see that the widows and orphans shall be cherished by the nation.

They will urge without ceasing the need for houses suitable to enshrine the spirit of home.

They will bear in their hearts the sorrows of the aged, the widowed mother, and the poor, that their lives shall not be without comfort.

They will endeavour to purge industry of the curse of unhealthy workshops, restore wages to the level of adequate maintenance, and eradicate the corrupting effects of monopoly and avarice.

They will press for the provision of useful employment or reasonable maintenance.They will have regard for the weak and those stricken by disease, for those who have fallen in the struggle of life and those who are in prison.

To this end they will endeavour to adjust the finances of the nation that the burden of public debt may be relieved and the maintenance of national administration be borne by those best able to bear it.

In all things they will abjure vanity and self–aggrandisement, recognising that they are the honoured servants of the people, and that their only righteous purpose is to promote the welfare of their fellow–citizens and the well–being of mankind.

Written by Rosslyn Mitchell and quoted in *The Clydesiders* by Robert Keith Middlemas (Hutchinson, 1965)

THE INDIVIDUAL AND FREEDOM

*'Socialism is an attempt to share as justly as we can
with one another the terms of human existence'*

Anthony Crosland
OPEN-AIR CAFES (1956)

Society's decisions impinge heavily on people's private lives as well as on their social or economic welfare; and they now impinge, in my view, in too restrictive and puritanical a manner. I should like to see action taken both to widen opportunities for enjoyment and relaxation, and to diminish existing restrictions on personal freedom.

The first of these requires, it is true, a change in cultural attitudes rather than government legislation. If this were to come about, much could be done to make Britain a more colourful and civilised country to live in. We need not only higher exports and old-age pensions, but more open-air cafés, brighter and gayer streets at night, later closing-hours for public houses, more local repertory theatres, better and more hospitable hoteliers and restaurateurs, brighter and cleaner eating-houses, more riverside cafés, more pleasure-gardens on the Battersea model, more murals and pictures in public places, better designs for furniture and pottery and women's clothes, statues in the centre of new housing estates, better-designed street-lamps and telephone kiosks, and so on *ad infinitum*. The enemy in all this will often be in unexpected guise; it is not only dark satanic things and people that now bar the road to the new Jerusalem, but also, if not mainly, hygienic, respectable, virtuous things and people, lacking only in grace and gaiety.

This becomes manifest when we turn to the more serious question of socially imposed restrictions on the individual's private life and liberty. There come to mind at once the divorce laws, licensing laws, prehistoric (and flagrantly unfair) abortion laws, obsolete penalties for sexual abnormality, the illiterate censorship of books and plays, and remaining restrictions on the equal rights of women. Most of these are intolerable, and should be highly offensive to socialists, in whose blood there should always run a trace of the anarchist and the libertarian, and not too much of the prig and the prude. If we really attach importance to the 'dignity of man', we must realise that this is as much affronted by a hypocritical divorce law which, as Matthew Arnold once wrote, neither makes divorce impossible nor makes it decent, as by the refusal to establish a joint production council in a factory. A time will come, as material standards rise, when divorce-law reform will increase the sum of human welfare more than a rise in the food subsidies (though no doubt the party managers will be less enthusiastic for it). Socialists cannot go on indefinitely professing to be concerned with human happiness and the removal of injustice, and then, when the programmes are decided, permitting the National Executive, out of fear of certain vocal pressure groups, to become more orthodox than the bench of bishops.

Much of this can at least claim the sanction of one powerful stream of socialist thought – that stemming from William Morris; though other, Nonconformist and Fabian, influences wear a bleaker and more forbidding air.

For one brought up as a Fabian, in particular, this inevitably means a reaction against the Webb tradition. I do not wish to be misunderstood. All who knew the Webbs have testified to their personal kindliness, gentleness, tolerance and humour; and no one who reads *Our Partnership* can fail to be intensely moved by the deep unaffected happiness of their mutual love. But many of their public virtues, so indispensable at the time, may not be as appropriate today. Reacting as they were against an unpractical, utopian, sentimental, romantic, almost anarchist tradition on the Left, they were no doubt right to stress the solid virtues of hard work, self-discipline, efficiency, research and abstinence: to sacrifice private pleasure to public duty, and expect that others should do the same: to put Blue Books before culture, and immunity from physical weakness above all other virtues.

And so they spent their honeymoon investigating trade societies in Dublin. And so Beatrice could write that 'owing to our concentration on research, municipal administration and Fabian propaganda, we had neither the time nor the energy, nor yet the means to listen to music and the drama, to brood over classic literature, to visit picture galleries, or to view with an informed intelligence the wonders of architecture'. And so Sidney withheld approval from the Soviet experiment until workers' control had been suppressed, and Beatrice until the anti-abortion law had been enacted, and she could write with approval of the serious, youthful Comsomols with their passion for self-discipline and self-improvement and of the emphasis on personal hygiene and self-control – 'there is no spooning in the Parks of Recreation and Rest'. And historically, without a doubt, this insistence on austerity was a vital service to a young and growing opposition movement.

But now we surely need a different set of values. Permeation has more than done its job. Today we are all incipient bureaucrats and practical administrators. We have all, so to speak, been trained at the LSE, are familiar with Blue Books and White Papers, and know our way around Whitehall. We realise that we must guard against romantic or utopian notions: that hard work and research are virtues: that we must do nothing foolish or impulsive: and that Fabian pamphlets must be diligently studied. We know these things too well. Posthumously, the Webbs have won their battle, and converted a generation to their standards. Now the time has come for a reaction: for a greater emphasis on private life, on freedom and dissent, on culture, beauty, leisure and even frivolity. Total abstinence and a good filing-system are not now the right signposts to the socialist Utopia: or at least, if they are, some of us will fall by the wayside.

The Future of Socialism by Anthony Crosland (Jonathan Cape, 1956)

John Smith
FREEDOM IS A MORAL GOAL (1993)

Let me assert my profound conviction that politics ought to be a moral activity and we should never feel inhibited in stressing the moral basis of our approach. Of course, we have to take matters further forward. We have to undertake the intellectual task of applying a moral principle in a way which results in a practical policy of benefit to our fellow citizens. And life is never free of dilemmas. But let us never be fearful of saying that we espouse a policy because it is, quite simply, the right thing to do. And let us not underestimate the desire, which I believe is growing in our society, for a politics based on principle.

What is more, I believe the tide of opinion is beginning to flow towards a recognition of the value of society and away from the nihilistic individualism of so much of modern conservatism.

Fifty years ago there was such a recognition as, in the throes of a world war, two major thinkers were reflecting on the needs of a nation. Beveridge, whose seminal report was the basis of the social action programme of the great post-war Labour Government, called for a war against the five giants of want, disease, ignorance, squalor, and idleness. At the same time, William Temple, Archbishop of Canterbury, published *Christianity and the Social Order* which strongly asserted the duty of the Christian churches to concern themselves with the application of Christian principles to the needs and problems of society.

Temple did not advocate a Christian social ideal: indeed he was sceptical about ideal states from Plato onwards. But he believed Christianity could provide something of far more value – namely principles which could guide our action. He identified three guiding social principles – freedom, fellowship and service.

Freedom, for Temple, meant freedom 'for' something as well as freedom 'from' something, and was the primary object of all political action. But he recognised that human beings are naturally and incurably social, and freedom is best expressed in fellowship. The combination of freedom and fellowship resulted in the obligation of service; service to family, to community and to nation.

Temple drew an important distinction between personality and individuality. 'Every person is an individual, but his individuality is what marks him off from others; it is a principle of division; whereas personality is social, and only in his social relationships can a man be a person . . . This point has great political importance: for these relationships exist in the whole network of communities and associations and fellowships. It is in these that the real wealth of human life consists.'

The theme that unites the writings of Tawney and Temple and which makes them so appealing to democratic socialists is their insistence on situating the individual in society. Individual freedom for them is only meaningful and achievable within society. This explanation of human experience is, of course, a core belief of democratic socialism. It provides an organising principle around which we believe our social order both political and economic can and should be built. It is the way in which we believe that individual freedom – our ultimate moral goal – can best be secured . . .

If, as I profoundly believe, the moral goal of our society is to extend and encourage individual freedom, then it is certainly not enough to rely simply on a minimal State charged with defending negative liberty – the freedom from coercion by the State. For as Tawney himself observed, 'A society, or a large part of it, may be both politically free and economically the opposite. It may be protected against arbitrary action by the agents of government, and be without the security from economic oppression which corresponds to civil liberty.'

What Tawney realised was that meaningful freedom depended on real ability. That for millions of people citizenship was empty and valueless if squalor and deprivation were the reality of a society only theoretically free. What was needed was positive liberty – the freedom to achieve that is gained through education, health care, housing and employment. An infrastructure of freedom that would require collective provision of basic needs through an enabling State. It is this richer conception of freedom for the individual in society that is the moral basis of democratic socialism . . .

The conclusion I reach is that the goal of individual freedom and the value of society, which we advocate as democratic socialists, is a theory of sustained intellectual force. When tested in the experience of humanity it can be found to be a better explanation of the lives and purposes of men and women than its rivals on the *laissez-faire* Right or the Marxist Left. We ought, therefore, in the battle of ideas which is at the centre of the political struggle, to be confident in the strength of our intellectual case.

But I believe we must also argue for our cause on the basis of its moral foundation. It is a sense of revulsion at injustice and poverty and denied opportunity, whether at home or abroad, which impels people to work for a better world, to become, as in our case, democratic socialists. The powerful contribution of Christian socialists in all the denominations of the Church has always focused on the moral purpose of political action. How true it is that the Labour Party has owed more to Methodism than to Marx. But it was that great Anglican, William Temple, who identified what he called 'the real wealth of human life', who saw that the individual was best fulfilled in the context of a strong community bound together in fellowship. That is a truth I want to reassert today with confidence and conviction. It is why I believe the Labour Party must be bold in demonstrating our commitment to enhance and extend individual freedom by building a society which is dynamic and responsive to the aspirations of all our people.

From *Reclaiming the Ground: Christianity and Socialism,*
edited by Christopher Bryant (Spire, 1993)

T.H. Green
LIBERATION FOR THE COMMON GOOD (1881)

We shall probably all agree that freedom, rightly understood, is the greatest of blessings; that its attainment is the true end of all our effort as citizens. But when we thus speak of freedom, we should consider carefully what we mean by it. We do not mean merely freedom from restraint or compulsion. We do not mean merely freedom to do as we like irrespectively of what it is that we like. We do not mean a freedom that can be enjoyed by one man or one set of men at the cost of a loss of freedom to others. When we speak of freedom as something to be so highly prized, we mean a positive power or capacity of doing or enjoying something worth doing or enjoying, and that, too, something that we do or enjoy in common with others. We mean by it a power which each man exercises through the help or security given him by his fellow-men, and which he in turn helps to secure for them. When we measure the progress of a society by its growth in freedom, we measure it by the increasing development and exercise on the whole of those powers of contributing to social good with which we believe the members of the society to be endowed; in short, by the greater power on the part of the citizens as a body to make the most and best of themselves. Thus, though of course there can be no freedom among men who act not willingly but under compulsion, yet on the other hand the mere removal of compulsion, the mere enabling a man to do as he likes, is in itself no contribution to true freedom . . .

If the ideal of true freedom is the maximum of power for all members of human society alike to make the best of themselves, we are right in refusing to ascribe the glory of freedom to a state in which the apparent elevation of the few is founded on the degradation of the many, and in ranking modern society, founded as it is on free industry, with all its confusion and ignorant licence and waste of effort, above the most splendid of ancient republics.

If I have given a true account of that freedom which forms the goal of social effort, we shall see that freedom of contract, freedom in all the forms of doing what one will with one's own, is valuable only as a means to an end. That end is what I call freedom in the positive sense: in other words, the liberation of the powers of all men equally for contributions to a common good.

From 'Lecture on Liberal Legislation and Freedom of Contract' in *Works* by T.H. Green (Longmans, 1911)

Ramsay MacDonald
DEVELOPING INDIVIDUALITY (1905)

The result is inevitable. The arts languish, the vulgar empire of plutocracy extends its gilded borders, luxurious indulgence takes the place of comfort, selfish pursuits that of public spirit, philanthropic effort that of just dealing.

We are accustomed to regard the present as a state of individualism, but no delusion could be more grotesque. Nothing is rarer in society today than individuality, and it is doubtful if ever there was less individuality amongst us than there is at the present moment. One has only to look on whilst the sons of the *nouveaux riches* spend their money, or whilst the crowds which our industrial quarters have disgorged enjoy themselves, to appreciate the meaningless monotony of our pleasure. From our furniture, made by the thousand pieces by machines, to our religion, stereotyped in set formulae and pursued by clockwork methods, individuality is an exceptional characteristic. In the production of wealth, owing to the differentiation of processes, there is less and less play for individuality, and as this more exclusively occupies the time and thought of both employers and employed, uniformity spreads its deadening hand over society, imitation becomes a social factor of increasing power, respectability becomes more securely enthroned as the mentor of conduct, and a drab level of fairly comfortable mediocrity is the standard to which we conform. Nothing is, indeed, more absurd than an argument in support of the present state of society, based on the assumption that as we move away from it in the direction of socialism we are leaving individuality and individual liberty behind.

From 'Socialism and Society' in *Ramsay MacDonald's Political Writings*,
edited by Bernard Baker (Allen Lane/the Penguin Press, 1972)

Robert Tressell
THE SOCIALIST VAN (1914)

On Sunday morning toward the end of July a band of about twenty–five men and women on bicycles invaded the town. Two of them, who rode a few yards in front of the others, had affixed to their handlebars a slender upright standard from the top of one of which fluttered a small flag of crimson silk with 'International Brotherhood and Peace', in gold letters. The other standard was similar in size and colour, but with a different legend: 'One for all and all for one.'

As they rode along they gave leaflets to the people in the streets and whenever they came to a place where there were many people they dismounted and walked about, distributing leaflets. They made several long halts during their progress along the Grand Parade, where there was a considerable crowd, and then they rode over the hill to Windley, which they reached just before opening time. There were little crowds waiting outside the several public houses, and a number of people passing through the streets on their way home from church and chapel. To all who would take them the strangers distributed leaflets, and also went through the side streets putting them under the doors and in the letter boxes. When they had exhausted their stock they remounted and rode back the way they came.

Meantime the news of their arrival had spread, and as they returned through the town they were greeted with jeers and booing. Presently someone threw a stone, and, as there happened to be plenty of stones just there, several others followed suit and began running after the retreating cyclists, throwing stones, hooting, and cursing.

The leaflet which had given rise to all this fury read as follows:

What is Socialism?
At present the workers with hand and brain produce continually food, clothing and all useful and beautiful things in great abundance.

But they labour in vain
for they are mostly poor and often in want. They find it a hard struggle to live. Their women and children suffer, and their old age is branded with pauperism. Socialism is a plan by which poverty will be abolished and all will be enabled to live in plenty and comfort, with leisure and opportunity for ampler life.

If you wish to hear more of this plan, come to the field at the Cross Roads on the hill at Windley, on Tuesday evening next at 8 p.m., and

Look out for the Socialist Van.

The cyclists rode away amid showers of stones without sustaining much damage. One had his hand cut and another, who happened to look round, was struck on the forehead, but these were the only casualties.

From *The Ragged-Trousered Philanthropist* by Robert Tressell (Paladin, 1991)

Oscar Wilde

SOCIALISM ENHANCES INDIVIDUALISM (1891)

Under the new conditions individualism will be far freer, far finer, and far more intensified than it is now. I am not talking of the great imaginatively realised individualism of such poets as I have mentioned, but of the great actual individualism latent and potential in mankind generally. For the recognition of private property has really harmed individualism, and obscured it, by confusing a man with what he possesses. It has led individualism entirely astray. It has made gain not growth its aim. So that man thought that the important thing was to have and did not know that the important thing is to be. *The true perfection of man lies, not in what man has, but in what man is.* Private property has crushed true individualism and set up an individualism that is false. It has debarred one part of the community from being individual by starving them. It has debarred the other part of the community from being individual by putting them on the wrong road and encumbering them. Indeed, so completely has man's personality been absorbed by his possessions that the English law has always treated offences against a man's property with far more severity than offences against his person, and property is still the test of complete citizenship. The industry necessary for the making of money is also very demoralising. In a community like ours, where property confers immense distinction, social position, honour, respect, titles, and other pleasant things of the kind, man, being naturally ambitious, makes it his aim to accumulate it long after he has got far more than he wants, or can use, or enjoy, or perhaps even know of. Man will kill himself by overwork in order to secure property, and really, considering the enormous advantages that property brings, one is hardly surprised. One's regret is that society should be constructed on such a basis that man has been forced into a groove in which he cannot freely develop what is wonderful, and fascinating, and delightful in him – in which, in fact, he misses the true pleasure and joy of living. He is also, under existing conditions, very insecure. An enormously wealthy merchant may be – often is – at every moment of his life at the mercy of things that are not under his control. If the wind blows an extra point or so, or the weather suddenly changes, or some trivial thing happens, his ship may go down, his speculations may go wrong, and he finds himself a poor man, with his social position quite gone. Now, nothing should be able to harm a man except himself. Nothing should be able to rob a man at all. What a man really has, is what is in him. What is outside of him should be a matter of no importance.

With the abolition of private property, then, we shall have true, beautiful, healthy individualism. Nobody will waste his life in accumulating things and the symbols for things. One will live. To live is the rarest thing in the world. Most people exist, that is all . . .

It will be a marvellous thing – the true personality of man – when we see it. It will grow naturally and simply, flower-like, or as a tree grows. It will not be at discord. It will never argue or dispute. It will not prove things. It will know everything. And yet it will not busy itself about knowledge. It will have wisdom. Its value will not be measured by material things. It will have nothing. And yet it will have everything, and whatever one takes from it, it will still have, so rich will it be. It will not be always meddling with others, or asking them to be like itself. It will love them because they will be different. And yet, while it will not meddle with others, it will help all, as a beautiful thing helps us by being what it is. The personality of man will be very wonderful. It will be as wonderful as the personality of a child . . .

Individualism then, is what through socialism we are to attain to.

From 'The Soul of Man Under Socialism'
in *Selected Essays and Poems* (Penguin, 1954)

John Mortimor
OSCAR WILDE REMEMBERED (1990)

It was with these thoughts in mind that I went back, not to Marx or even to Shaw, but to Oscar Wilde, who once wrote a long political essay, I dimly remembered, called 'The Soul of Man Under Socialism'. He undertook this work in 1891, a year in which he published four books, wrote *Salome* and became a famous West End dramatist with *Lady Windermere's Fan*. As you would expect, his thoughts on politics are brilliant, paradoxical, based on aesthetic values and occasionally maddening. It's a piece of prose which I would like all those blue-suited and efficient characters on the Labour front bench to take home and read in bed. Strangely enough, when they put out their lights, they may start dreaming of a better world.

'The chief advantage that would result from the establishment of socialism is undoubtedly the fact that socialism would relieve us from that sordid necessity of living for others which, in the present condition of things, presses so hardly upon almost everybody . . . The majority of people spoil their lives by an unhealthy and exaggerated altruism – are forced indeed, so to spoil them.' What Wilde is saying is the reverse of Thatcherism: there is no virtue at all in feeling sorry for the poor, by flattering ourselves for our humane concern or doling out small sums in charity. It's an essential function of government to abolish the conditions which make such self-indulgence possible. The end of poverty, the proper provision of housing, the more equal distribution of wealth, the organisation of health care and so on are the basic services which a government can perform. Once done, this will save us all from having to go round feeling sorry for each other, signing deeds of covenant or going on sponsored swims. But this is not an end in itself, it's merely an essential part of any decent government service. You could, if you wished, call it socialism, but socialism is not an end in itself. 'Socialism,' says Wilde, 'will be of value simply because it leads to individualism.' And what is individualism? Simply the right of us all to make the most of our lives, to improve their quality and take full advantage of our powers of enjoyment. It is to have open to us whatever can widen our horizons, the consolations of religion, the stimulus of the arts, the right to a decent system of education and the enjoyment of a countryside rescued from the destructive deprivations of the last ten years.

Of course Wilde overstates his case, and puts it with all the theatricality of a man who lectured in a velvet coat, knee breeches and diamond-buckled shoes. But in a way, this essay, exaggerated as it is, provides a useful antidote to the new Tory idea of freedom. Government activity, so runs the Thatcherite creed, should be reduced to a minimum so we are all set free to make money. Government activity must be increased, says Wilde, to solve those basic problems which prevent us living fulfilled and satisfactory lives. And among those restrictions on complete and successful living he lists the pursuit of property and an obsession with personal enrichment. It's not only the rich who should be relieved of such concerns. 'There is only one class of the community,' Wilde says in one of his better epigrams, 'that thinks more about money than the rich and that is the poor. The poor can think of nothing else. That is the misery of being poor.'

So, as they read these thoughts which are no doubt meant to shock the bourgeois, and even the left-wing bourgeois, two aims may present themselves to the thoughtful member of a new Labour Government. They are two ideals which may well be unattainable, but there is nothing wrong with unattainable ideals if they lead to some small improvement in the state of the nation. The first is to remove the demeaning and soul-destroying results of social injustice. Let's get that cured, Wilde said, so at least we may not have to waste our lives feeling sorry for each other. And then, and always, let's aim for a rise in the standard of living, that standard to be judged not solely, or indeed at all, by money.

From *The Alternative – Politics for Change*, edited by Ben Pimlott,
Anthony Wright and Tony Flowers (W.H. Allen, 1990)

R.H. Tawney
CAPITALISM AND RELIGION (1922)

Circumstances alter from age to age, and the practical interpretation of moral principles must alter with them. Few who consider dispassionately the facts of social history will be disposed to deny that the exploitation of the weak by the powerful, organised for purposes of economic gain, buttressed by imposing systems of law, and screened by decorous draperies of virtuous sentiment and resounding rhetoric, has been a permanent feature in the life of most communities that the world has yet seen. But the quality in modern societies, which is most sharply opposed to the teaching as ascribed to the founder of the Christian faith, lies deeper than the exceptional failures and abnormal follies against which criticism is most commonly directed. It consists in the assumption, accepted by most reformers with hardly less *naïveté* than by the defenders of the established order, that the attainment of material riches is the supreme object of human endeavour and the final criterion of human success. Such a philosophy, plausible, militant, and not indisposed, when hard pressed, to silence criticism by persecution, may triumph or may decline. What is certain is that it is the negation of any system of thought or morals which can, except by a metaphor, be described as Christian. Compromise is as impossible between the Church of Christ and the idolatry of wealth, which is the practical religion of capitalist societies, as it was between the church and the State idolatry of the Roman Empire.

'Modern capitalism,' writes Mr Keynes, 'is absolutely irreligious, without internal union, without much public spirit, often, though not always, a mere congeries of possessors and pursuers.' It is that whole system of appetites and values, with its deification of the life of snatching to hoard, and hoarding to snatch, which now, in the hour of its triumph, while the plaudits of the crowd still ring in the ears of the gladiators and the laurels are still unfaded on their brows, seems sometimes to leave a taste as of ashes on the lips of a civilisation which has brought to the conquest of its material environment resources unknown in earlier ages, but which has not yet learned to master itself. It was against that system, while still in its supple and insinuating youth, before success had caused it to throw aside the mask of innocence, and while its true nature was unknown even to itself, that the saints and sages of earlier ages launched their warnings and their denunciations. The language in which theologians and preachers expressed their horror of the sin of covetousness may appear to the modern reader too murkily sulphurous; their precepts on the contracts of business and the disposition of property may seem an impracticable pedantry. But rashness is a more agreeable failing than cowardice, and, when to speak is unpopular, it is less pardonable to be silent than to say too much.

From *Religion and the Rise of Capitalism* by R.H. Tawney (Penguin, 1922)

E.P. Thompson
HUMAN POTENTIAL (1960)

Human nature is neither originally evil nor originally good; it is, in origin, *potential*. If human nature is what men make history *with*, then at the same time it is human nature which they make. And human nature is potentially *revolutionary*; man's will is not a passive reflection of events, but contains the power to rebel against 'circumstances' (or the hitherto prevailing limitations of 'human nature') and on that spark to leap the gap to a new field of possibility. It is the aim of socialism, not to sublimate the contest between 'evil' and 'good' into an all-perfect paternal state (whether 'Marxist' or Fabian in design), but to end the condition of all previous history whereby the contest has always been rigged *against* the 'good' in the context of an authoritarian or acquisitive society. Socialism is not only one way of organising production; it is also a way of producing 'human nature'. Nor is there only *one*, prescribed and determined, way of making socialist human nature; in building socialism we must discover the way, and discriminate between many alternatives, deriving the authority for our choices not from absolute historicist laws nor from reference to biblical texts but from real human needs and possibilities, disclosed in open, never-ceasing intellectual and moral debate. The aim is not to create a socialist State, towering above man and upon which his socialist nature *depends*, but to create a 'human society or socialised humanity' where (to adapt the words of More) man, and not money, 'beareth all the stroke.'

From *Out of Apathy* edited by Norman Birnbaum (Stevens & Sons Ltd, 1960)

William Morris
THE REBIRTH OF SOCIETY (1887)

Well, now I will try to draw these discursive remarks to a head, and will give you a more concise and complete idea of the society into which I would like to be reborn.

It is a society which does not know the meaning of the words rich and poor, or the rights of property, or law or legality, or nationality: a society which has no consciousness of being governed: in which equality of condition is a matter of course, and in which no man is rewarded for having served the community by having the power given him to injure it.

It is a society conscious of a wish to keep life simple, to forgo some of the power over nature won by past ages in order to be more human and less mechanical, and willing to sacrifice something to this end. It would be divided into small communities varying much within the limits allowed by due social ethics, but without rivalry between each other, looking with abhorrence at the idea of a holy race.

Being determined to be free, and therefore contented with a life not only simpler but even rougher than the life of slave-owners, division of labour would be habitually limited: men (and women too, of course) would do their work and take their pleasure in their own persons, and not vicariously: the social bond would be habitually and instinctively felt, so that there would be no need to be always asserting it by set forms: the family of blood-relationship would melt into that of the community and of humanity. The pleasures of such a society would be founded on the free exercise of the senses and passions of a healthy human animal, so far as this did not injure the other individuals of the community and so offend against social unity: no one would be ashamed of humanity or ask for anything better than its due development.

But from this healthy freedom would spring up the pleasures of intellectual development, which the men of civilisation so foolishly try to separate from sensuous life, and to glorify at its expense. Men would follow knowledge and the creation of beauty for their own sakes, and not for the enslavement of their fellows, and they would be rewarded by finding their most necessary work grow interesting and beautiful under their hands without their being conscious of it. The man who felt keenest the pleasure of lying on the hillside under a rushen hut among the sheep on a summer night, would be no less fit for the enjoyment of the great communal hall with all its splendours of arch and column, and vault and tracery. Nor would he who took to heart the piping of the wind and washing of the waves as he sat at the helm of the fishing-boat, be deadened to the beauty of art-made music. It is workmen only and not pedants who can produce real vigorous art.

And amidst this pleasing labour, and the rest that went with it, would disappear from the earth's face all the traces of the past slavery. Being no longer driven to death by anxiety and fear, we should have time to avoid disgracing the earth with filth and squalor, and accidental ugliness would disappear along with that which was the mere birth of fantastic perversity. The utterly base doctrine, as Carlyle has it, that this world is a cockney nightmare, would be known no more.

From 'The Society of the Future' in *The Political Writings of William Morris*, edited by A.L. Morton (Lawrence & Wishart, 1979)

George Orwell
EARTHLY PARADISE (1946)

A socialist or a communist . . . is a person who believes the 'earthly paradise' to be possible. Socialism is in the last analysis an optimistic creed and not easy to square with the doctrine of original sin . . . At this moment it is difficult for utopianism to take shape in a definite political movement. The masses everywhere want security much more than they want equality, and do not generally realise that freedom of speech and of the Press are of urgent importance in themselves. But the desire for an earthly paradise has a very long history behind it.

If one studied the genealogy of ideas for which writers like Koestler and Silone stand, one would find it leading back through utopian dreamers like

William Morris and the mystical democrats like Walt Whitman, through Rousseau, through the English Diggers and Levellers, through the peasant revolts of the Middle Ages, and back to the early Christians and the slave revolts of antiquity. The pamphlets of Gerrard Winstanley, the Digger from Wigan, whose experiments of primitive communism were crushed by Cromwell, are in some ways strangely close to modern left-wing literature.

The 'earthly paradise' has never been realised, but as an idea it never seems to perish, despite the ease with which it can be debunked . . . Underneath it lies the belief that human nature is fairly decent to start with, and is capable of indefinite development. This belief has been the main driving force of the socialist movement, including the underground sects who prepared the way for the Russian revolution, and it could be claimed that the utopians, at present a scattered minority, are the true upholders of socialist tradition.

From a book review in the *Manchester Evening News*

William McIlvanney
SOCIALISM AND HUMANITY (1991)

From my first acquaintance with Marxism, I felt it was doomed in its own absolutist error. It does not seek so much to discover human nature as to re-invent it. It does not seek merely to grow through time, but to negate it. It would liberate humanity into the contradiction of itself. Formidably intelligent as Marx's arguments are, their conclusions seem to me about as rational as achieving immortality by committing suicide.

. . . What Marxism is after is certain and reachable and is supposed to be finitely realisable in a time-scale that is, in any humanly experienceable way, infinite (as the great white whale is finite in the infinity of the sea). Socialism is trying to move towards that which may never be finally found, like the Kraken, though we can imagine it. And if we can imagine it, I would think we demean ourselves by not at least trying to realise it. It seems to me one of the greatest nobilities of which our imagination is capable, because it is simultaneously the least selfish and the most fulfilling. While Marxism is a demand for absolute justice which our individual natures cannot honestly answer, socialism is an attempt to share as justly as we can with one another the terms of human existence. The first says: you must be other than you are and force other people to do likewise. The second says: you must be the most that you can be while still allowing others to be the most that they can be. Only one of these demands is human. The other is a denial of our humanity.

From *Surviving the Shipwreck* by William McIlvanney (Mainstream, 1991)

Arnold Wesker
FULL OF LIVING (1959)

BEATIE: He's *not* trying to change me Mother. You can't change people, he say, you can only give them some love and hope they'll take it. And he's tryin' to teach me and I'm tryin' to understand – do you see that Mother?

MRS BRYANT: I don't see what that's got to do with music though.

BEATIE: Oh my God! (*Suddenly*) I'll show you. (*Goes off to front room to collect pick-up and a record.*) Now sit you down gal and I'll show you. Don't start ironing or reading or nothing, just sit there and be prepared to learn something. (*Appears with pick-up and switches on.*) You aren't too old, just you sit and listen. That's the trouble you see, we ent ever prepared to learn anything, we close our minds the minute anything unfamiliar appear. *I* could never listen to music. I used to like some on it but then I'd lose patience, I'd go to bed in the middle of a symphony, or my mind would wander 'cos the music didn't mean anything to me so I'd go to bed or start talking. 'Sit back woman,' he'd say, 'listen to it. Let it happen to you and you'll grow as big as the music itself.'

MRS BRYANT: Blust he talk like a book.

BEATIE: An' sometimes he talk as though you didn't know where the moon or the stars was. (*Beatie puts on record of Bizet's L'Arlésienne Suite.*) Now listen. This is a simple piece of music, it's not highbrow but it's full of living. And that's what he say socialism is. 'Christ,' he say. 'Socialism isn't talking all the time, it's living, it's singing, it's dancing, it's being interested in what go on around you, it's being concerned about people and the world.' Listen Mother. (*She becomes breathless and excited.*) Listen to it. It's simple isn't it? Can you call that squit?

MRS BRYANT: I don't say it's all squit.

From *Roots* by Arnold Wesker (Penguin, 1959)

J.A. Symonds
THESE THINGS SHALL BE (*c.*1912)

These things shall be! a loftier race
Than e'er the world hath known shall rise
With flame of freedom in their souls,
And light of science in their eyes.

They shall be gentle, brave, and strong,
To spill no drop of blood, but dare
All that may plant man's lordship firm
On earth and fire, and sea, and air.

Nation with nation, land with land,
Unarm'd shall live as comrades free,
In ev'ry heart and brain shall throb
The pulse of one fraternity.

New arts shall bloom of loftier mould,
And mightier music thrill the skies,
And every life shall be a song,
When all the earth is paradise.

These things – they are no dreams – shall be
For happier men when we are gone:
Those golden days for them shall dawn,
Transcending aught we gaze upon.

From *The Socialist Sunday School Tune Book* (1912)

Rex Warner
FUTURE

I see the houses of the future, and men upstanding,
men not fearing the sack.
Women work with men and love is voluntary,
love is delightful.

Hate is no more against those who withhold bread;
those people have gone.
Love is no more the antidote for terror,
but is recreation.

What is happening will be clear to the men of the future;
for deceit will not be needed.
But our here and now to them will look like a dream,
sad, furious, fatal.

William Blake
JERUSALEM (1804)

And did those feet in ancient time
Walk upon England's mountains green?
And was the holy Lamb of God
On England's pleasant pastures seen?

And did the Countenance Divine
Shine forth upon our clouded hills?
And was Jerusalem builded here
Among these dark Satanic mills?

Bring me my bow of burning gold!
Bring me my arrows of desire!
Bring me my spear! O clouds unfold!
Bring me my chariot of fire!

I will not cease from mental fight,
Nor shall my sword sleep in my hand,
Till we have built Jerusalem
In England's green and pleasant land.

From *Complete Writings*, edited by Sir Geoffrey Keynes (London, 1966)

COMMUNITY

'The watchword of socialism is not class consciousness but community consciousness'

Neil Kinnock

NO SUCH THING AS SOCIETY (1988)

'No such thing as society,' she says.
No obligation to the community.
No sense of solidarity.
No principles of sharing or caring.
'No such thing as society.'
No sisterhood, no brotherhood.
No neighbourhood.
No honouring other people's mothers and fathers.
No succouring other people's little children.
'No such thing as society.'
No number other than one.
No person other than me.
No time other than now.
No such thing as society, just 'me' and 'now'.
That is Margaret Thatcher's society.

From a speech to the Labour Party Conference, Blackpool, in *Thorns and Roses: Speeches 1983–1991* by Neil Kinnock (Hutchinson, 1992)

John Stuart Mill

PRIVATE WAR (1869)

At this point, in the enumeration of the evils of society, the mere levellers of former times usually stopped: but their more far-sighted successors, the present socialists, go farther. In their eyes the very foundation of human life as at present constituted, the very principle on which the production and repartition of all material products is now carried on, is essentially vicious and anti-social. It is the principle of individualism, competition, each one for himself and against all the rest. It is grounded on opposition of interests, not harmony of interests, and under it everyone is required to find his place by a struggle, by pushing others back or being pushed back by them. Socialists consider this system of private war (as it may be termed) between everyone and everyone, especially fatal in an economical point of view and in a moral. Morally considered, its evils are obvious. It is the parent of envy, hatred, and all uncharitableness; it makes everyone the natural enemy of all others who cross his path, and everyone's path is constantly liable to be crossed. Under the present system hardly any one can gain except by the loss or disappointment of one or of many others. In a well-constituted community every one would be gained by each other's loss and lose by each other's gain, and our greatest gains come from the worst source of all, from death, the death of those who are nearest and should be dearest to us. In its purely economical operation the principle of individual competition receives as unqualified condemnation from the social reformers as in its moral. In the competition of labourers they see the cause of low wages; in the competition of producers the cause of ruin and bankruptcy; and both evils, they affirm, tend constantly to increase as population and wealth make progress; no person (they conceive) being benefited except the great proprietors of land, the holders of fixed money incomes, and a few great capitalists, whose wealth is gradually enabling them to undersell all other producers, to absorb the whole of the operations of industry into their own sphere, to drive from the market all employers of labour except themselves, and to convert the labourers into a kind of slaves or serfs, dependent on them for the means of support, and compelled to accept these on such terms as they choose to offer. Society, in short, is travelling onwards, according to these speculators, towards a new feudality, that of the great capitalists

From 'Chapters on Socialism' in *On Liberty and Other Writings,*
edited by Stefan Collini (Cambridge University Press, 1989)

Bishop Westcott
SOCIALISM VERSUS INDIVIDUALISM

The term socialism has been discredited by its connection with many extravagant and revolutionary schemes, but it is a term which needs to be claimed for nobler uses. It has no necessary affinity with any forms of violence, or confiscation, or class selfishness, or financial arrangement. I shall therefore venture to employ it apart from its historical associations as describing a theory of life, and not only a theory of economics. In this sense socialism is the opposite of individualism, and it is by contrast with individualism that the true character of socialism can best be discerned. Individualism and socialism correspond with opposite views of humanity. Individualism regards humanity as made up of disconnected or warring atoms; socialism regards it as an organic whole, a vital unity formed by the combination of contributory members mutually interdependent.

It follows that socialism differs from individualism both in method and in aim. The method of socialism is co-operation, the method of individualism is competition. The one regards man as working with man for a common end, the other regards man as working against man for private gain. The aim of socialism is the fulfilment of service, the aim of individualism is the attainment of some personal advantage, riches, or place, or fame. Socialism seeks such an organisation of life as shall secure for everyone the most complete development of his powers; individualism seeks primarily the satisfaction of the particular

147

wants of each one in the hope that the pursuit of private interest will in the end secure public welfare.

If men were perfect, with desires and powers harmoniously balanced, both lines of action would lead to the same end. As it is, however, experience shows that limitations must be placed upon the self-assertion of the single man. The growing sense of dependence as life becomes more and more complex necessarily increases the feeling of personal obligation which constrains us each to look to the circumstances of others. At the same time in the intercourse of a fuller life we learn that our character is impoverished in proportion as we are isolated, and we learn also that evil or wrong in one part of society makes itself felt throughout the whole.

. . . Socialism, as I have defined it, is not, I repeat, committed to any one line of action, but everyone who accepts its central thought will recognise certain objects for immediate effort. He will seek to secure that labour shall be acknowledged in its proper dignity as the test of manhood, and that its reward shall be measured, not by the necessities of the indigent, but by its actual value as contributing to the wealth of the community. He will strive to place masses of men who have no reserve of means in a position of stability and to quicken them by generous ideas. He will be bold to proclaim that the evils of luxury and penury cannot be met by palliatives. He will claim that all should confess in action that every power, every endowment, every possession, is not of private use, but a trust to be administered in the name of the Father for their fellow-men.

From *Socialism in England*

Alan Bleasdale

LOOKING AFTER NUMBER ONE

SNOWY: I can take it y'know, Loggo. I can take it 'cos I know my beliefs are right. I've been brought up by me dad to support what's worth supportin' –
LOGGO: I didn't know y' dad followed Everton.
SNOWY: All I'm saying is, if y' don't fight, if y' know, if . . . like I mean, it was easy to be a socialist when I was growin' up in the sixties, an' even f' most of the seventies. Everyone was a friggin' socialist then. It was fashionable. But it's not now . . . Everythin's gone sour, everyone's lockin' the door, turnin' the other cheek, lookin' after number one. *But now's the time when we should all be together.* Now's the time when we *need* to be together, 'cos . . . 'cos well we're not winnin' anymore. *Don't you see that?* (*He pauses*) Like, that's all I'm sayin'.
CHRISSIE: (*Gently*) Of course we see it.
JIMMY: And the last thing we need is t' be told about it, f' Christ's sake.
CHRISSIE: 'Cos deep down, most of us know it. But y' don't look that far, not

148

these days. Not when y' scared Snowy. And when y' scared, unless y' very special, y' think about y'self – an' yours. Y' think about feedin' the kids, an' payin' the rent, an' the effect it's havin' on y' tart – an' even what Christmas is going to be like this year. (*He shrugs*) I'm a married man with two kids, an' y' beliefs go right out of the window when y' debtors knock at your door. (*There is a pause*) And what's more I shouldn't be here now. The sniffers've been round our house twice this past fortnight.

SNOWY: But y' need the money.

CHRISSIE: Got it in one.

From *Boys from the Blackstuff – Jobs for the Boys* by Alan Bleasdale

Dennis Potter and Melvyn Bragg
AN INTERVIEW (1994)

You do feel the state of decay has deeply set in, don't you?

I do. With great regret and pity, and a feeling of shame of self. But it's rescuable, just. It's up to people to stand up and shout a bit. Not to turn it into cynicism, which I'm afraid is what is happening. Politics is still crucially important. Our choices are vital, and we've got to make them and not just say, 'Oh, they're all the same'. They *are* all the same in certain ways, alas – a political animal is such an animal. But lurking somewhere behind their rhetoric and their spittle are important choices that we should make.

Do you think the overall sense of decay that you've talked about stems from political decay, or that political decay stems from other powerful symptoms?

Both. They interlace. The press and politics. The commercialisation of every-thing means you're putting commercial value upon everything and you turn yourself from a citizen into a consumer, and politics is a commodity to be sold. Look what's happening at the BBC. Look what's happening to television in general. Look who owns it.

The arguments of respectable, liberal commentators about size, economies of scale, and so on, are all nonsense. A programme costs what a programme costs. It can be made by a tiny company. It's a question of ownership of the means of communications, 'the mass media' in J.B. Priestley's phrase; of political control. How can we have a mature democracy when newspapers and television are beginning to be so interlaced in ownership? Where are our freedoms to be guaranteed? Who is going to guarantee them? Look at the power that Murdoch has. Look at the effects of all these takeovers.

The world of television or radio when we came into it, I'm not saying that world wasn't paternalistic, and I'm not saying it can be preserved as it was, and I'm not saying there mustn't be change, but that world was based upon a set of assumptions that are now almost derisible, laughable. Like in politics, certain statements become derisible. We're destroying ourselves by not making those statements. Just as we're destroying our television. Week by week, day by day, I see it.

My first television programme was in 1960, a documentary about the Forest of Dean. My first television plays were in 1965, when I had this burst of energy through illness, when I reinvented myself, quite consciously. I was so out of it, I had lost my job, I had two small kids and a third on the way, and I wrote this television play and they liked it, thank God, and commissioned another. I was given the space to grow, and I gave my working life to it as a result, and I have stayed with television to a large extent because of that.

Whereas if I was starting now, where would I get that chance; who would cosset and look after me? Where is the single play now? And the series – you can call the shot numbers in advance. Formula-ridden television is because of sales. They'll soon be able to tell every five seconds who's switching off. The pressure upon creators – whether they're writers, directors, designers, actors, producers, whatever – will be to maximise the audience at any given point, which is the very antithesis of discovering something you didn't know. It's the very antithesis of the kind of broadcasting on television which was such a glory in British life.

But given what was done in the sixties and seventies on television, and given the power and influence of television, and given the fact that people came through from good schools and burgeoning universities – let's be a bit Panglossian about that – given that, why do you think it turned so sharply in the mid-eighties?

Because there needed to be some stripping out of things, there needed to be change. We were conscious of the need for a change in British politics, like the 1945 Government in a way. There was a genuine radicalism in the air, coming from the Right. But then everything was given its price-tag, and the price-tag became the only gospel. And that gospel is very thin gruel indeed. If you start measuring humankind in those terms, everything else becomes less important, or laughable – all the things that bind us as a community. And they're partly right-wing things.

Sometimes I get out of bed and I don't know whether I'm right-wing or left-wing, to be honest, because I feel the pull of both. I feel the pull of tradition, and I love my land, I love England, and when I'm abroad, I genuinely feel homesick. I've always loved my country, but not drums and trumpets and billowing Union Jacks and busby soldiers and the monarchy and pomp and circumstance, but something about our people that I come from and therefore respond to. And I expect other people to do it of their own backgrounds and nations and cultures, too.

But those things are very difficult to put prices on and to quantify in the terminology of Mrs Thatcher and the current Government. They use phrases like 'community care' when they mean 'Close that costly thing and put that madman onto the street'. And then if it's in front of their noses they'll do another makeshift measure and claim that things are getting better, or that the per-head spending has gone up. So what? It may have done, but what is actually happening when a young person in many, many a town in this country sees no prospect of a job?

Then they will moralise, that's the worst thing, and say, 'Oh, crime is everything to do with the criminal.' What is a life of not expecting to get work? What is a life of only expecting cynicism in political conversation? What is a life that sees no horizon further than the latest video nasty and cable TV and the Murdochs and the *Sun*?

Just pick up a copy of the *Sun*. Is this Britain? Is this what we've done to ourselves? How can the people who work on that paper go home and face their families without any sense of shame? I'd be ashamed to the pit of my guts if I were forced to do it, and some of them are, to be fair, forced to do it, because they don't want to be unemployed. They need to earn. Some of them do things that they are appalled by. I know that, I've met some of them. But my God, what a system.

From *Dennis Potter: Seeing the Blossom – Two Interviews, a Lecture and a Story*
(Faber & Faber, 1994)

Brian Barry
PRIVATE SOLUTIONS? (1988)

What can we learn from the opposition of socialism to capitalism and individualism? I think that both contrasts fit together with the following definition of socialism: 'A socialist society is one in which the citizens of that society are able, by acting together, to control the undesirable consequences of individual actions.' Thus conceived, socialism is, above all, a theory of citizenship: it is concerned with empowering citizens to act collectively in pursuit of the interests and ideals that they share with one another and that can be realised only by collective action . . .

Acting through the market, we can do nothing to change a grotesquely unjust distribution of income, to create an adequate system of income-maintenance, to prevent industries from polluting and farmers from destroying the countryside, or to provide ourselves with properly funded public services of all kinds. Only in our capacity as citizens can we, acting collectively through local and national governments, bring about the outcomes that we want.

But do we really want them? I think it must be conceded that it is possible to create a society in which the response to market failure is not a swing to socialism, but an exacerbation of individual efforts to stay ahead by making and spending yet more money. Does the public health service have long waiting lists and inadequate facilities? Buy private insurance. Has public transport broken down? Buy a car for each member of the family above driving age. Has the countryside been built over or the footpaths eradicated? Buy some elaborate exercise machinery and work out at home. Is air pollution intolerable? Buy an air-filtering unit and stay indoors. Is what comes out of the tap foul to the taste and chock-full of carcinogens? Buy bottled water. And so on. We know it can all happen because it has: I have been doing little more than describing Southern California.

Now it is worth noticing two things about the private substitutes that I have described. The first is that in the aggregate they are probably much more expensive than would be the implementation of the appropriate public policy. The second is that they are extremely poor replacements for the missing outcomes of good public policy. Nevertheless, it is plain that the members of a society can become so alienated from one another, so mistrustful of any form of collective action, that they prefer to go it alone.

Let's not feel too sorry for the inhabitants of Southern California. Most of them have enough money to carry out the project of extreme privatisation in style – and anyway there's all that sunshine. What is much less of a joke is the prospect of the same thing in a country with a third of the income and even less than a third of the sunshine.

Can it happen here? The object of the present Government is undoubtedly to create the conditions for its happening. By systematically reducing the quality of public services of all kinds, it hopes to turn people away from them and encourage them to seek solutions individually. There is, it seems to me, no guarantee that this strategy will fail. As I said before, I do not regard socialism as having any built-in prophecies. Perhaps, however perverse it may be, most people will get locked into pursuing private solutions to public deficiencies. But I hope not because this would entail all of us living more limited and impoverished lives.

From 'The Continuing Relevance of Socialism' by Brian Barry in *Thatcherism*, edited by Robert Skidelsky (Chatto & Windus, 1988)

Raymond Williams

THINKING SOCIALLY (1961)

An equally important effect of the 'consumer' description is that, in materialising an individual figure, it prevents us thinking adequately about the true range of uses of our economic activity. There are many things, of major importance, which we do not use or consume individually, in the ordinary sense, but socially. It is a poor way of life in which we cannot think of social use as one criterion of our economic activity, yet it is towards this that we are being pushed by the 'consumer' emphasis, but the supposed laws of the market, and by the system of production and distribution from which these derive. It is beginning to be widely recognised that a serious state of unbalance between provision for social and individual needs now exists and seems likely to increase. It is easy to get a sense of plenty from the shop windows of contem-porary Britain, but if we look at the schools, the hospitals, the roads, the libraries, we find chronic shortages far too often. Even when things are fac-tually connected, in direct daily experience, as in the spectacular example of the flood of new cars and the ludicrous inadequacy of our road system, the spell of this divided thinking seems too powerful to break. Crises of this kind seem certain to dominate our economy in the years ahead, for even when late, very late, we begin thinking about the social consequences of our individual patterns of use, to say nothing about social purposes in their own right, we seem to find it very difficult to think about social provision in a genuinely social way. Thus we think of our individual patterns of use in the favourable terms of spending and satisfaction, but of our social patterns of use in the unfavourable terms of deprivation and taxation. It seems a fundamental defect of our society that social purposes are largely financed out of individual incomes, by a method of rates and taxes which make it very easy for us to feel that society is a thing that continually deprives and limits us — without this system we could all be profitably spending. Who has not heard that impassioned cry of the modern barricade: *but it's my money you're spending on all this; leave my money alone*? And it doesn't help much to point out that hardly any of us could get any money, or even live for more than a few days, except in terms of a highly organised social system which we too easily take for granted. I remember a miner saying to me, of someone we were discussing: 'He's the sort of man who gets up in the morning and presses a switch and expects the light to come on'. We are all, to some extent, in this position, in that our modes of thinking habitually suppress large areas of our real relationships, including our real dependences on others. We think of my money, my light, in these naive terms, because parts of our very idea of society are withered at root. We can hardly have any conception, in our present system, of financing of social purposes from the social product, a method which would continually show us, in real terms, what our society is and does. In a society whose products depend almost entirely on intricate and continuous co-operation and social organisation, we expect to consume as if we were isolated individuals, making our own way. We are then forced into stupid comparison of individual consumption and social taxation – one desirable and to be extended, the other regrettably necessary and to be limited. From this kind of thinking the physical unbalance follows inevitably.

Unless we achieve some realistic sense of community, our true standard of living will continue to be distorted.

From *The Long Revolution* by Raymond Williams (Chatto & Windus, 1961)

Herbert Morrison
CALL FOR FELLOWSHIP (1943)

From the very beginning of its history – indeed before its real political history began with the formation of the Labour Representation Committee in 1900 – the Labour movement has been animated by a vision of a unified society reshaped according to the highest conceptions of man's reason and conscience – a vision embracing not only the present and future of our own country but that of the entire human race. The pioneers of the movement in its early twentieth-century form were men of a lofty moral and social idealism.

That idealism was backed by the driving force of determined millions who knew they were ill used by the economic system and were resolved to better their condition. But the party has never grown, and can never grow, merely from an instinctive thrust for more of this world's goods, animated by no broad conception of universal brotherhood or of a life enriched in far more than the material sense.

My colleague, Ernest Bevin, recently quoted a great labour leader, John Burns, as saying that 'the real tragedy of the working class is the poverty of our desires'. That was true. In future it must be different. We must not accept for ourselves as a party or for the nation poor desires and limited aims. Abundant life means something far more than, indeed something essentially different from, an abundance of material things. It means more than bread and circuses, more than minimums and movies. It means freedom and fellowship, leisure and the capacity to enjoy it, plenty and the will to share it, an active part in the control of all the affairs which touch men's daily lives; it must mean also soldierly strength and readiness for sacrifice, not only sacrifice of our own lives for our country but sacrifice of some of our own country's immediate and narrower aims and interests in the cause of a wider fellowship.

From *Looking Ahead* by Herbert Morrison (Hodder & Stoughton, 1943)

William Temple
SOCIAL FELLOWSHIP (1942)

No man is fitted for an isolated life; everyone has needs which he cannot supply for himself; but he needs not only what his neighbours contribute to the equipment of his life but their actual selves as the complement of his own. Man is naturally and incurably social.

Recent political theories have given ostensible emphasis to this truth and have then, as a rule, gone far to ignore it. Certainly our social organisation largely ignores it. For this social nature of man is fundamental to his being. I am not first someone on my own account who happens to be the child of my parents, a citizen of Great Britain, and so forth. If you take all these social relationships away, there is nothing left. A man is talking nonsense if he says: 'Well, if I had been the son of someone else . . . etc.' He *is* his parents' son; what he is supposing is not that *he* should be someone else's son, but that *he* should not exist and someone else should exist instead. By our mutual influence we actually constitute one another as what we are. This mutual influence finds its first field of activity in the family; it finds other fields later in school, college, trade union, professional association, city, county, nation, Church . . .

Now man is a child of God, destined for eternal fellowship with Him, though a sinful child who in many ways frustrates his own destiny. Further, as children of God, men and women are members of one family, and their true development is that of an ever richer personal experience in an ever wider and deeper fellowship. If, then, an economic system is abundantly effective in producing and distributing material goods, but creates or intensifies divisions and hostilities between men, that system is condemned, not on economic but on moral grounds; not because it fails to deliver the goods, but because it is a source of wrong personal relationships.

From *Christianity and the Social Order* by William Temple (Penguin, 1942)

Sidney Webb
FELLOWSHIP IS LIFE (1923)

Finally, let me remind you that there is a higher need even than government, whether it be the government of a city or the government of our tempers or the government of our tongues. It is not upon its plans or its programmes – not even upon its principles or its ideals – that a political party is ultimately judged. It is not upon them or any of them that its measure of success in the continuous appeal to the judgment of the average citizen finally depends. The success of the Labour Party in this country depends, more than on anything else, upon the spirit in which we hold our faith, the spirit in which we present our proposals, the spirit in which we meet our opponents in debate, the spirit in which we fulfil our own obligations, the spirit in which, with inevitable backslidings, we live our own lives. We shall not achieve much, whatever changes we can bring about, unless what we do is done in the spirit of fellowship. For we must always remember that the founder of British socialism was not Karl Marx but Robert Owen, and that Robert Owen preached not 'class war' but the ancient doctrine of human brotherhood – the hope, the faith, the living fact of human fellowship – a faith and a hope reaffirmed in the words of that other great British socialist – William Morris – in *The Dream of John Ball*. 'Forsooth, brothers, fellowship is heaven, and lack of fellowship is hell; fellowship is life, and lack of fellowship is death;

and, the deeds that ye do upon the earth, it is for fellow-ship's sake that ye do them; and the life that is in it, that shall live on and on for ever, and each one of you part of it, while many a man's life upon the earth from the earth shall wane.'

From 'The Labour Party on the Threshold' (Fabian Tract no. 207)
by Sidney Webb (1923)

J.M. Ludlow
PARTNERSHIPS (1848)

The word 'society', in the languages from which it is derived, means the same thing as 'partnership'. And I really think that many misconceptions on the subject would be cleared away, if we could accustom ourselves to think of society simply as the great partnership, either of one nation in itself, or of mankind at large, according as we look upon it from a special or a general point of view. One thing is clear, that the modern idea and word of 'socialism' could never have sprung up, but from the forgetfulness of this great fact of human partnership. Socialism is but the recoil of individualism, of that splitting up of society under a thousand influences of sceptical and vicious selfishness in the last century, through which indeed nations seemed to have become mere aggregations of units, heaped together without cohesion, like the shingle on the sea–beach, instead of being built up into glorious palaces and temples of brotherhood and worship. If men really felt themselves to be partners in the great business of life, they would not need to be reminded that they should be so. And thus the mere word of socialism – which means nothing of itself but the science of making men partners, the science of partnership – conveys to us a great lesson and a great warning . . .

A partnership always has an object in view; some benefit, to be common to all the members. That object, and not chance or fancy, is the sole foundation from which it springs; there can be no partners but for a purpose. And the purpose again can be but one of common benefit – a benefit which can only be attained by joining the efforts of several in one. No man enters into a partnership, but for the sake of bettering himself, of adding in some shape or other to his wealth, or his influence, or his pleasure, or his sense of duty fulfilled; and no man remains in partnership but as a means of so bettering himself. And thus society must be felt to be a blessing, for men enter into it, and for men to remain in it. It is not the giving up of a part of one's liberty as the price of certain advantages. For, indeed, Louis Blanc has added something to the truth of our conception of the word 'liberty', when he has shown us that it includes the idea of power. It is increase of power to do that which man seeks to do, and to obtain that which he seeks to obtain; that is the real end of society, as of every partnership. There may be fetters and burdens connected with the relation which were not felt before, and yet those fetters and burdens arise not out of the relation itself, but from a cause, the very opposite to it -- from the spirit of individual selfishness jarring still against the higher spirit of fellowship and community of purpose. It is because the partners are not partners enough – because they are not sufficiently impressed with the need of co-operation, not sufficiently willing to merge individual interests in the pursuit of the common object, that they quarrel and fall out with one another, and feel their union as a galling chain. The more harmoniously they do act together, the more they will feel their power, their true freedom, increased and multiplied. Then, the confidence which they have in one another, allows each to devote himself the more entirely to his own branch of the business, to the purchases or to the sales, to the books or to the works.

And thus it is with society. So long as we look upon it only as a system of mutual checks and chains, hemming in on all sides I know not what so-called natural rights (which, if closely inquired into, would very likely be found nothing more than depraved and unnatural rights) still more when we openly rail at the tyranny of society, and speak of it as a mere mass of corruption and injustice – we can never be really free within its bosom, we can never work successfully towards its ends. True, all the partners may not fill such places as they ought to fill, enjoy such share of the common profit as they ought to enjoy; the deed of settlement may contain useless and ill-devised clauses, which clog and hamper the partnership business instead of promoting its success. But still, it is a partnership; it is the union of men bent together for a common purpose, and whose true interest is not to quarrel and break up the concern, but to learn to manage it better – nay, to work each man the more wisely and zealously, the more the common business appears likely to lose by the folly or indolence of another partner – though not without endeavouring by all possible means, by open reproof if necessary, to bring him round to a sense of duty, nor without remembering that the party in fault may have to be turned out wholly, sooner than that the whole concern should go to ruin.

From *Politics for the People* by J.M. Ludlow (1848)

Maureen
(a low-paid, part-time worker from Northern Ireland)

WHAT THE WORLD NEEDS

A little more kindness,
A little less needs,
A little more giving,
A little less greed,
A little more gladness,
A little less care,

A little more faith,
And a little more prayer.
A little more 'We',
A little less 'I',
A little more laughter,
A little less sigh,
A little more sunshine
Brightening the view,
A lot more friends
Exactly like you!

Anonymous

COMMUNITY

Oh happy time, when all mankind
Shall competition's evil see:
And seek with one united mind
The blessings of community.

When social love's benignant flow
Shall peace on earth, goodwill restore;
And charity, like ocean's flow,
Connect and compass every shore.

Then will the claims of wealth and state,
This goodly world no more deface;
Then war and rapine, strife and hate,
Among mankind will have no place.

The will mankind, in common share
The gifts their industry supplies,
And prove, escaped from selfish care
The joys of heaven beneath the skies.

From *Songs for Co-operative Women* from the Women's Co-operative Guild

Sidney Webb
THINKING IN COMMUNITIES (1901)

This time it is not a new continent that the ordinary man has discovered, but a new category. We have become aware, almost in a flash, that we are not merely individuals, but members of a community, nay, citizens of the world. This new self-consciousness is no mere intellectual fancy, but a hard fact that comes home to us in our daily life. The labourer in the slum-tenement, competing for employment at the factory gate, has become conscious that his comfort and progress depend, not wholly or mainly on himself, or on any other individual, but upon the proper organisation of his trade union and the activity of the factory inspector. The shopkeeper or the manufacturer sees his prosperity wax or wane, his own industry and sagacity remaining the same, according to the good government of his city, the efficiency with which his nation is organised, and the influence which his empire is able to exercise in the councils, and consequently in the commerce, of the world. Hence the ordinary elector, be he workman or manufacturer, shopkeeper or merchant, has lost his interest in the individual 'rights', or abstract 'equality', political or religious. The freedom that he now wants is not individual but corporate freedom – freedom for his trade union to bargain collectively, freedom for his co-operative society to buy and sell and manufacture, freedom for his municipality to supply all the common needs of the town, freedom, above all, from the narrow insularity which keeps his nation backing, 'on principle', out of its proper place in the comity of the world. In short, the opening of the twentieth century finds us all, to the dismay of the old fashioned individualist, thinking in communities.

From 'Twentieth-century Politics: a Policy of National Efficiency'
(Fabian Tract no. 108) by Sidney Webb (1901)

Ramsay MacDonald
COMMUNITY CONSCIOUSNESS (1905)

The socialist appeal, therefore, is to all who believe in social evolution, who agree that the problem which society has now to solve is that of the distribution of wealth, who trust in democracy, who regard the State not as antagonistic to but as an aspect of, individuality, and who are groping onwards with the co-operative faith guiding them. That appeal may find some people in poverty, and they may follow because it offers them economic security, but it will find others in wealth, and they will follow because it brings order where there is now chaos, organisation where there is now confusion, law where there is now anarchy, justice where there is now injustice.

Socialism marks the growth of society, not the uprising of a class. The consciousness which it seeks to quicken is not one of economic class solidarity, but one of social unity and growth towards organic wholeness. The watchword of socialism, therefore, is not class consciousness but community consciousness.

From 'Socialism and Society' in *Ramsay MacDonald's Political Writings,* edited by Bernard Barker (Allen Lane/Penguin Press, 1972)

Glenda Jackson
EVERYBODY'S SCHOOL (1991)

I am a product of the welfare state. It was that socialist dream made reality by a socialist government that gave me all my opportunities. I was educated at a local school – a state school. That meant we had to pay to go there. My parents paid, so did their next-door neighbours and the people next door to them. In fact the whole of my street paid. They paid through their taxes. They paid for me to go to school. But they didn't just pay for me; they also paid for the children next door and the children next door to them and the children next door to them. And they did that because it wasn't just my school, it was our school, it was everybody's school. And thanks to that same welfare state I was given a second educational opportunity via the Royal Academy of Dramatic Art. And forty years later I stand here addressing conference yet without state education it's doubtful I'd be addressing envelopes. What I am today is thanks to those people and that street and those schools.

From a speech to the Labour Party Annual Conference, 1991

Robert Tressell
COMMUNITY RESPONSIBILITY (1914)

All through the winter, the wise, practical, philanthropic, fat persons whom the people of Mugsborough had elected to manage their affairs – or whom they permitted to manage them without being elected – continued to grapple, or to pretend to grapple, with the 'problem' of unemployment and poverty. They continued to hold meetings, rummage and jumble sales, entertainments and special services. They continued to distribute the rotten cast-off clothing and boots, and the nourishment tickets. They were all so sorry for the poor, especially for the 'dear little children'. They did all sorts of things to help the children. In fact, there was nothing that they would not do for them except levy a halfpenny rate. It would never do to do that. It might pauperise the parents and destroy parental responsibility. They evidently thought that it would be better to destroy the health or even the lives of the 'dear little children' than to pauperise the parents or undermine parental responsibility. These people seemed to think that the children were the property of their parents. They did not have sense enough to see that the children are not the property of their parents at all, but the property of the community. When they attain to manhood and womanhood they will be, if mentally or physically inefficient, a burden on the community, and if they are healthy, educated and brought up in good surroundings, they will become useful citizens, able to render valuable service, not merely to their parents, but to the community. Therefore the children are the property of the community, and it is the business and to the interest of the community to see that their constitutions are not undermined by starvation.

From *The Ragged-Trousered Philanthropist* by Robert Tressell (Paladin, 1991)

T.H. Marshall
CITIZENSHIP VERSUS A CLASS SYSTEM (1950)

Citizenship is a status bestowed on those who are full members of a community. All who possess the status are equal with respect to the rights and duties with which the status is endowed. There is no universal principle that determines what those rights and duties shall be, but societies in which citizenship is a developing institution create an image of an ideal citizenship against which achievement can be measured and towards which aspiration can be directed. The urge forward along the path thus plotted is an urge towards a fuller measure of equality, an enrichment of the stuff of which the status is made and an increase in the number of those on whom the status is bestowed.

Social class, on the other hand, is a system of inequality. And it too, like citizenship, can be based on a set of ideals, beliefs and values. It is therefore reasonable to expect that the impact of citizenship on social class should take the form of a conflict between opposing principles. If I am right in my contention that citizenship has been a developing institution in England at least since the latter part of the seventeenth century, then it is clear that its growth coincides with the rise of capitalism, which is a system, not of equality, but of inequality. Here is something that needs explaining. How is it that these two opposing principles could grow and flourish side by side in the same soil? What made it possible for them to be reconciled with one another and to become, for a time at least, allies instead of antagonists? The question is a pertinent one, for it is clear that, in the twentieth century, citizenship and the capitalist class system have been at war.

From *Citizenship and Social Class* by T.H. Marshall
and Tom Bottomore (Pluto Press, 1992)

David Marquand
COMMUNITY LOYALTY (1990)

'Altruism' does not capture the full flavour of words like 'comradeship', 'loyalty' and 'duty' which lie at the heart of any notion of community. The dictionary definition of altruism is 'regard for others as a principle of action; unselfishness'. There is something a little watery about the concept, perhaps because it goes too wide and insufficiently deep. 'Regard for others': which others? 'Unselfish': but *is* it unselfish to discharge one's obligations to the community which has helped to make one's self what it is? Communitarian loyalty is both stronger and narrower than this. It implies loyalty to the other members of the community to which one belongs, not to everyone: and it carries with it a flavour of obligation which altruism lacks. Altruism is freely chosen by the sovereign, atomistic, impermeable individual of the reductionist model; and what the sovereign individual can freely choose, he can freely unchoose when his mood changes. In a community, the individual is not sovereign, or not, at any rate, in the same way. A community is like home – the place where, 'when you have to go there, they have to take you in'. Membership of it is not altogether involuntary. You can, in Hirschman's language, 'exit' from it. But if you do, you deny or lose part of your nature.

From 'A Language of Community' by David Marquand in *The Alternative – Politics for Change,* edited by Ben Pimlott, Anthony Wright and Tony Flower (W.H. Allen & Co, 1990)

Richard Hoggart and Raymond Williams
WORKING-CLASS ATTITUDES (1959)
(Revised transcript of a recorded conversation)

RH: I think working-class life may change when a town reaches more than a certain size. I talked about this once with Asa Briggs who comes from a smallish industrial township in the West Riding, a wool town. He is the same age and a scholarship boy; the family had a corner shop which, I believe, failed in the '30s. The points he made about working-class attitudes in his township seemed more applicable to your Welsh village than to my big city, Leeds.

His, and many like it, were very tight townships with their life based on wool or some ancillaries to wool. They had a sort of unity. Even physically, the most striking difference between the bosses' houses, the foremen's and the workers' was one of size – they all had a similar style, a common comeliness and dignity. The communities had a kind of organic quality, closer and more varied relations between the social groups than we had.

I've noticed too how many of the men have an air of great self-respect. The trade turned out experts – this man knew how to feel the differences between types of wool, this one to keep the machines going well and so on. You can see much the same air in a main-line express driver of the old type. He's got a craft and he is important. If you go into the pubs in the West Riding mill towns you're struck by how many of the men have this sort of air.

RW: Yes, and that's how I remember the men of my own village. They were important, and felt themselves important, because they lived there and knew each other. They'd call nobody 'Sir', in any ordinary circumstances, and I notice this difference in southern England at least, where so many people seem to take up a servant's attitude quite naturally: I still can't stand it when people call me 'Sir' on the bus – at least they do when I've got my suit on. But I remember the men at home – a whole attitude in a way of dress. Good clothes, usually, that you bought for life. The big heavy overcoat, good jacket, good breeches, leggings, then a cardigan, a waistcoat, a watchchain, and all of it open, as a rule, right down to the waist. Layers of it going in, and of course no collar. But standing up, quite open. They weren't, really, people with a sense of inferiority.

RW: . . . the other consciousness, that of being working class, is more complicated. Basically, I think, it centred about the railway. There, as a new element, you have a group of men conscious of their identity in a different way. And in fact, at the two stations, you get the growth of political and trade-union attitudes of a quite mature urban kind.

RH: That's extraordinarily interesting. You think it only came in with the railway?

RW: Well, the self-government tradition in the chapels disposed many people to democratic feeling; feeling, really, rather than thinking. Someone like my father who grew up in a farm labourer's family, outside the tradition that brought conscious trade union attitudes, still got, I think, the feelings that matter. There was just enough local and practical democracy, but even more there was this sense that to be a man in this place was to be important; that this mattered more than any sort of grading on a social basis. Of course when he came back from the first war he was much more definite politically, and then on the railway it was the Labour Party, the union, the under-standing of what a strike was, what it implied.

RH: The differences seem to me striking. Leeds in my day had just under half a million people. A great many of the working people seemed to belong to families which had originally come in from the surrounding countryside between, I suppose, 1840 and 1880. Once there they began to live in new ways, segregated into districts. As we know, their districts grew up round the works, near canals, rivers, railway yards. The better-class districts were up the hill or on the right side of the wind. Generally one gets the impression, looking at this sort of city, that this physical separation illustrates less obvious separations between the various social groups. You don't have the sort of relations I called 'organic' when I mentioned the mill towns. What you have in a town like Leeds – or Sheffield or Manchester – is much more a sense of great blocks of people. Of course each block would be shot through with all sorts of distinctions and differences. Among working people you had extended families, often overlapping; and particular neighbourhood loyalties; and you had distinctions between say the transport men, the heavy engineering men, those who laboured for the corporation and so on and so on. The distinctions were very fine and very complicated. But still you could see first this large rough distinction – that industrially the area was a block, or a pool, of general labour for the city's industries – the human equivalent of the private reservoirs at the side of some of the big works. In our area there were a lot of men who hadn't served an apprenticeship, who weren't skilled workers – or not really skilled – but who could turn their hands to a number of jobs within related heavy industries. They felt two main kinds of connections, with their neighbourhood and with the industries they worked in; but the neighbourhood connections were stronger for most. They felt they belonged to a district more than to a trade – though not in the way country workers feel they belong to a village. We talked about 'our' kind of people in 'our' kind of area. You see this in the Institute's study of Bethnal Green too. Still – they were villages of a kind, and remarkably tiny villages. You knew exactly where your boundaries were.

RW: The most difficult bit of theory, that I think both of us have been trying to get at, is what relation there is between kinds of community, that we call working class, and the high working-class tradition, leading to democracy, solidarity in the unions, socialism . . . All I'd say is that certain major principles, that matter for our future, have in fact come out of the high working-class tradition, supported by many aspects of ordinary working-class life. I mean the sense of community, of equality, of genuine mutual respect: the sense, too, of fairness, when the humanity of everyone in the society is taken as basic, and must not be outraged by any kind of exploitation.

From *New Left Review*, No. 1, January–February 1960

Peter Townsend

WAR SOLIDARITY (1958)

During the war I lived in London . . . I remember many days spent in improvised classrooms in the school crypt and nights curled up on a mattress under an iron bedstead, or huddled at the foot of the basement stairs with my mother and grandmother and the other tenants in our large, gloomy Victorian house. There was less reserve between neighbours and everyone seemed to be in and out of one another's house, papering over pin-pricks of light in blackened windows, claiming access to stairways and roofs, keeping meaning-less records of alerts and all-clears, drinking cups of tea at all hours and, increasingly as time went on, arguing about the sort of Britain they wanted after the war.

I was not old enough to take much of an interest in proposals for social change but I was aware of the lowering of social barriers and of the popular support for social reform. This had a profound influence on me and, so it seems now, on many others of my generation. At the start of the war my mother was on tour in Blackpool and some evacuees from Liverpool were lodged temporarily in our boarding-house. A poorly dressed woman with leaden eyes climbed off the bus with a tearful baby and, without a thought for the landlady and two sharp-nosed women guests, undid her blouse and pulled out one of her breasts to comfort the child. I remember how shocked the three women were by her unselfconscious behaviour and, more important, how shocked they and many others were too by the poverty of the evacuees. In the early part of the war the upheavals of evacuation caused many people to understand for the first time how the other half lived, and what the years of unemployment had wrought. Here were two nations confronted.

The rich were chastened by this sudden revelation of social misery and the young wanted to put an end to it. Involvement in the problems of others, and a respect for them, as well as mere patriotism, made people prepared to accept sacrifices. National assistance was liberalised, welfare foods and all kinds of benefits for mothers were introduced, stiff taxation was accepted and the most envied rationing system of the war raised the living standards of the poor. Experts who had been arguing seriously whether the number of 'unemploy-ables' in the population was half a million or one million were shamed into silence. Other experts who had predicted widespread war neurosis and panic to get out of the cities were humbled by the calm and steadiness of the people. Infant and child mortality fell sharply, morbidity was amazingly low and, despite the apparent rigours of rationing, the submarine blockade, the bombing and everything else, a near-miracle occurred – there was in 1942 a greater sense of national well-being than in any year of the thirties.

Although social objectives which had been sought from one Royal Commission to another were now secured within weeks and months few people were satisfied. The guilt of the Thirties had to be erased. The Beveridge Report successfully competed with the battles in Russia and North Africa for the front pages of the daily press. A Coalition Government produced the first White Paper on a National Health Service, more remarkable, in some respects, than the plan finally agreed; *The Times* even complained in the middle of the war that the Government was dragging its feet in putting forward proposals for social reform; and a Tory who had been one of the Foreign Office spokesmen in Parliament at the time of Munich actually piloted through the Education Act of 1944. These were measures of the agreement that existed. A new post-war society seemed ready to emerge.

The details of the plan seemed not to matter. The will was there and that was enough. The public was determined that there must be no return to pre-war conditions and sought a Government which could maintain the momentum of social change. Looking back now at the popular feeling generated by the events of the war years it is difficult to understand how anyone could have been surprised by the Labour Party's victory. A transformation had taken place. In the Britain of 1945 it seems possible to detect the two human impulses which, as I understand it, are necessary to any socialist society. Tracing what has happened to these two provides, in a sense, the theme of this essay. There was an attitude of trust, tolerance, generosity, goodwill – call it what you like – towards others; a pervasive faith in human nature. Then there was a prevailing mood of self-denial, a readiness to share the good things in life and to see that others got the same privileges as oneself; an urge to give everyone, including the poor, the sick, the old and the handicapped, the chance of having certain elementary rights or freedoms so that they could achieve individual self-respect. Am I wrong in supposing that these were the really important attitudes struck by society then, despite the effects of a long war? After all, millions of people were thankful to be safely home once more, and their memories were still fresh with the sufferings of the victims of the war.

Perhaps I exaggerate. Perhaps I am being sentimental about the carry-over of a popular mood from the period of the blitz. Whatever the truth, many others, now in their late twenties and thirties, felt much the same. From wartime experiences of evacuation, sleeping in shelters, civil defence, farming and forestry camps during school holidays and finally service in the armed forces, many of us gained a sense of fair shares of common effort, of mixing with people of different class and of planning for the future which came at the most impressionable age and which could at times be intoxicating.

From 'A Society for People' by Peter Townsend in *Conviction*,
edited by Norman Mackenzie (MacGibbon & Kee, 1958)

Anne Phillips
FRATERNITY (1984)

In the gloom of present-day politics, socialists may well lose themselves in nostalgic dreams of fraternity. We feel ourselves hemmed in by a world of self-interest, and experience the daily weakening of those bonds of class and community which gave the socialist movement so much of its strength. The world we now inhabit seems markedly individualist; we cast around in trepidation for some surviving signs of collective feeling.

We talk forlornly of the old back-to-backs with their bustling street life, compare them wistfully with anonymous tower blocks. We recall the mining communities where workers shared their poverty and danger, then shudder at the new towns with their semi-detacheds and their holidays in Spain. We have, perhaps, fond memories of the extended family where each generation played its role, and we shake our heads at its nuclear substitute with granny condemned to an old people's home. Self-help, self-interest, self-protection – these seem the catch-words of today. Fraternity, solidarity, even co-operation, look sadly out of place.

Socialists do their best to resist nostalgia, but even the strongest will quail before such images . . .

Those who mourn the lost community are often on shaky ground, with an over-romantic view of the past and unnecessarily bleak picture of the present. The mining communities were, after all, never typical of working-class existence, the back-to-back terraces contained all the frustrations of poverty as well as the comforts of belonging; on numerous criteria (the proportion of old people in institutions, the number of young people who leave their home town in search of work) communities are now *more* stable and caring than they used to be. And as far as fraternity itself is concerned, we should surely start with the admission that solidarity is not socialist in all its forms, that there are versions of it that repel as well as ones that attract. When we hear talk of the old boys' network, or the clannishness of the old school tie, we do not thrill to these exhibitions of community spirit. Solidarity can divide as well as unite, and some of what we have lost we should be glad to leave behind.

Fraternity in particular has a richly archaic ring and I want to argue we should leave it that way. Trade unionists, we know, are still brothers and send fraternal greetings, but now that one trade unionist in three is a woman such language has come increasingly under fire. Our ears are now more finely tuned to the tensions of sexual division, and when the longing for unity is expressed in terms of men, it begins to strike a discordant note. However grand the 'brotherhood of man' once sounded, today it is out of date. When we review the problem of solidarity, we should beware of slogans that seek to unite in the name of division.

I want in this essay to reassess the tradition of fraternity, arguing against any simple strategy of rehabilitation. As a model of solidarity it is flawed and partial, celebrating the unity of men and exclusion of women. As a basis for future action it is increasingly anachronistic, ignoring major changes that have occurred in the composition of the labour force . . .

In criticising the concept, I am not proposing we abandon all it represents. Like so much in our lives, politics demands a certain romance, and the harsh logic of self-interest is rarely enough to move us. There are reasons why we thrill to those moments of unity, and reasons why we despair when they seem to elude us. But if we hope to build solidarity on a firm foundation, we have to start from a clear understanding of the differences that divide us. We will never secure alliances between men and women, black people and white people, white-collar workers and those in manual trades if we try to deny the conflicts that rage between us. Unity premised on simple similarity can be powerful but in the end restrictive – attractive but in the end destructive. We are not all the same, and the pretence that we are will not help us to change our world . . .

If I am right in thinking that such work-based unity is beginning to lose its power, then we have to look to alternative sources of strength and solidarity.

Socialists had good reasons for believing that solidarity is created at work, but bad reasons for claiming this as the only site of political strength. If the women's movement has shown anything, it is that there are other kinds of unity and other forms of power. Think of the way the women of Greenham Common have transformed the debate over nuclear weapons, and compare this with the empty slogans of those who say that 'only workers' power will stop the bomb'. Of course a few women camped outside an army base will not change history; of course the women who take such actions are atypical; of course the majority of women would find it impossible to join them there. Yet women *have* identified with Greenham Common on a massive scale – and opinion polls show how radicalising this experience has been.

Greenham Common is not a prototype for all future action, any more than was the bonding of manual workers in the past. That lesson rather is that there are many different ways of working for a better future, many and varied forms of solidarity. We should, I believe, abandon the search for a single model, discard our last dogmas on the typical 'worker'. Capitalism has not created a homogeneous working class and, for the foreseeable future, is unlikely to do so. What brings us together *may* be similarities in our work lives, but it may equally be similarities in our home lives. Sometimes it will simply be a common commitment to social or economic change, cutting across differences in the way we live and the jobs we do. We should not act as if the only solidarity worth its name is the one that unites through every aspect of our existence. Rather, we should think of socialist unity as a complicated – maybe even painful – construction from many *different* solidarities, some of which will inevitably be in conflict.

The argument I am putting here may seem a negative one, but it can form the basis for more positive steps. The crucial starting point is not to glorify the past. Some of the old traditions were tainted and divisive; some of what we feel we have lost is better left behind. Whatever solidarity we build on for the future must rest on a new foundation. Not the false fraternity that constrains us to a family likeness, but that more complex unity that stems from recognising and facing those conflicts that can divide us.

From 'Fraternity' by Anne Phillips in *Fabian Essays in Socialist Thought*, edited by Ben Pimlott (Heinemann, 1984

DEVELOPING A COMMON PURPOSE

'Individually we cannot do enough, though individual effort matters enormously. Together we can, quite literally, move mountains'

G.D.H. Cole

DEFINING THE COMMUNITY (1920)

Community is the broadest and most inclusive of the words which we have to define. By a 'community' I mean a complex of social life, a complex including a number of human beings living together under conditions of social relationship, bound together by a common, however constantly changing, stock of conventions, customs, and traditions, and conscious to some extent of common social objects and interests. It will be seen at once that this is a very wide and elastic form of definition, under which a wide variety of social groups might be included. It is, indeed, of the essence of community that its definition should be this elastic; for 'community' is essentially a subjective term, and the reality of it consists in the consciousness of it among its members. Thus a family is, or may be, a community, and any group which is, in a certain degree, self-contained and self-subsistent is or may be a community. A medieval university, a monastic brotherhood, a co-operative colony – these and many more may possess those elements of social comprehensiveness which give a right to the title of community.

But, if the word is wide and inclusive enough in one aspect, it is essentially limited in another. In order to be a community, a group must exist for the good life and not merely for the furtherance of some specific and partial purpose. Thus, a cricket club, or a trade union, or a political party is not a community, because it is not a self-contained group of complete human beings, but an association formed for the furtherance of a particular interest common to a number of persons who have other interests outside it. A community is thus essentially a social unit or group to which human beings belong, as distinguished from an association with which they are only connected.

Yet, despite this wholeness and universality which are of the nature of community, it is not the case that a man can belong to one community only. A community is an inclusive circle of social life; but round many narrow circles of family may be drawn the wider circles of the city, and round many circles of city the yet wider circle of the province or the nation, while round all the circles of nation is drawn the yet wider and more cosmopolitan circle of world civilisation itself. No one of these wider circles necessarily absorbs the narrower circles within it: they may maintain themselves as real and inclusive centres of social life within the wider communities beyond them. A man is not less a member of his family or a citizen of his city for being an Englishman or a cosmopolitan. Membership of two communities my lead, for the individual, to a real conflict of loyalties; but the reality of the conflict only serves to measure the reality of the communal obligation involved . . .

. . . It is plain, then, that our thing, 'a community', does not necessarily involve any particular form of social organisation, or indeed any social organisation at all. It is not an institution or a formal association, but a centre of feeling, a group felt by its members to be a real and operative unity. In any community larger than the family, however, this feeling of unity, with its accompanying need for common action, almost necessarily involves conscious and formal organisation. The feeling of unity makes it easy for the members of a community to associate themselves together for the various purposes which they have in common, and, where the community is free from external hindrances, such association surely arises and is devoted to the execution of these common purposes. Where a community is not free, and an external power hinders or attempts to prevent organisation, association still asserts itself, but instead of directing itself to the fulfilment of the various social needs of the group, almost every association is diverted to subserve the task of emancipating the community from external hindrances.

From *The Social Theory* by G.D.H. Cole (Methuen, 1920)

R.H. Tawney
ORGANISING ON THE BASIS OF FUNCTION (1920)

The conditions of a right organisation of industry are, therefore, permanent, unchanging, and capable of being apprehended by the most elementary intelligence, provided it will read the nature of its countrymen in the large outlines of history, not in the bloodless abstractions of experts. The first is that it should be subordinated to the community in such a way as to render the best service technically possible, that those who render that service faithfully should be honourably paid, and those who render no service should not be paid at all, because it is of the essence of a function that it should find its meaning in the satisfaction not of itself, but of the end which it serves. The second is that its direction and government should be in the hands of persons who are responsible to those who are directed and governed, because it is the condition of economic freedom that men should not be ruled by an authority which they cannot control. The industrial problem, in fact, is a problem of right, not merely of material misery, and because it is a problem of right it is most acute among those sections of the working classes whose material misery is least. It is a question, first of function, and secondly of freedom.

A function may be defined as an activity which embodies and expresses the idea of social purpose. The essence of it is that the agent does not perform it merely for personal gain or to gratify himself, but recognises that he is responsible for its discharge to some higher authority. The purpose of industry is obvious. It is to supply man with things which are necessary, useful or beautiful, and thus to bring life to body or spirit. In so far as it is governed by this end, it is among the most important of human activities. In so far as it is diverted from it, it may be harmless, amusing, or even exhilarating to those who carry it on, but it possesses no more social significance than the orderly business of ants and bees, the strutting of peacocks, or the struggles of carnivorous animals over carrion. Men have normally appreciated this fact, however unwilling or unable they may have been to act upon it; and therefore from time to time, in so far as they have been able to control the forces of violence and greed, they have adopted various expedients for emphasising the social quality of economic activity. It is not easy, however, to emphasise it effectively, because to do so requires a constant effort of will, against which egotistical instincts are in rebellion, and because, if that will is to prevail, it must be embodied in some social and political organisation, which may itself become so arbitrary, tyrannical and corrupt as to thwart the performance of function instead of promoting it. When this process of degeneration has gone far, as in most European countries it had by the middle of the eighteenth century, the indispensable thing is to break the dead organisation up and to clear the ground. In the course of doing so, the individual is emancipated and his rights are enlarged; but the idea of social purpose is discredited by the discredit justly attaching to the obsolete order in which it is embodied.

It is not surprising, therefore, that in the new industrial societies which arose on the ruins of the old regime the dominant note should have been the insistence upon individual rights, irrespective of any social purpose to which their exercise contributed . . .

. . . No doubt it is better that individuals should have absolute rights than that the State or the Government should have them; and it was the reaction against the abuses of absolute power by the State which led in the eighteenth century to the declaration of the absolute right of the individuals. The most obvious defence against the assertion of one extreme was the assertion of the other. Because governments and the relics of feudalism had encroached upon the property of individuals it was affirmed that the right of property was absolute; because they had strangled enterprise, it was affirmed that every man had a natural right to conduct his business as he pleased. But, in reality, both the one assertion and the other are false, and, if applied to practice, must lead to disaster. The State has no absolute rights; they are limited by its commission. The individual has no absolute rights; they are relative to the function which he performs in the community of which he is a member, because, unless they are so limited, the consequences must be something in the nature of private war. All rights, in short, are conditional and derivative, because all power should be conditional and derivative. They are derived from the end or purpose of the society in which they exist. They are conditional on being used to contribute to the attainment of that end, not to thwart it. And this means in practice that, if society is to be healthy, men must regard themselves not as the owners of rights, but as trustees for the discharge of functions and the instruments of a social purpose . . .

So the organisation of society on the basis of function, instead of on that of rights, implies three things. It means, first, that proprietary rights shall be maintained when they are accompanied by the performance of service and abolished when they are not. It means, second, that the producers shall stand in a direct relation to the community for whom production is carried on, so that their responsibility to it may be obvious and unmistakable, not lost, as at present, through their immediate subordination to shareholders whose interest is not service but gain. It means, in the third place, that the obligation for the maintenance of the service shall rest upon the professional organisation of those who perform it, and that, subject to the supervision and criticism of the consumers, those organisations shall exercise so much voice in the government of industry as may be needed to secure that the obligation is discharged. It is obvious, indeed, that no change of system or machinery can avert those causes of social *malaise* which consist in the egotism, greed, or quarrelsomeness of human nature. What it can do is to create an environment in which those are not the qualities which are encouraged. It cannot secure that men live up to their principles. What it can do is establish their social order upon principles to which, if they please, they can live up and not live down. It cannot control their actions. It can offer them an end on which to fix their minds. And, as their minds are, so, in the long run and with exceptions, their practical activity will be . . .

Viewed from that angle issues which are insoluble when treated on the basis of rights may be found more susceptible of reasonable treatment. For a purpose is, in the first place, a principle of limitation. It determines the end for which, and therefore the limits within which, an activity is to be carried on. It divides what is worth doing from what is not, and settles the scale upon which what is worth doing ought to be done. It is, in the second place, a principle of unity, because it supplies a common end to which efforts can be directed, and submits interests, which would otherwise conflict, to the judgment of an overruling object. It is, in the third place, a principle of apportionment or distribution. It assigns to the different parties of groups engaged in a common undertaking the place which they are to occupy in carrying it out. Thus it establishes order, not upon chance or power, but upon a principle, and bases remuneration not upon what men can with good fortune snatch for themselves nor upon what, if unlucky, they can be induced to accept, but upon what is appropriate to their function, no more and no less, so that those who perform no function receive no payment, and those who contribute to the common end receive honourable payment for honourable service . . .

The famous lines in which Piccarda explains to Dante the order of Paradise are a description of a complex and multiform society which is united by overmastering devotion to a common end. By that end all stations are assigned and all activities are valued. The parts derive their quality from their place in the system, and are so permeated by the unity which they express that they themselves are glad to be forgotten, as the ribs of an arch carry the eye from the floor from which they spring to the vault in which they meet and interlace. Such a combination of unity and diversity is possible only to a society which subordinates its activities to the principle of purpose. For what that principle offers is not merely a standard for determining the relations of different classes and groups of producers, but a scale of moral values.

From *The Sickness of an Acquisitive Society* by R.H. Tawney (Fabian pamphlet, 1920)

Sidney Webb

THE INDIVIDUALIST TOWN COUNCILLOR (1890)

The development of socialistic institutions is gradual, persistent, and carried out by legislative enactments. Whatever may be the case in other countries, no one acquainted with English politics can reasonably fear that this feature will not continue. No student of society, whether socialist or individualist, can doubt that any important organic changes will necessarily be (1) democratic, and thus acceptable to a majority of the people and prepared for in the minds of all; (2) gradual, and thus causing no dislocation, however rapid may be the rate of progress; (3) not regarded as immoral by the mass of people, and thus not subjectively demoralising to them; and in this country, at any rate (4), constitutional and peaceful.

If socialism is thus neither a Utopia nor a specially violent method of revolution, what, it may be asked, are its distinctive features? It is not easy to reply in a single sentence. The ideas denoted by socialism represent the outcome of a gradual change of thought in economics, ethics and politics. The socialist is distinguished from the individualist, not so much by any special shibboleth as by a complete difference as to the main principles of social organisation. The essential contribution of the century to sociology has been the supersession of the individual by the community as the starting point of social investigations. Socialism is the product of this development, arising with it from the contemporary industrial evolution. On the economic side, socialism implies the collective administration of rent and interest, leaving to the individual only the wages of his labour, of hand or brain. On the political side, it involves the collective control over, and ultimate administration of, all the main instruments of wealth production. On the ethical side, it expresses the real recognition of fraternity, the universal obligation of personal service, and the subordination of individual ends to the common good . . .

It may be summed up that the progress of socialism in England has hitherto been, and is still being accomplished, in four leading directions, viz:

1. Constantly increasing restrictions upon the private ownership of land and capital. (Factory Acts, etc.)

2. Gradual supersession of private industrial ventures by public administration. (National telegraphs, municipal tramways, parochial schools.)

3. Progressive absorption by taxation of unearned incomes (rent and inter-est), and 'rent of ability'. (Income tax, taxes on real property etc.)

4. The supplementing of private charity by public organisation, aiming at raising the condition of the 'residuum'. (Public education, improved dwellings, etc.)

Philanthropic reformers will be surprised to find some of these measures classed as socialistic. They, as well as many socialists, have been so accustommed to think of socialism merely as an ideal, that they do not recognise the steps by which the ideal is being gradually realised. Wherever rent and interest are being absorbed under public control for public purposes, wherever the collective organisation of the community is being employed in place of individual effort, wherever, in the public interest, the free use of private land or capital is further restrained – there one more step towards the complete realisation of the socialist ideal is being taken. Society is reforming itself on collectivist, not on individualist principles, and although the advocates of each particular change intend no further alteration, the result is nevertheless an increasing social momentum in the same general direction . . .

Our unconscious acceptance of this progressive socialism is a striking testimony to the change which has come over the country of Godwin and Malthus. The 'practical man', oblivious or contemptuous of any theory of the social organism or general principles of social organisation, has been forced by the necessities of the time, into an ever deepening collectivist channel. Socialism, of course, he still rejects and despises. The individualist town councillor will walk along the municipal pavement, lit by municipal gas and cleansed by municipal brooms with municipal water, and seeing by the municipal clock in the municipal market, that he is too early to meet his children coming from the municipal school hard by the county lunatic asylum and municipal hospital, he will use the national telegraph system to tell them not to walk through the municipal park but to come by the municipal tramway to meet him in the municipal reading room, by the municipal art gallery, museum and library, where he intends to consult some of the national publications in order to prepare his next speech in the municipal town hall, in favour of the nationalisation of canals and the increase of the Government control over the railway system. 'Socialism, sir,' he will say, 'don't waste the time of a practical man by your fantastic absurdities. Self-help, sir, individual self-help, that's what's made our country what it is.'

From *Socialism in England* by Sidney Webb (1890)

John Stuart Mill

CHANGING THE INDIVIDUALIST CULTURE (1908)

In those days I had seen little further than the old school of political economists into the possibilities of fundamental improvement in social arrangements. Private property, as now understood, and inheritance, appeared to me, as to them, the *dernier mot* of legislation: and I looked no further than to mitigating the inequalities consequent on these institutions, by getting rid of primogeniture and entails. The notion that it was possible to go further than this in removing the injustice – for injustice it is, whether admitting of a complete remedy or not – involved in the fact that some are born to riches and the vast majority to poverty, I then reckoned chimerical, and only hoped that by universal education, leading to voluntary restraint on population, the portion of the poor might be made more tolerable. In short, I was a democrat, but not the least of a socialist. We were now much less democrats than I had been, because so long as education continues to be so wretchedly imperfect, we dreaded the ignorance and especially the selfishness and brutality of the mass: but our idea of ultimate improvement went far beyond democracy, and would class us decidedly under the general designation of socialists. While we repudiated with the greatest energy that tyranny of society over the individual which most socialist systems are supposed to involve, we yet looked forward to a time when society will no longer be divided into the idle and the industrious; when the rule that they who do not work shall not eat, will be applied not to paupers only, but impartially to all; when the division of the produce of labour, instead of depending, as in so great a degree it now does, on the accident of birth, will be made by concert on an acknowledged principle of justice; and when it will no longer either be, or thought to be, impossible for human beings to exert themselves strenuously in procuring benefits which are not to be exclusively their own, but to be shared with the society they belong to. The social problem of the future we considered to be, how to unite the greatest individual liberty of action, with a common ownership in the raw material of the globe, and an equal participation of all in the benefits of combined labour. We had not the presumption to suppose that we could already foresee, by what precise form of institutions these objects could most effectually be attained, or at how near or how distant a period they would become practicable. We saw clearly that to render any such social transformation either possible or desirable, an equivalent change of character must take place both in the uncultivated herd who now compose the labouring masses, and in the immense majority of their employers. Both these classes must learn by practice to labour and combine for generous, or at all events for public and social purposes, and not, as hitherto, solely for narrowly interested ones. But the capacity to do this has always existed in mankind, and is not, nor is ever likely to be, extinct. Education, habit, and the cultivation of the sentiments, will make a common man dig or weave for his country, as readily as fight for his country. True enough, it is only by slow degrees, and a system of culture prolonged through successive generations, that men in general can be brought up to this point. But the hindrance is not in the essential constitution of human nature. Interest in the common good is at present so weak a motive in the generality, not because it can never be otherwise, but because the mind is not accustomed to dwell on it as it dwells from morning till night on things which tend only to personal advantage. When called into activity, as only self-interest now is, by the daily course of life, and spurred from behind by the love of distinction and the fear of shame, it is capable of producing, even in common men, the most strenuous exertions as well as the most heroic sacrifices. The deep-rooted selfishness which forms the general character of the existing state of society, is *so* deeply rooted, only because the whole course of existing institutions tends to foster it; and modern institutions in some respects more than ancient, since the occasions on which the individual is called on to do anything for the public without receiving its pay, are far less frequent in modern life than in the smaller commonwealths of antiquity. These considerations did not make us overlook the folly of premature attempts to dispense with the inducements of private interest in social affairs, while no substitute for them has been or can be provided: but we regarded all existing institutions and social arrangements as being (in a phrase I once heard from Austin) 'merely provisional', and we welcomed with the greatest pleasure and interest all socialistic experiments by select individuals (such as the co-operative societies), which, whether they succeeded or failed, could not but operate as a most useful education of those who took part in them, by cultivating their capacity of acting upon motives pointing directly to the general good, or making them aware of the defects which render them and others incapable of doing so.

From *Autobiography* by John Stuart Mill (Longmans, Green & Co, 1908)

G.D.H. Cole
THE STATE AND SOVEREIGNTY (1917)

The State seems to be the community, and can plausibly be put forward as the community, simply because it does claim to be the supreme representative of the community, and because it does at present hold a position of such power as to make its influence in the community superior to that of any other association. But all this is merely a question of fact. The fact that the State claims to be the community, and in fact exercises the greatest part of the community's power, does nothing to prove that the State is rightfully the community, or its sole representative, or that it has an absolute claim upon the individual's loyalty and service . . .

The theory of State sovereignty falls to the ground, if this view of the fundamental nature of the State is correct. State sovereignty, if the phrase has any meaning at all, implies, not indeed that the State ought to interfere in every sphere of human action, but that the State has ultimately a right to do so. It regards the State as the representative of the community in the fullest sense, and as the superior both of the individual 'subject' and of every other form of association. It regards the State as the full and complete representative of the individual, whereas, if the view just put forward is correct, the State only represents the individual in his particular aspect of 'neighbour', 'user' and 'enjoyer'. The advocates of State sovereignty, if they do not regard the State as being the community, do at least regard it as 'sustaining the person of the community', whereas our whole view is that the person of the community cannot truly be sustained by any single form of organisation . . .

Our view, then, of the nature and rights of vocational and other forms of association is profoundly modified by the view we have taken of the nature of the State. We now see such associations as natural expressions and instruments of the purposes which certain groups of individuals have in common, just as we see the

State, both in national and in local government, as the natural expression and instrument of other purposes which the same individuals have in common when they are grouped in another way. Similarly, our whole view of the relation of the State to other forms of association is profoundly modified, and we come to see the State, not as the 'divine' and universally sovereign representative of the community, but as one among a number of forms of association in which men are grouped according to the purposes which they have in common. Men produce in common, and all sorts of association, from the medieval guild to the modern trust and the modern trade union, spring from their need to co-operate in production: they use and enjoy in common, and out of their need for common action and protection in their use and enjoyment spring the long series of States, the various phases of co-operation, the increasing developments of local government. They hold views in common, and out of their common opinions spring propagandist and doctrinaire associ-ations of every sort: they believe in common, and out of their need for fellowship and worship spring churches, connections and covenants.

In all this diversity of human association, the State can claim an important place, but not a solitary grandeur. States exist for the execution of that very important class of collective actions which affect all the members of the communities in which they exist equally and in the same way. For other classes of action, in respect of which men fall into different groups, other forms of association are needed, and these forms of association are no less sovereign in their sphere than the State in its sphere. There is no universal sovereign in the community, because the individuals who compose that community cannot be fully represented by any form of association. For different purposes, they fall into different groups, and only in the action and inter-action of these groups does sovereignty exist. Even so, it is an incomplete sovereignty; for all the groups, which together make up society, are imperfectly representative of that general will which resides in the community alone.

From *Self-Government in Industry* by G.D.H. Cole (G. Bell, 1917; Hutchinson, 1972)

Robert Owen

A NEW VIEW OF SOCIETY (1813)

The members of any community may by degrees be trained to live without idleness, without poverty, without crime, and without punishment. Train any population rationally, and they will be rational. Furnish honest and useful employments to those so trained, and such employments they will greatly prefer to dishonest or injurious occupations. It is beyond all calculation the interest of every government to provide that training and that employment: and to provide both is easily practicable.

The first is to be obtained by a national system for the formation of character;

the second, by governments preparing a reserve of employment for the surplus working classes, when the general demand for labour throughout the country is not equal to the full occupation of the whole: that employment to be on useful national objects.

The national plan for the formation of character should include all the modern improvements of education, without regard to the system of any one individual; and should not exclude the child of any one subject in the empire.

Can any question be brought forward of deeper interest to the community than that which affects the formation of character and the well-being of every individual within the empire? A question too which, when understood, will be found to offer the means of amelioration to the revenues of these kingdoms, far beyond any practical plan now likely to be devised. Yet, important as are considerations of revenue, they must appear secondary when put in competition with the lives, liberty, and comfort of our fellow subjects, which are now hourly sacrificed.

From *A New View of Society and Other Writings* by Robert Owen (Dent, 1927)

William Morris
HOW I BECAME A SOCIALIST (1894)

I am asked by the editor to give some sort of a history of the above conversion, and I feel that it may be of some use to do so, if my readers will look upon me as a type of a certain group of people, but not so easy to do clearly, briefly, and truly. Let me, however, try. But first, I will say what I mean by being a socialist, since I am told that the word no longer expresses definitely and with certainty what it did ten years ago. Well, what I mean by socialism is a condition of society in which there should be neither rich nor poor, neither master nor master's man, neither idle nor overworked, neither brain-sick brain workers, nor heart-sick hand workers, in a word, in which all men would be living in equality of condition, and would manage their affairs unwastefully, and with the full consciousness that harm to one would mean harm to all – the realisation at last of the meaning of the word COMMONWEALTH.

From *William Morris: Selected Writings and Designs*, edited by Asa Briggs (1962)

William Temple
OBJECTIVES FOR CITIZENS (1942)

To many it appears evident that we have allowed the making of profits, which is necessary as a means to the continuance of the industry, to get into the first place which properly belongs to the supply of human needs – the true end of industry. We have inverted the 'natural order'. Instead of finance existing to facilitate production and production existing to supply needs, the supply of needs is made the means to profitable production; and production itself is controlled as much as it is facilitated by finance.If that is true, it is the duty of Christians to become aware of it and to demand a remedy. It cannot be said that it is their duty as Christians to know what the remedy is, for this involves many technical matters. But they are entitled to call upon the Government to set before itself the fol-lowing objectives and pursue them as steadily and rapidly as opportunity permits:

1. Every child should find itself a member of a family housed with decency and dignity, so that it may grow up as a member of that basic community in a happy fellowship unspoilt by underfeeding or overcrowding, by dirty and drab surroundings or by mechanical monotony of environment.

2. Every child should have the opportunity of an education till years of maturity, so planned as to allow for his peculiar aptitudes and make possible their full development. This education should throughout be inspired by faith in God and find its focus in worship.

3. Every citizen should be secure in possession of such income as will enable him to maintain a home and bring up children in such conditions as are described in paragraph 1 above.

4. Every citizen should have a voice in the conduct of the business or industry which is carried on by means of his labour, and the satisfaction of knowing that his labour is directed to the well-being of the community.

5. Every citizen should have sufficient daily leisure, with two days of rest in seven, and, if an employee, an annual holiday with pay, to enable him to enjoy a full personal life with such interests and activities as his tasks and talents may direct.

6. Every citizen should have assured liberty in the forms of freedom of worship, of speech, of assembly, and of association for special purposes.

As a background to these six points we need to insist on the principle laid down by the four religious leaders in their Foundations of Peace (*The Times*, 21 December 1940): 'The resources of the earth should be used as God's gifts to the whole human race, and used with due consideration for the needs of the present and future generations.'

Utopian? Only in the sense that we cannot have it all tomorrow. But we can set ourselves steadily to advance towards that six-fold objective. It can all be summed up in a phrase: *the aim of a Christian social order is the fullest possible development of individual personality in the widest and deepest possible fellowship.*

From *Christianity and the Social Order* by William Temple (Penguin, 1942)

Richard Titmuss

GENEROSITY TOWARDS STRANGERS (1970)

What is unique as an instrument of social policy among the countries we have surveyed is the National Health Service and the values it embodies. Attitudes to and relationships with the National Blood Transfusion Service among the general public since 1948 can only be understood within the context of the Health Service. The most unsordid act of British social policy in the twentieth century has allowed and encouraged sentiments of altruism, reciprocity and social duty to express themselves; to be made explicit and identifiable in measurable patterns of behaviour by all social groups and classes. In part, this is attributable to the fact that, structurally and functionally, the Health Service is not socially divisive; its universal and free access basis has contributed much, we believe, to the social liberties of the subject in allowing people the choice to give or not to give blood for unseen strangers.

Of course, in probing the deeper human motives for giving and return-giving, for altruism and self-love, it would be facile to suggest that socialised medicine was wholly responsible. We have not said that at all. What we do suggest, however, is that the ways in which society organises and structures its social institutions – and particularly its health and welfare systems – can encourage or discourage the altruistic in man; such systems can foster integration or alienation; they can allow the 'theme of the gift' (to recall Mauss's words) – of generosity towards strangers – to spread among and between social groups and generations. This, we further suggest, is an aspect of freedom in the twentieth century which, compared with the emphasis on consumer choice in material acquisitiveness, is insufficiently recognised. It is indeed little understood how modern society, technical, professional, large-scale organised society, allows few opportunities for ordinary people to articulate giving in morally practical terms outside their own network of family and personal relationships . . .

From our study of the private market in blood in the United States we have concluded that the commercialisation of blood and donor relationships represses the expression of altruism, erodes the sense of community, lowers scientific standards, limits both personal and professional freedoms, sanctions the making of profits in hospitals and clinical laboratories, legalises hostility between doctor and patient, subjects critical areas of medicine to the laws of the marketplace, places immense social costs on those least able to bear them.

From *The Gift Relationship: from Human Blood to Social Policy*
by Richard M. Titmuss (George Allen & Unwin, 1970)

A.H. Halsey
A FRATERNAL SOCIETY (1978)

Past failures to achieve fair and equal social distribution have driven some to apathy, others to a belief in a violent seizure of power and the imposition of an authoritarian social order, and still others to denial of the possibility or even desirability of an egalitarian society. These are the roads to tyranny. Our experiences of industrial, nationalist, and racial conflict continually demonstrate the need for a new sense of equality to replace old class-restrictive liberties and status-crippled fraternities. We have still to provide a common experience of citizenship in childhood and old age, in work and play, and in health and sickness. We have still, in short, to develop a common culture to replace the divided cultures of class and status.

Our society cannot stand on such shifting foundations. To strengthen them, we need principles and practices of social distribution which are acknowledged to be just by the great majority. And in a world of growing visibility of reference groups, these principles will be seen as just only if they actually are just. The implication is that in a political democracy which secures our liberties, the paramount principle of distribution must be equality. Equality of opportunity is not enough. It is a state of affairs we have still not reached but which is, in any case, a step towards a society that could be more ruthlessly stratified than the one we live in now. Nor is it enough to eliminate all irrelevant discriminations of skin, colour, sex, cultural background, or family upbringing. We need full equality of the basic material conditions of social life. If poverty remains in Britain this is not because the technical means to its abolition are missing: it is because of an inadequate sense of moral implication in the lives of compatriots. It is a failure not of economic production, but of fraternal distribution. The guarantee of the material essentials for freedom from want does not require even a radically egalitarian policy. The fraternity nurtured in the kind of family experienced by the majority, extended by standards of schooling that most parents expect, and embodied in the political definitions of citizenship which were proclaimed during and after the Second World War, would put an end to poverty, once and for all.

Beyond this readily attainable minimum of a fraternal society, R.H. Tawney's conception still stands: because men are men, social institutions – property rights, and the organisation of industry, and the system of public health and education – should be planned, as far as is possible, to emphasise and strengthen, not the class differences which divide, but the common humanity which unites them.

From *Change in British Society* by A.H. Halsey (Oxford University Press, 3rd ed., 1986)

E.P. Thompson
WRITING BY CANDLELIGHT (1980)

I have said that you cannot change a political culture without changing the character of the people, and perhaps this is what has at last been done. The freeborn Briton has been bred out of the strain, and the stillborn Britperson has been bred in. The people have been drugged into an awe of office, and into that diminished reality-sense known as 'normality'. They can look at a nicely groomed expert on TV who is telling them about weapons of genocide, and they can suppose that this is 'authorised' by 'responsible persons' and in the normal course of things. An operation has been done on our culture and the guts have been taken out.

Maybe it was time. The freeborn Brit was full of self-congratulation, and other nations found him a hypocrite and bore. At home he used to strut about and rant of 'birthright' and of 'transmitting British liberties to posterity in their pristine purity'. In the eighteenth century, if a gentleman had cause to take issue with the Crown, and had reason to expect arrest, the style was to seat oneself in one's study and be taken while reading the Magna Carta to one's son. No one has a son or daughter who would put up with that sort of camp now.

Yet they did, those exhibitionists and hams, have a point of sorts. They stood in a certain position. They had a certain stance towards authority. The position was that the State was for them, they were not for the State. The stance was that of vigilance; they suspected authority's every move. They thought that the best State was weak, and that it was under weak central power that consensual order is best maintained.

'Pristine purity' makes one wrinkle one's nose. Yet it does so happen that we *are* their posterity, and that they *did* hand something down. And might we not also have some kind of a duty – I am sorry to use such a heavy word – to pass on down the line what we have inherited, in the way of rights and rules upon power? If we, with our universal literacy and high technology and great institutes of learning and comfortable homes, should seem to respect ourselves less, as citizens in the face of authority, than seventeenth-century petty gentry and yeomen, than tradesmen and artisans in the 1790s, than Clerkenwell bakers or Chartist working women and men – might we not have to wrinkle the nose at ourselves?

As I left my typewriter and walked down the lane this evening, multitudes of starlings were settling in the autumn trees. The air was full of chittering and hissing, as if the whole sky was saying 'sus-sus-sus'. The scene was menacing, as if an energy was out of control. Myriads of black wings swirled around the television aerials, like images of violence flocking towards the screens.

I must say, in honesty, that I can see no reason why we should be able to bar that foul storm out. I doubt whether we can pass our liberties on and I am not even confident that there will be a posterity to enjoy them. I am full of doubt.

All that I can say is that, since we have had the kind of history that we have had, it would be contemptible in us not to play out our old roles to the end.

From *Writing by Candlelight* by E.P. Thompson (Merlin Press, 1980)

David Marquand
ACTIVE CITIZENSHIP (1990)

'We do not learn to read or write, to ride, or swim, by being merely told how to do it,' wrote John Stuart Mill, that strange amalgam of civic republican and liberal individualist, 'but by doing it.' We learn the habits of community by practising them; we become responsible by taking responsibility. Where High Tory communitarians see the community as a matter of blood, soil and inheritance, a centre-left communitarian would see it as a construct, made and remade by the free and conscious decision of its members. The values of a centre-left communitarian would be civic republican values, the values of active citizenship, as opposed to passive subjecthood. But such values cannot be instilled from on high. They have to be learned; and they can be learned only in action. Centre-left communitarians will therefore seek the widest possible diffusion of responsibility and power – not only in what is conventionally thought of as the political sphere, but in what Mill called 'the business of life', at work, in the school system, in the health service, indeed wherever discussion and debate can help to determine collective purposes, and, in doing so, to give the participants a chance to experience the disciplines of collective choice.

Unlike the revisionist social democrats of the 1960s and 1970s, centre-left communitarians would not deploy public power only, or even mainly, through the central state. But where the neo-liberals tried to resolve the crisis of central-state social democracy by narrowing the scope of public power, centre-left communitarians would do so by widening access to it; and where neo-liberals draw in the frontiers of politics and citizenship, centre-left communitarians would extend them.

From 'A Language of Community' by David Marquand in *The Alternative – Politics for Change,* edited by Ben Pimlott, Anthony Wright and Tony Flower
(W.H. Allen & Co, 1990)

Sheila Rowbotham
A SELF-HELP COMMUNITY (1979)

I am not suggesting that the idea of mutual self-help is new or limited to the women's movement in the last decade. Indeed it has an ancient genealogy from the creation of friendly societies and co-operatives to the cycling clubs, workers' Esperanto groups, nurseries and socialist Sunday schools of the late nineteenth and early twentieth century. Mutual self-help was an integral part of the creation of a new culture of fellowship in the movement towards a socialist common-wealth. Moreover there has been a recent growth of an enormous variety of forms of self-help which relate to personal and social problems, like playgroups, One o'Clock clubs, Gingerbread, Parents Anonymous, Alcoholics Anonymous, Stigma along with voluntary organisations from the Samaritans, Citizens Advice to radical therapy and co-counselling. There has been a similar development of community projects, the law centres for example.

These movements assert the possibility of people changing themselves, and helping one another through co-operating. They are concerned about our social lives. Some carry an alternative to the monopoly of the State over welfare and question the partiality of the law. Some of the forms of organising in the women's movement relate to these self-help groups and can best be seen within this more general context. I am not suggesting that we can evolve to socialism through self-help or that all forms of self-help are necessarily radical or that self-help cannot coexist with a new form of labour reformism. It is evident that the coercive power of the State must be contested, that several class interests can use similar forms of organising and that some strands of the right can assert self-activity as well as the left. With the active support of working-class people in a community, mutual self-help forms provide a potential means of distinguishing between the coercive aspects of the State machinery and those activities of the State which are necessary to people in their everyday life. They raise the possibility of welfare control. Self-help community activity is not a substitute for the equally important radical struggles within the welfare state sector. But they can indicate ways of questioning the role of professionals and the means of creating more direct forms of control over welfare resources.

From *Beyond the Fragments: Feminism and the Making of Socialism*
by Sheila Rowbotham, Lynne Segaland Hilary Wainwright (Merlin Press, 1979)

The Commission on Social Justice
MAKING A GOOD SOCIETY (1994)

It is far easier to destroy than to create a sense of community. Building a good society is about far more than the success of its component parts. A good society depends not just on the economic success of 'I', the individual, but the social commitment of 'We', the community.

This is a notion that the deregulators have scorned for more than a decade. The credo of market individualism reduces relationships to contracts; it turns citizens into buyers and sellers in the marketplace. This is no basis for a stable thriving society, as the condition of the UK demonstrates. As the Archbishop of Canterbury has put it: 'One-eyed individualism and the privatisation of morality exacts a high price in personal and public dimensions of life alike.' For fifteen years we have been the subject of a more or less clinical experiment in free market economics and the results are plain for all to see: the social institutions on which a free society rests are in a state of advanced decay.

Investors argue that investment in social institutions is as important as investment in economic infrastructure. At the heart of social justice is not just the idea that we owe something to each other, but the belief that we gain from giving to each other. The pioneering socialist and social scientist R.H. Tawney was already insisting on this fundamental principle in the 1920s:

> No individual can create by his isolated actions a healthy environment, or establish an education system with a wide range of facilities, or organise an industry in such a manner as to diminish economic insecurity . . . Yet these are the conditions which make the difference between happiness and misery, and sometimes indeed, between life and death. In so far as they exist they are the source of a social income, received in the form not of money, but of increased well-being.

. . . The ideas of reciprocal responsibility and social well-being are at the core of this chapter. The American economist and sociologist Robert D. Putnamm calls this *social capital*, the 'networks, norms and trust that facilitate co-ordination and co-operation for mutual benefit'. Social capital consists of the institutions and relationships of a thriving civil society – from networks of neighbours to extended families, community groups to religious organisations, local businesses to local public services, youth clubs to parent-teacher associations, playgroups to police on the beat. Where you live, who else lives there, and how they live their lives – co-operatively or selfishly, responsibly or destructively – can be as important as personal resources in determining life chances . . .

The moral and social reconstruction of our society depends on our willingness to invest in social capital. We badly need to mend a social fabric that is so obviously torn apart. Social capital is a good in itself; it makes life possible. But social capital is also essential for economic renewal; the two go together. As Putnamm argues, economic prosperity depends not only on economic but also on social resources. Social capital can encourage new investment as well as making existing investment go further; it is the glue that bonds the benefits of economic and physical capital into marginalised communities . . .

It is difficult to exaggerate the change in thinking and working required of central government and civil servants, away from a top-down approach towards one rooted in the needs and skills of local communities. The Fabian notion, that governments know better than citizens what they need, cannot stand. The future lies in a new partnership, where national and local governments share power with their citizens, enabling local people to use the skills which are now being wasted. Much of the local outreach work of the Belfast Action Teams, for instance, demonstrates how social capital can be nurtured through vital links made between local communities and civil servants seconded to the teams. The quality of personal contact with the community is a key resource: much depends on engaging people who understand the problems communities face and are open-minded about how to tackle them.

We found on our own visits to Meadowell in Newcastle and to the Miles Platting and Ancoats Development Trust in Manchester that community action has been encouraged by a number of small but tangible projects that have an immediate effect on people's quality of life – from the purchase of a coach for youth outings to the development of play facilities and youth clubs for children and adolescents. But it is the local people who make the investment work . . . Changing the attitude of people towards themselves is as important as changing the attitude of others to the estate.

The experience of Meadowell in the initial stage revealed the importance of local people having hands-on experience, and not just a say. The Planning-for-Real exercises which took place there and in other community development projects helped to give local people real power over the planning process. Because of its considerable power for good as well as bad, the planning system must be central to community development. Planning authorities, both local and national, have profoundly affected life in Britain over the past fifty years

Deregulators dislike the planning system, which they see as an encumbrance on the free operation of the market. It does indeed give political power to people who lack market power: it is one important way in which economically marginalised people can be given a seat at the bargaining table with powerful economic interests, from supermarket chains to housing developers to multinational companies. Planning gain can help local people get what they actually want, rather than what they are assumed to need; and local communities must also be given the chance to say what they do not want. 'Value-added' comes most obviously in a wider choice of housing. Community approval for local, regional and strategic development plans increases com-munity 'ownership' of development strategies, and builds local trust and commitment. 'Citizens' plans' represent the ultimate step in the development of community expertise and confidence, but people will only make the effort to develop them if they are convinced that it is worth while, and that their views will be listened to.

From *Social Justice: Strategies for National Renewal*, the Report of the Commission on Social Justice (Vintage, 1994)

Herbert Morrison
DEFENDING CO-OPERATION

Behind our various measures what is the broad point of view and what is the purpose? It is the co-operative and socialist conception that the function of both national and local government is to use the State and the municipality to do things collectively for the individual citizens which are in themselves beneficial, and which individuals could not well do for themselves. Let me give a simple illustration of this point of view.

If each individual citizen of our towns was to construct and maintain that portion of the pavement and carriageway outside his house, we should face him with an impossible task, and our pavements and highways would be very patchy affairs. So we have created local authorities among whose duties is the construc-tion and maintenance of highways. That is to say, experience has taught us that if we leave such matters to individual householders, either the job would not be done at all, or it would be done in a very patchy and uncertain manner.

We have created local authorities through which we do for ourselves collectively things of that kind which we could not successfully achieve if we acted individually. Here, unrealised though it is by ninety-nine people out of a hundred, is the essence of the socialist and co-operative idea which is behind, not only those simple and accepted activities of civic administration, but which is also at the basis of the policy of His Majesty's Government.

And here let me say that I am no opponent of healthy competition. I enjoy it. Indeed within socialised industries we must go out of our way to stimulate and preserve healthy competition and lively emulation. Socialised industries must not be a happy hunting ground for the go-slows, for the dunderheads, for people on the look-out for a Utopia of idleness. But I do say that you can't run a country, or an industry, on competition alone. You need co-operation, too. We've heard too much about 'nature, red in tooth and claw'. There is a lot of friendliness and co-operation in nature, even in the jungle, and the human race would not have advanced to where it is now if it had not relied more on co-operation than on conflict. And anyway capitalism itself has been making great efforts to eliminate competition . . .

The human race has a long way to go yet. Individually we cannot do enough, though individual effort matters enormously. Together we can, quite literally, move mountains. We can bring into the service of our civilisation great forces and great resources – if we act collectively.

That is the wider and more virile idea and conception of citizenship behind the socialist idea and the programme of the Labour Party. That is the background to our belief in certain forms of national ownership and control – not only do we ask ourselves what benefits collective effort can bring us; we also, by the same token, look for what we can ourselves add to the common effort and to the common good.

So you see, there is underlying the work of this great Parliament a common philosophy of public service. The modern, rational socialist idea is behind it all.

From *Peaceful Revolution* by Herbert Morrison (Allen & Unwin, 1949)

Anonymous
IF IT WISNAE FOR THE UNION

Chorus
Too ra loo ra loo ra loo
I'll tell ye something awfu' true,
Ye wouldna' hae your telly the noo,
If it wisnae for the Union.

I had a boss in Aberdeen,
The nicest fella ever I've seen,
But I think he thought I wis awfa green,
Afore I joined the Union.

I had a boss they called Colquhoun,
The nicest fella in Glesga Toon.
Except for keeping yer wages doon,
Afore we joined the Union.

I had a boss his name wis Black,
He told me I could call him Jack,
He wis helluva good a gi'en ye the sack,
Afore we joined the Union.

Too ra loo ra loo ra loo,
I'll tell you something else that's true,
The boss would hae us black and blue,
If it wisnae for the Union.
I had a lass in Inverness,
And she wis one o' the very best,
But we couldnae afford tae marry unless
I went and joined the Union.

Too ra loo ra loo ra loo
There's twenty-four hours in a day it's true,
And we'd ha' worked the twenty-two,
If it wisnae for the Union.

Men and women listen tae me,
It's time tae rise up aff yer knee,
So raise the flag of Unity,
And forward with the Union.

Alan Bleasdale

ACTING FOR OTHERS

GEORGE: But that's what I'm telling you, that's why you've got to take them out, Ritchie. I mean, you know me, I was never one for taking men out if there was an option, especially if you had to take them back disillusioned and empty-handed.

RITCHIE: You know the score, dad.

GEORGE: But men can't work under those conditions.

RITCHIE: I know, dad. But look, times are hard now, let's face it. And most of them don't want to come out because they're thinking of their few bob.

GEORGE: Money before safety.

RITCHIE: That's the way it is.

JOHN: It's different now, dad. These days, y' go out on strike –

RITCHIE: Whatever the reasons –

JOHN: . . . before y' get out of the gates, management are havin' sing-songs an' wearing party hats.

RITCHIE: (*Indicating*) With 'Goodbye Boys' written on the front.

JOHN: Come back next week to get your cards.

GEORGE: But what are the men thinking about? Y' not goin' to tell me that they're safeguardin' their future – 'cos they've got none whatever way it goes – so they may as well do what's right an' honest.

> (*He coughs, Anna looks up*)

RITCHIE: (*Holding his hands up*) Look dad, I stood there yesterday, right, John . . .

JOHN: Yeah.

RITCHIE: . . . said to them I said, look – this workshop is a deathtrap, one of youse is going to get killed and it won't be a finger or a thumb next time, it'll be two hundredweight of bloody mincemeat lyin' there. They just looked at me.

JOHN: They just stood there, lookin' around, wonderin' who they'd like it to be.

RITCHIE: On the floor.

JOHN: As long as it wasn't them.

RITCHIE: I tell y', dad, honest to God – I look around sometimes at some of the fellers I'm supposed to be fightin' for . . . they don't seem to care or understand about anythin' that hasn't got tits or comes out of a barrel. I mean that.

GEORGE: No, no, no. You're wrong!

RITCHIE: I mean it.

MRS MALONE: (*Flaring – starts clearing the table*) And I won't have that kind of defeatist talk at my table. Go and eat jelly with the bairns, go on. And on your way to work in the morning, buy the *Daily Mail.*

JOHN: Ah come on mam, we were just –

MRS MALONE: Talking soft – that's what you were doing, having had it soft most of your lives.

    (*The brothers exchange glances*)

MRS MALONE: Talk to me about hardship and want. Talk to me about no shoes on your feet. Have you any idea what no shoes on your feet means?

JOHN: It means getting y' feet wet when it rains.

RITCHIE: And your socks go mouldy.

JOHN: It means the '30s mam, and soup kitchens and hunger marches. You with your father marchin' from the North-east, and my dad with his. It means people standing together and fighting. And it means another time and age.

MRS MALONE: And the only reason things got better was because men like your father, who refused to be slave labour and cannon fodder, who said 'No, I won't go down the docks every morning and stand in a stinking pen, and no I won't beg for half a day's work and come crawling home defeated.'

    (*She leaves the table and goes into the kitchen. She continues her speech when she comes back in.*)

MRS MALONE: And what's it got better for? So the likes of you can sit back and say you can't do nothing and let it all happen to us again?

    (*She storms out of the room, having cleared the contents of the table, except for George's soup bowl*)

JOHN: What did you let her read Karl Marx for, dad?

GEORGE: Dickens.

RITCHIE: Pardon?

GEORGE: *Tale of Two Cities.* We are the most important part of the nation. We are the ones who do the work.

From *Boys from the Blackstuff – George's Last Ride* by Alan Bleasdale

Socialist Sunday Schools

THE SOCIALIST TEN COMMANDMENTS (*c.*1920)

I   Love your schoolfellows, who will be your fellow-workmen in life.

II   Love learning, which is the food of the mind, and be grateful to your teacher as to your parents.

III   Make every day holy by good and useful deeds and kindly actions.

IV   Honour good men, be courteous to all, bow down to none.

V   Do not hate or speak evil of anyone, do not be revengeful, but stand up for your rights and resist oppression.

VI   Do not be cowardly, be a friend to the weak and love justice.

VII   Remember that all the good things of the earth are produced by labour, whoever enjoys them without working for them is stealing the bread of the workers.

VIII Observe and think in order to discover the Truth. Do not believe what is contrary to reason, and never deceive yourself or others.

IX   Do not think that he who loves his own country must hate and despise other nations, or wish for war, which is a remnant of barbarism.

X   Look forward to the day when all men will be free citizens of one fatherland and live together as brothers, in peace and righteousness.

Socialism is the hope of the World.

From *Socialist Sunday Schools: Aims, Objects and Organisation*

Hamish Henderson
FREEDOM COME ALL YE (*c.*1960)

Roch the wind in the clear day's dawin'
Blaws the cloods heilster-gowdie ower the brae
But there's mair nor a roch wind blawin'
Through the great glen o' the warld the day.
It's a thocht that wid gar oor rottans
A' they rogues that gang gallus fresh and gay
Tak the road and seek ither loanings
For their ill ploys tae sport an' play.

Nae mair will the bonny callants
Merch tae war when oor braggarts croosely craw
Nor wee weans frae pit-heid and clachan
Mourn the ships sailin' doon the Broomielaw.
Broken families in lands we've herriet

Will curse Scotland the Brave nae mair, nae mair
Black and white, ane till ither merrit,
Mak' the vile barracks o' their maisters bare.

Oh come all ye at hame wi' freedom
Never heed whit the hoodies croak for doom
In yer hoose a' the bairns o' Adam
Will find breid, barley bree and painted room.
When MacLean meets wi' his freens in Springburn
A' the roses and geans will turn tae bloom
An' the black boy fae yont Nyanga
Dings the fell gallows o' the burghers doon.

From *Chapbook: Scotland's Folk-life Magazine*, vol. 3, no. 6

Idris Davies
TONYPANDY (1945)

And meanwhile, Dai, with your woollen muffler
Tight around your pit-scarred neck,
Remind us of the gratitude we owe you,
We who so easily pass you by.

Remind us of your long endurance,
Those bitter battles the sun has never seen,
And remind us of the struggles you have waged
Against the crude philosophy of greed.

And remind all who strut with noses high in the air,
How the proudest of nations would falter without you,
And remind us when we lie on fireside cushions
Of the blood that is burnt within the flame.
And remind us when we kneel to the unknown God
And turn and cry to the cold infinite heavens,
Remind us of the toil of the blistered hands
And the courage and the comradeship of men.

From 'Tonypandy' in *The Collected Poems of Idris Davies*,
edited by Islwyn Jenkins (Gomer Press, 1972)

Jennie Lee
OUR BANNER (1945)

'Now don't you be picking holes in our banner,' said Mrs O, and she was laughing as she said it. The great red banner with the gold lettering has not been seen for a long time, but it will be brought out for our meeting on the first Sunday in May. I shall look at it carefully to see if Mrs O was chaffing when she said that some of the letters may be a little off the straight. I don't expect it to be exactly copperplate, not now that I know how and when it was made. Mrs O made it. That takes you back to before the 1926 miners' strike, to the time when there were the nine children at home and only a collier's wage to support them and Mrs O ill in bed and the red banner spread across her bed so that she could sew the lettering.

Talking of the banner and the time when it was made led on to talk of other things. Mrs O was no longer smiling. Not at this point, for she had come to the day when her father and mother, with nothing but the old age pension to live on, could not keep alive without help from somewhere. There was nothing for it but to appeal to the Board of Guardians. When the time came for them to appear before the guardians they were nervous. It is not pleasant to have to go before strangers and lay bare the intimacies of your life. There was not much Mrs O could do to help, but to buck them up before the interview she said she would stand treat for a bottle of beer. 'If it is all the same to you,' said her father, 'I won't bring the bottle home. I shall have a glass with the rest of the company at the club.'

That is how it was. But he was seen affluently drinking beer. At the interview his claim was turned down. One of the guardians said a man who could afford beer was in no need of relief. Bewildered and bruised, the old couple made their way home. Their daughter, anxious about them, went to see what was happening. She found her mother leaning against a wall, weeping. That weeping figure drove the guardian responsible for the tears out of public life. At every one of his meetings the daughter was there to accuse him, denounce him, never letting go.

At this point, as Mrs O told her story, there was a glint in her eye. She was fighting. She was hitting back. 'They kept coming to my husband,' she said, 'asking him to do something to stop me going to the meetings, but he said, "No, I shall do nothing to prevent her, for what she says is the truth, and it is her own father and mother".' So the son-in-law stood in behind the daughter and the whole local Labour movement closed in around both. As a team they did more than drive that guardian out of public life. They broke the back of local reaction. Mrs O herself was elected a member of the old Board of Guardians as one of a group of newly elected Labour members.

So you see if there is any laughing about our old banner it will have to be the right people who do the laughing and for the right reasons. Its reappearance is important. It is going to be needed. That is how working people will feel about their banners all over Great Britain this coming weekend. At the meetings we shall try to make mention of every nation and every race, for that is the meaning of May Day. The Union Jack may be all very well for certain things, but it is not broad enough for the main purpose of our times. It takes the Red Flag for that.

Mrs O has set me thinking of the early struggle of others like her. How well I remember that last talk I had with old Mrs Bob Smillie. Bob was struggling to get the miners' union established and recognised. Again and again his union activities led to victimisation. At one time the home circumstances were desperate. It was the old story of one precarious wage and a young family to be somehow fed and clothed. This day there had again been a row at the pit. Bob lost his temper, was ring-leader as usual, and was sacked as usual. Brave men have their moments of panic. Bob had his on the way home. How would they manage? What would she say when she saw him coming back in the middle of the forenoon? 'So instead of coming right in,' said Mrs Smillie to me, 'he chappit at the door, and when I went to open it he was standing there like a muckle laddie. "Am out," was all he said. "Never mind, Bob," says I, "if they've put ye out, I'll tak ye in!"'

From 'Our Banner' by Jennie Lee in Tribune 21,
edited by Elizabeth Thomas (Tribune Publications, 1958)

J.B. Priestley
THE ENGLISH SPIRIT (1934)

Ours is a country that has given the world something more than millions of yards of calico and thousands of steam engines. If we are a nation of shopkeepers, then what a shop! There is Shakespeare in the window, to begin with; and the whole establishment is blazing with geniuses. Why, these little countries of ours have known so many great men and great ideas that one's mind is dazzled by their riches. We stagger beneath our inheritance. But let us burn every book, tear down every memorial, turn every cathedral and college into an engineering shop, rather than grow cold and petrify, rather than forget that inner glowing tradition of the English spirit. Make it, if you like, a matter of pride. Let us be too proud, my mind shouted, to refuse shelter to exiled foreigners, too proud to do dirty little tricks because other people can stoop to them, too proud to lose an inch of our freedom, too proud, even if it beggars us, to tolerate social injustice here, too proud to suffer anywhere in this country an ugly mean way of living. We have led the world, many a time before today, on good expeditions and bad ones, on piratical raids and on quests for the Hesperides. We can lead it again. We headed the procession when it took what we see now to be the wrong turning, down in the dark bog of greedy industrialism, where money and machines are of more importance than men and women. It is for us to find the way out again, into the sunlight. We may have to risk a great deal, perhaps our very existence. But rather than live on meanly and savagely, I concluded, it would be better to perish as the last of the civilised peoples.

From *English Journey* by J.B. Priestley (William Heinemann Ltd, in association with Victor Gollancz Ltd, 1934)

DEMOCRACY

*'For really I think that the poorest he that is in England hath a life to
live, as the greatest he; and therefore, sir, I think it's clear, that every
man that is to live under a government ought first by his own consent to
put himself under that government'*

The Putney Debates
THE RIGHT TO VOTE (1647)

COWLING: Since the Conquest the greatest part of the kingdom was in vassalage.

PETTY: We judge that all inhabitants that have not lost their birthright should have an equal voice in elections.

RAINBOROUGH: I desired that those that had engaged in it might be included. For really I think that the poorest he that is in England hath a life to live, as the greatest he; and therefore truly, sir, I think it's clear, that every man that is to live under a government ought first by his own consent to put himself under that government; and I do think that the poorest man in England is not at all bound in a strict sense to that government that he hath not had a voice to put himself under; and I am confident that, when I have heard the reasons against it, something will be said to answer those reasons, insomuch that I should doubt whether he was an Englishman or no, that should doubt of these things.

IRETON: . . . For my part, I think it is not right at all. I think that no person hath a right to an interest or share in the disposing of the affairs of the kingdom, and in determining or choosing those that shall determine what laws we shall be ruled by here – no person hath a right to this, that hath not a permanent fixed interest in this kingdom, and those persons together are properly the represented of this kingdom, and consequently are [also] to make up the representers of this kingdom, who taken together do comprehend whatsoever is of real of permanent interest in the kingdom. And I am sure otherwise I cannot tell what any man can say why a foreigner coming in amongst us – or as many as will coming in amongst us, or by force or otherwise settling themselves here, or at least by our permission having a being here – why they should not as well lay claim to it as any other. We talk of birthright. Truly [by] birthright there is thus much claim. Men may justly have by birthright, by their very being born in England, that we should not seclude them out of England, that we should not refuse to give them air and place and ground, and the freedom of the highways and other things, to live amongst us – not any man that is born here, though by his birth there come nothing at all (that is part of the permanent interest of this kingdom) to him. That I think is due to a man by birth. But that by a man's being born here he shall have a share in that power that shall dispose of the lands here, and of things here, I do not think it a sufficient ground . . .

RAINBOROUGH: I do hear nothing at all that can convince me, why any man that is born in England ought not to have his voice in election of burgesses. It is said that if a man have not a permanent interest, he can have no claim; and [that] we must be no freer than the laws will let us be, and that there is no [law in any] chronicle will let us be freer than that we [now] enjoy. Something was said to this yesterday. I do think that the main cause why Almighty God gave men reason, it was that they should make use of that reason, and that they should improve it for that end and purpose that God gave it them. And truly, I think that half a loaf is better than none if a man be hungry: [this gift of reason without other property may seem a small thing], yet I think there is nothing that God hath given a man that any [one] else can take from him. And therefore I say, that either it must be the Law of God or the law of man that must prohibit the meanest man in the kingdom to have this benefit as well as the greatest. I do not find anything in the Law of God, that a lord shall choose twenty burgesses, and a gentleman but two, or a poor man shall choose none: I find no such thing in the Law of Nature, nor in the Law of Nations.

The Putney Debates, quoted in *Puritanism and Liberty* by A.S.P. Woodhouse
(Dent, 1974)

Thomas Paine
NATURAL RIGHTS (1791)

If any generation of men ever possessed the right of dictating the mode by which the world should be governed forever, it was the first generation that existed; and if that generation did not do it, no succeeding generation can show any authority for doing it, nor set any up. The illuminating and divine principles of the equal rights of man (for it has its origin from the maker of man) relates, not only to the living individuals, but to generations of men succeeding each other. Every generation is equal in rights to the generations which preceded it, by the same rule that every individual is born equal in rights with his contemporary.

Every history of the creation, and every traditionary account, whether from the lettered or unlettered world, however they may vary in their opinion or belief of certain particulars, all agree in establishing one point, *the unity of man*; by which I mean that man is all of *one degree,* and consequently that all men are born equal and with equal natural rights, in the same manner as if posterity had been continued by *creation* instead of *generation,* the latter being only the mode by which the former is carried forward; and consequently every child born into the world must be considered as deriving its existence from God. The world is as new to him as it was to the first man that existed, and his natural right in it is of the same kind.

The Mosaic account of the creation, whether taken as divine authority, or merely historical, is fully up to this point, *the unity or equality of man.* The expressions admit of no controversy. 'And God said, let us make man in our own image. In the image of God created he him; male and female created he them.' The distinction of sexes is pointed out, but no other distinction is even implied. If this be not divine authority, it is at least historical authority, and shows that the equality of man, so far from being a modern doctrine, is the oldest upon record .

. .

Hitherto we have spoken only (and that but in part) of the natural rights of man. We have now to consider the civil rights of man, and to show how the one originates out of the other. Man did not enter into society to become *worse* than he was before, nor to have less rights than he had before, but to have those rights better secured. His natural rights are the foundation of all his civil rights. But in order to pursue this distinction with more precision, it is necessary to mark the different qualities of natural and civil rights.

A few words will explain this. Natural rights are those which always appertain to man in right of his existence. Of this kind are all the intellectual rights, or rights of the mind, and also all those rights of acting as an individual for his own comfort and happiness, which are not injurious to the rights of others. Civil rights are those which appertain to man in right of his being a member of society. Every civil right has for its foundation some natural right pre-existing in the individual, but to which his individual power is not, in all cases, sufficiently competent. Of this kind are all those which relate to security and protection.

From this short review, it will be easy to distinguish between that class of natural rights which man retains after entering into society and those which he throws into common stock as a member of society.

The natural rights which he retains are all those in which the power to execute is as perfect in the individual as the right itself. Among this class, as is before mentioned, are all the intellectual rights, or rights of the mind: consequently, religion is one of those rights. The natural rights which are not retained are all those in which, though the right is perfect in the individual, the power to execute them is defective. They answer not his purpose. A man, by natural right, has a right to judge in his own cause; and so far as the right of the mind is concerned, he never surrenders it: but what availeth it him to judge, if he has not power to redress? He therefore deposits this right in the common stock of society, and takes the arm of society, of which he is a part, in preference and in addition to his own. Society *grants* him nothing. Every man is a proprietor in society, and draws on the capital as a matter of right.

From 'The Rights of Man' by Thomas Paine, in *Political Writings,*
edited by Bruce Kuklick (Cambridge University Press, 1989)

William Wordsworth
THE WILL OF ALL (1792)

Hatred of absolute rule, where will of one
Is law for all, and of that barren pride
In them who, by immunities unjust,
Betwixt the sovereign and the people stand,
His helper and not theirs, laid stronger hold
Daily upon me, mixed with pity too
And love; for where hope is, there love will be
For the abject multitude. And when we chanced
One day to meet a hunger-bitten girl,
Who crept along fitting her languid self
Unto a heifer's motion, by a cord
Tied to her arm, and picking thus from the lane
Its sustenance, while the girl with her two hands
Was busy knitting in a heartless mood
Of solitude, and at the sight my friend
In agitation said, "'Tis against *that*
Which we are fighting,' I with him believed
Devoutly that a spirit was abroad
Which could not be withstood, that poverty
At least like this would in a little time
Be found no more, that we should see the earth
Unthwarted in her wish to recompense
The industrious, and the lowly child of toil,
All institutes for ever blotted out
That legalised exclusion, empty pomp
Abolished, sensual state and cruel power,
Whether by edict of the one or few;
And finally, as sum and crown of all,
Should see the people having a strong hand
In making their own laws; whence better days
To all mankind . . .

From 'The Prelude' by William Wordsworth, in *A Parallel Text*,
edited by J.C. Maxwell (Harmondsworth, 1971)

Joseph Priestley
THE HAPPINESS OF ALL (1768)

The sum of what hath been advanced upon this head, is a maxim, than which nothing is more true, that *every government, whatever be the form of it, is originally, and antecedent to its present form, an equal republic*; and, consequently, that every man, when he comes to be sensible of his natural rights, and to feel his own importance, will consider himself as fully equal to any other person whatever. The consideration of riches and power, however acquired, must be entirely set aside, when we come to these first principles. The very idea of property, or right of any kind, is founded upon a regard to the general good of the society, under whose protection it is enjoyed; and nothing is properly *a man's own*, but what general rules, which have for their object the good of the whole, give to him. To whomsoever the society delegates its power, it is delegated to them for the more easy management of public affairs, and in order to make the more effectual provision for the happiness of the whole. Whoever enjoys property, or riches in the State, enjoys them for the good of the State, as well as for himself; and whenever those powers, riches, or rights of any kind, are abused, to the injury of the whole, that awful and ultimate tribunal, in which every citizen hath an equal voice, may demand the resignation of them . . . Magistrates, therefore, who consult not the good of the public, and who employ their power to oppress the people, are a public nuisance, and their power is abrogated *ipso facto* . . .

From *On the First Principles of Government* by Joseph Priestley (London, 1768)

First Chartist Petition
DEMAND FOR THE VOTE *(Rejected 12 July 1839)*

Unto the Honourable the Commons of the United Kingdom of Great Britain and Ireland in Parliament assembled, the Petition of the undersigned, their suffering countrymen,

HUMBLY SHOWETH

That we, your petitioners, dwell in a land where merchants are noted for enterprise, whose manufactures are very skilful, and whose workmen are proverbial for their industry.

The land is goodly, the soil rich, and the temperature wholesome; it is abundantly furnished with the materials of commerce and trade; it has numerous and convenient harbours; in facility of internal communication it exceeds all others.

For three-and-twenty years we have enjoyed a profound peace.

Yet, with all these elements of national prosperity, and with every disposition and capacity to take advantage of them, we find ourselves overwhelmed with public and private suffering.

We are bowed down under a load of taxes; which, notwithstanding, fall greatly short of the wants of our rulers; our traders are trembling on the verge of bankruptcy; our workmen are starving; capital brings no profit and labour no remuneration; the home of the artificer is desolate, and the warehouse of the pawnbroker is full; the workhouse is crowded and the manufactory is deserted.

We have looked on every side, we have searched diligently in order to find out the causes of a distress so sore and so long continued.

We can find none in nature, or in Providence.

Heaven has dealt graciously by the people; but the foolishness of our rulers has made the goodness of God of none effect.

The energies of a mighty kingdom have been wasted in building up the power of selfish and ignorant men, and its resources squandered for their aggrandisement

The good of a party has been advanced to the sacrifice of the good of the nation; the few have governed for the interests of the few, while the interest of the many has been neglected or insolently and tyrannously trampled upon.

It was the fond expectation of the people that a remedy for the greater part, if not for the whole, of their grievances, would be found in the Reform Act of 1832.

They were taught to regard that Act as a wise means to a worthy end; as the machinery of an improved legislation, when the will of the masses would be at length potential.

They have been bitterly and basely deceived.

The fruit which looked so fair to the eye has turned to dust and ashes when gathered.

The Reform Act has effected a transfer of power from one dominating faction to another, and left the people as helpless as before.

Our slavery has been exchanged for an apprenticeship to liberty, which has aggravated the painful feeling of our social degradation, by adding to it the sickening of still deferred hope.

We come before your Honourable House to tell you, with all humility, that this state of things must not be permitted to continue; that it cannot very long continue without very seriously endangering the stability of the throne and the peace of the kingdom; and that if by God's help and all lawful and constitutional appliances, an end can be put to it, we are fully resolved that it shall speedily come to an end.

We tell your Honourable House that the capital of the master must no longer be deprived of its due reward; that the laws which make food dear, and those which, by making money scarce, make labour cheap, must be abolished; that taxation must be made to fall on property, not on industry; that the good of the many, as it is the only legitimate end, so it must be the sole study of the Government.

As a preliminary essential to those and other requisite changes, as means by which alone the interests of the people can be effectually vindicated and secured we demand that those interests be confided to the keeping of the people.

When the State calls for defenders, when it calls for money, no consideration of poverty or ignorance can be pleaded in refusal or delay of the call.

Required, as we are, universally, to support and obey the laws, nature and reason entitle us to demand, that in the making of the laws, the universal voice shall be implicitly listened to.

We perform the duties of freemen; we must have the privileges of freemen.

Quoted in *Revolution from 1789 to 1906* by Raymond Postgate (Gloucester, 1962)

William Cobbett
PARLIAMENTARY REFORM (1831)

It may be asked, Will a reform of the Parliament give the labouring man a cow or a pig; will it put bread and cheese into his satchell instead of infernal cold potatoes; will it give him a bottle of beer to carry to the field instead of making him lie down upon his belly to drink out of the brook; will it put upon his back a Sunday coat and send him to church, instead of leaving him to stand lounging about shivering with an unshaven face and a carcass half covered with a ragged smock-frock, with a filthy cotton shirt beneath it as yellow as a kite's foot? Will parliamentary reform put an end to the harnessing of men and women by a hired overseer to draw carts like beasts of burden; will it put an end to the practice of putting up labourers to auction like negroes in Carolina or Jamaica; will it put an end to the system which caused the honest labourer to be fed worse than the felons in the jails; will it put an end to the system which caused almost the whole of the young women to incur the indelible disgrace of being on the point of being mothers before they were married owing to that degrading poverty which prevented the fathers themselves from obtaining the means of paying the parson and the clerk: will parliamentary reform put an end to the foul, the beastly, the nasty practice of separating men from their wives by force, and committing to the hired overseer the bestial superintendence of their persons day and night; will parliamentary reform put an end to this which was amongst the basest acts which the Roman tyrants committed towards their slaves? The enemies of reform jeeringly ask us, whether reform would do these things for us; and I answer distinctly that IT WOULD DO THEM ALL!

From *Cobbett's Weekly Political Register*, 1 April 1831

William Lovett
DEMOCRACY AND REPRESENTATION (*c.*1836)

Is the *Landholder*, whose interests lead him to keep up his rents by unjust and exclusive laws, a fit representative for working men?

Are the whole host of *Money-makers, Speculators*, and *Usurers*, who live on the corruptions of the system, fit representatives for the sons of labour?

Are the immense numbers of *Lords, Earls, Marquises, Knights, Baronets, Honourables*, and *Right Honourables*, who have seats in that house, fit to represent our interests? Many of whom have the certainty before them of being the *hereditary legislators* of the other house, or are the craving expectants of place or emolument; persons who cringe in the gilded circle of a court, flutter among the gaieties of the ballroom, to court the passing smile of Royalty, or whine at Ministers of the day; and when the interests of the people are at stake in the Commons are often found the revelling debauchees of fashion, or the duelling wranglers of a gambling-house?

Are the multitude of *Military* and *Naval Officers* in the present House of Commons, whose interest it is to support that system which secures them their pay and promotion, and whose only utility, at any time, is to direct one portion of our brethren to keep the other in subjection, fit to represent our grievances?

Have we fit representatives in the multitude of *Barristers, Attorneys*, and *Solicitors*, most of them seeking places, and all of them having interests depending on the dissensions and corruptions of the people? – persons whose prosperity depends on the obscurity and intricacy of the laws, and who seek to perpetuate the interests of *'their order'* by rendering them so abstruse and voluminous that none but *law conjurers* like themselves shall understand them – persons whose *legal* knowledge (that is, of fraud and deception) often procures them seats in the Government, and the highest offices corruption can confer?

Is the *Manufacturer* and *Capitalist*, whose exclusive monopoly of the combined powers of wood, iron, and steam enables them to cause the destitution of thousands, and who have an interest in forcing labour down to the *minimum* reward, fit to represent the interests of working men?

Is the *Master*, whose interests it is to purchase labour at the cheapest rate, a fit representative for the *Workman*, whose interest it is to get the most he can for his labour?

Yet such is the only description of persons composing that house, and such the interests represented, to whom we, session after session, address *our humble petitions*, and whom we in our ignorant simplicity imagine will generously sacrifice their hopes and interests by beginning the great work of political and social reformation.

Working men, inquire if this be not true, and then if you feel with us, stand apart from all projects, and refuse to be the tools of any party, who will not, as *a first and essential measure*, give to the working classes *equal political and social rights,* so that they may send their own representatives from the ranks of those who live by labour into that house, to deliberate and determine along with *all other interests,* that the interests of the labouring classes – of those who are the foundation of the social edifice – shall not be daily sacrificed to glut the extravagances of the pampered few. If you feel with us, then you will proclaim it in the workshop, preach it in your societies, publish it from town to village, from county to county, and from nation to nation, that there is no hope for the sons of toil, till those who feel with them, who sympathise with them, and whose interests are identified with theirs, have *an equal right to determine what laws shall be enacted or plans adopted for justly governing this country.*

From *Life and Struggles* by William Lovett (1920)

Mary Wollstonecraft
THE REPRESENTATION OF WOMEN (1792)

The preposterous distinctions of rank, which render civilisation a curse, by dividing the world between voluptuous tyrants and cunning duties of wives and mothers, by religion and reason, I cannot help lamenting that women of a superior cast have not a road open by which they can pursue more extensive plans of usefulness and independence. I may excite laughter, by dropping a hint, which I mean to pursue, some future time, for I really think that women ought to have representatives, instead of being arbitrarily governed without having any direct share allowed them in the deliberations of government.

But, as the whole system of representation is now, in this country, only a convenient handle for despotism, they need not complain, for they are as well represented as a numerous class of hard-working mechanics, who pay for the support of royalty when they can scarcely stop their children's mouths with bread. How are they represented whose very sweat supports the splendid stud of an heir-apparent, or varnishes the chariot of some female favourite who looks down on shame? Taxes on the very necessaries of life, enable an endless tribe of idle princes and princesses to pass with stupid pomp before a gaping crowd, who almost worship the very parade which costs them so dear. This is mere gothic grandeur, something like the barbarous useless parade of having sentinels on horse-back at Whitehall, which I could never view without a mixture of contempt and indignation . . .

Would men but generously snap our chains, and be content with rational fellowship instead of slavish obedience, they would find us more observant daughters, more affectionate sisters, more faithful wives, more reasonable mothers – in a word, better citizens. We should then love them with true affection, because we should learn to respect ourselves; and the peace of mind of a worthy man would not be interrupted by the idle vanity of his wife, nor the babes sent to nestle in a strange bosom, having never found a home in their mother's.

From *A Vindication of the Rights of Woman* by Mary Wollstonecraft, edited by Miriam Kramnick (Harmondsworth, 1975)

Harriet Taylor Mill
WOMEN AND THE VOTE (1851)

That women have as good a claim as men have, in point of personal right, to the suffrage, or to a place in the jury-box, it would be difficult for any one to deny. It cannot certainly be denied by the United States of America, as a people or as a community. Their democratic institutions rest avowedly on the inherent right of every one to a voice in the government. Their Declaration of Independence, framed by the men who are still their great constitutional authorities – that document which has been from the first, and is now, the acknowledged basis of their policy – commences with this express statement:

We hold these truths to be self-evident: that all men are created equal; that they are endowed by their Creator with certain inalienable rights; that among these are life, liberty, and the pursuit of happiness; that to secure these rights, governments are instituted among men, deriving their just powers from the consent of the governed.

We do not imagine that any American democrat will evade the force of these expressions by the dishonest or ignorant subterfuge, that 'men', in this memorable document, does not stand for human beings, but for one sex only; that 'life, liberty, and the pursuit of happiness' are 'inalienable rights' of only one moiety of the human species; and that 'the governed', whose consent is affirmed to be the only source of just power, are meant for that half of mankind only, who, in relation to the other, have hitherto assumed the character of governors. The contradiction between principle and practice cannot be explained away . . .

When a prejudice, which has any hold on the feelings, finds itself reduced to the unpleasant necessity of assigning reasons, it thinks it has done enough when it has re-asserted the very point in dispute, in phrases which appeal to the pre-existing feeling. Thus, many persons think they have sufficiently justified the restriction on women's field of action, when they have said that the pursuits from which women are excluded are *unfeminine*, and that the *proper sphere* of women is not politics or publicity, but private and domestic life.

We deny the right of any portion of the species to decide for another portion, or any individual for another individual, what is and what is not their 'proper sphere'. The proper sphere for all human beings is the largest and highest which they are able to attain to. What this is, cannot be ascertained, without complete liberty of choice . . .

The real question is, whether it is right and expedient that one-half of the human race should pass through life in a state of forced subordination to the other half. If the best state of human society is that of being divided into two parts, one consisting of persons with a will and a substantive existence, the other of humble companions to these persons, attached, each of them to one, for the purpose of bringing up *his* children, and making *his* home pleasant to him; if this is the place assigned to women, it is but kindness to educate them for this; to make them believe that the greatest good fortune which can befall them, is to be chosen by some man for this purpose; and that every other career which the world deems happy or honourable, is closed to them by the law, not of social institutions, but of nature and destiny.

When, however, we ask why the existence of one-half the species should merely be ancillary to that of the other – why each woman should be a mere appendage to a man, allowed to have no interests of her own, that there may be nothing to compete in her mind with his interests and his pleasure; the only reason which can be given is, that men like it. It is agreeable to them that men should live for their own sake, women for the sake of men: and the qualities and conduct in subjects which are agreeable to rulers, they succeed for a long time in making the subjects themselves consider as their appropriate virtues.

From *On the Enfranchisement of Women* by Harriet Taylor Mill (Virago, 1983)

James Keir Hardie
VOTES FOR WOMEN (1913)

The ferment among women is far and away the most important event in the history of the world. So far as I know this is the first time in which women have come boldly forward, claiming equal rights with men, with their corresponding duties and responsibilities. Just what they may mean cannot be foretold. The one thing certain is that things can never again be what they have been. Under the influence of the Women's Movement the existing relationships are bound in process of time to undergo great changes. Let anyone who doubts this try to picture what is likely to emerge out of a state of society in which women have fought their way to economic freedom and have ceased to be dependent upon men. That one fact of itself must change the whole basis upon which society now rests.

For men and women alike socialism means economic freedom, but men may as well realise the fact, sooner rather than later, that freedom must come to all or it cannot come to any. So long as there is a class or a sex which is not free that fact anchors all the rest of society in a like bondage. It is a law of the universe from which there is no escape. If this be so then, the cause of women is the cause of humanity. Political equality will, as in the case of men, precede economic equality. Votes for women will not only be a recognition of the equality of the sexes, but will also enable women to stand with men in the greater fight for economic freedom.

From an article in the first edition of *Labour Women*

John Strachey
DEBTS TO THE PAST (1956)

We sometimes celebrate the pioneers of trade unionism, and co-operation, with more sentiment than knowledge or understanding. But, for all that, can we ever too greatly honour these men and women? For they laid the essential basis of modern democracy. In the mire of Tolpuddle and the murk of Rochdale, in a hundred other British back streets and country lanes, the social atoms began to fuse. These for the most part anonymous men and women then and there began a long, painful process by which the hitherto helpless wage earners were to forge for themselves the organisations and institutions which could alone enable them to appear as actors instead of patients on the pages of history. Nor was that development accomplished without almost unbelievably stubborn perseverance and immense self-sacrifice. The sheer doggedness, level-headedness and good sense of the nineteenth- and early twentieth-century British workers in using the means that were open to them constituted a kind of heroism no less noble, and far more fruitful, than that of their continental comrades who died upon the barricades. For they gave social and economic content to the political democracy which, by the middle of the twentieth century, had been established in Britain.

From *Contemporary Capitalism* by John Strachey (Gollancz, 1956)

Sidney Webb

THE IMPORTANCE OF CONSENT (1923)

For the Labour Party, it must be plain, socialism is rooted in political democracy; which necessarily compels us to recognise that every step towards our goal is dependent on gaining the assent and support of at least a numerical majority of the whole people. Thus, even if we aimed at revolutionising every-thing at once, we should necessarily be compelled to make each particular change only at the time, and to the extent, and in the manner in which ten or fifteen million electors, in all sorts of conditions, of all sorts of temperaments, from Land's End to the Orkneys, could be brought to consent to it. How anyone can fear that the British electorate, whatever mistakes it may make or may condone, can ever go too fast or too far is incomprehensible to me. That, indeed, is the supremely valuable safeguard of any effective democracy.

From *The Labour Party on the Threshold* (Fabian Tract no. 207)
by Sidney Webb (1923)

Sidney Webb and Beatrice Webb
INFORMING THE ELECTORATE (1920)

Today it seems, in the Labour and socialist world, that the vital question is who should give orders and who should obey them – whether the government of industry shall be 'from above' or 'from below'. In the ensuing years of ever-increasing socialisation this controversy will become largely meaningless. Paradoxical as this may seem today, we venture on the prediction that, from the stand point of personal authority, it will matter far less than at present exactly how the executive command is apportioned. In industry no less than in political administration, the combination of Measurement with Publicity is today already undermining personal autocracy. The deliberate intensification of this *searchlight of published knowledge* we regard as the cornerstone of successful democracy. The need for final decision will remain not merely in emergencies but also as to policy; and it is of high importance to vest the responsibility for a decision, according to the nature of the case, in the right hands. But a great deal of the old autocracy, once deemed to be indispensable in government departments and capitalist industry alike, is ceasing to be necessary to efficiency, and will, accordingly, as democracy becomes more genuinely accepted, gradually be dispensed with. A steadily increasing sphere will, except in matters of emergency, be found for consultation among all grades and sections concerned, out of which will emerge judgments and decisions arrived at, very largely, by common consent. This common consent will be reached by the cogency of accurately ascertained and authoritatively reported facts, driven home by the silent persuasiveness of the public opinion of those concerned. The works committee, the district council, the national board, the social Parliament itself, will have before them, not merely the spontaneous promptings of their members' minds, and not even only the information provided by their own officials, but much more. To such committees and councils there will come, as a matter of course, a stream of reports from independent and disinterested experts . . .

Democracy cannot afford to dispense with complication in its administrative machinery, because only by an extensive variety of parts, and a deliberately adjusted relation among those parts, can there be any security for the personal freedom and independence in initiative of the great mass of individuals, whether as producers, as consumers or as citizens. It is only by systematically thinking out the function that each person has to perform, the sphere that must be secured to each group or section, the opportunities in which each must be protected, and the relation in which each must stand to the others and to the whole, that in any highly developed society the ordinary man can escape a virtual, if not a nominal, slavery. Those impatient democrats who will not take the trouble to understand the problem, and who petulantly demand, at the same time, the elaborations and refinements of civilisation and the anarchy and simplicity of the primitive age, cannot in the nature of things ever be gratified. The condition of any genuine democracy, of the wide diffusion of any effective freedom, is such a systematic complication of social machinery as will negative alike the monarchical and the capitalist dictatorships, and prevent the rise of any other. The price of liberty – of individual variety and specialisation 'in widest commonalty spread' – is the complication of a highly differentiated and systematically co-ordinated social order.

From *A Constitution for the Socialist Commonwealth of Great Britain* by Sidney Webb and Beatrice Webb (Longmans, Green & Co, 1920)

Ramsay MacDonald
THE CONSENT OF ACTIVE MINDS (1919)

The socialist spirit is that of liberty, of discussion. It is historical and not cataclysmic. It is objective as well as subjective; it can understand as well as feel. It can admire even when it does not agree. Such admiration is part of the capacity to transform society, because that transformation depends upon a relationship between the mind of that reformer and his social circumstances . .

Above all it discards lightning changes as the way to realise itself. It knows that no system of government or of society can rest upon anything but common consent – the consent of passive minds, or the consent of active minds. The latter kind of consent is the only one it values. The idea of a revolution transforming the structure of society by the will of a minority must seem as utopian to it as the ideas of the Owenites and of all who sought to create an oasis of peace in the wilderness of the capitalist system. It believes in democracy, not only as a moral creed which alone is consistent with its views of humanity, but because it is the only practical creed. It knows that, revolutions or no revolutions, public consent is the basis of all social order and that the good builder makes his foundations sound before he puts up his storeys.

It knows that opinion must always precede reconstruction, but it also knows that the harvest of socialism does not ripen in a night and has therefore to be gathered at one cutting, but that every day brings something to fruition, that the moments as they go bring us nearer to socialism by their products of socialist thought and experiment which have to be seized and embodied in the transforming structure of society, not in a bunch, but bit by bit. It believes in the class conflict as a descriptive fact, but it does not regard it as supplying a political method. It strives to transform through education, through raising the standards of mental and moral qualities, through the acceptance of programmes by reason of their justice, rationality and wisdom. It trusts to no regeneration by trick or force. Founding itself on the common sense of everyday experience, it knows that, come enthusiasm or depression, impatience or lethargy, the enlightened State can be built up and maintained only by enlightened citizens. It walks with the map of socialism in front of it and guides its steps by the compass of democracy.

From *Parliament and Revolution* (National Labour Press, 1919)

Michael Foot
MY KIND OF PARTY (1982)

For the men and women who made the Labour Party constitution, and who insisted on seeking to establish a Labour Party inside Parliament as well as outside in the country, were not mistaken. They understood the place Parliament occupied in the history of the British people and the importance which our people attach to what Tawney called 'the elementary decencies' of parliamentary government.

They understood that Parliament was where disputes could be settled by consent instead of force. They understood that the Left in politics, so much more than the Right, with its traditional resort to actual fighting, had a vested interest in settling arguments peaceably. They understood maybe – William Lovett had an inkling of it – that what was achieved without resort to force would last much longer and better; that the socialism won by such means might be the only kind worth having; that the words *democratic socialism* should never be separated, that one was impossible without the other.

From *The Observer* (January 1982)

Aneurin Bevan
DEMOCRATIC SOCIALISM (1952)

The philosophy of democratic socialism is essentially cool in temper. It sees society in its context with nature and is conscious of the limitations imposed by physical conditions. It sees the individual in his context with society and is therefore compassionate and tolerant. Because it knows that all political action must be a choice between a number of possible alternatives it eschews all absolute proscriptions and final decisions. Consequently it is not able to offer the thrill of the complete abandonment of private judgment, which is the allure of modern Soviet communism and of fascism, its running mate. Nor can it escape the burden of social choice so attractively suggested by those who believe in *laissez-faire* principles and in the automatism of the price system. It accepts the obligation to choose among different kinds of social action and in so doing to bear the pains of rejecting what is not practicable or less desirable.

Democratic socialism is a child of modern society and so of relativist philosophy. It seeks the truth in any given situation, knowing all the time that if this be pushed too far it falls into error. It struggles against the evils that flow from private property, yet realises that all forms of private property are not necessarily evil. Its chief enemy is vacillation, for it must achieve passion in action in the pursuit of qualified judgments. It must know how to enjoy the struggle, while recognising that progress is not the elimination of struggle but rather a change in its terms.

From *In Place of Fear* by Aneurin Bevan (MacGibbon & Kee, 1961)

Neil Kinnock
DEMOCRATIC SOCIALISM – A RATIONAL CHOICE (1983)

Democratic socialism if it is to succeed must appear and appeal as a source of efficiency and justice as much to the affluent and secure as to the impoverished and insecure. The business of transforming society needs the support of the confident as well as the disadvantaged.

Decent instincts of care for the weakened are central to our socialist values, but the material advantages for all must also play a major part. Democratic socialism must emphasise the interest of payer and user alike in attaining a society with universally dependable and accessible health treatment – the serenity of good homes, the security of pensions and benefits, the freedom from the ugliness and pain of poverty and from the menace of crime and the merit of a free and fair education system of high quality. Democratic socialists must show the *utility* of democratic socialism for all as well as its desirability for the enlightened and its absolute necessity for the needy.

From *The New Statesman* (October 1983)

DEMOCRACY AND THE ECONOMY

'If we develop and extend our democracy, we can make the corporate economy serve the community's needs'

John Stuart Mill
ASSESSING PROPERTY (1867)

Private property, in every defence made of it, is supposed to mean the guarantee of individuals of the fruits of their own labour and abstinence. The guarantee to them of the fruits of the labour and abstinence of others, transmitted to them without any merit or exertion of their own, is not of the essence of the institution, but a mere incidental consequence, which when it reaches a certain height, does not promote, but conflicts with the ends which render private property legitimate. To judge of the final destination of the institution of property, we must suppose everything rectified, which causes the institution to work in a manner opposed to that equitable principle, of proportion between remuneration and exertion, on which in every vindication of it that will bear the light, it is assumed to be grounded. We must also suppose two conditions realised, without which neither communism nor any other laws or institutions could make the condition of the mass of mankind other than degraded and miserable. One of these conditions is universal education; the other, a due limitation of the numbers of the community. With these, there could be no poverty even under the present social institutions; and these being supposed, the question of socialism is not, as generally stated by socialists, a question of flying to the sole refuge against the evils which now bear down on humanity, but a mere question of comparative advantages, which futurity must determine. We are too ignorant either of what individual agency in its best form, or socialism in its best form, can accomplish, to be qualified to decide which of the two will be the ultimate form of human society.

If a conjecture may be hazarded, the decision will probably depend mainly on one consideration, viz., which of the two systems is consistent with the greatest amount of human liberty and spontaneity. After the means of subsistence are assured, the next in strength of the personal wants of human beings is liberty; and (unlike the physical wants, which as civilisation advances become more moderate and more amenable to control) it increases instead of diminishing in intensity as the intelligence and the moral faculties are more developed. The perfection both of social arrangements and of practical morality would be to secure to all persons complete independence and freedom of action, subject to no restriction but that of not doing injury to others; and the education which taught or the social institutions which required them to exchange the control of their own actions for any amount of comfort or affluence, or to renounce liberty for the sake of equality, would deprive them of one of the most elevated characteristics of human nature. It remains to be discovered how far the preservation of this characteristic would be found compatible with the communistic organisation of society. No doubt, this, like all the other objections to the socialist schemes, is vastly exaggerated. The members of the association need not be required to live together more than they do now, nor need they be controlled in the disposal of their individual share of the produce, and of the probably large amount of leisure which, if they limited their production to things really worth producing, they would possess. Individuals need not be chained to an occupation, or to a particular locality. The restraints of communism would be freedom in comparison with the present condition of the majority of the human race. The generality of labourers in this and most other countries have as little choice of occupation or freedom of locomotion, are practically as dependent on fixed rules and on the will of others as they could be on any system short of actual slavery, to say nothing of the entire domestic subjection of one half the species, to which it is the signal honour of . . . socialism that they assign equal rights, in all respects, with those of the hitherto dominant sex.

From *Principles of Political Economy, Book II*

William Morris
THE DAMAGE CAUSED BY PROFIT (1884)

And, again, that word art leads me to my last claim, which is that the material surroundings of my life should be pleasant, generous, and beautiful; that I know is a large claim, but this I will say about it, that if it cannot be satisfied, if every civilised community cannot provide such surroundings for all its members, I do not want the world to go on; it is a mere misery that man has ever existed. I do not think it possible under the present circumstances to speak too strongly on this point. I feel sure that the time will come when people will find it difficult to believe that a rich community such as ours, having such command over external Nature, could have submitted to live such a mean, shabby, dirty life as we do.

And once for all, there is nothing in our circumstances save the hunting of profit that drives us into it. It is profit which draws men into enormous unmanageable aggregations called down, for instance; profit which crowds them up when they are there into quarters without gardens or open spaces; profit which won't take the most ordinary precautions against wrapping a whole district in a cloud of sulphurous smoke; which turns beautiful rivers into filthy sewers, which condemns all but the rich to live in houses idiotically cramped and confined at the best, and at the worst in houses for whose wretchedness there is no name.

I say it is almost incredible that we should bear such crass stupidity as this; nor should we if we could help it. We shall not bear it when the workers get out of their heads that they are but an appendage to profit–grinding, that the more profits that are made the more employment at high wages there will be for them, and that therefore all the incredible filth, disorder, and degradation of modern civilisation are signs of their prosperity. So far from that, they are signs of their slavery. When they are no longer slaves they will claim as a matter of course that every man and every family should be generously lodged; that every child should be able to play in a garden close to the place his parents live in; that the houses should by their obvious decency and order be ornaments to Nature, not

217

disfigurements of it; for the decency and order above mentioned when carried to the due pitch would most assuredly lead to beauty in building. All this, of course, would mean the people – that is, all society – duly organised, having in its own hands the means of production, to be *owned* by no individual, but used by all as occasion called for its use, and can only be done on those terms; on any other terms people will be driven to accumulate private wealth for themselves, and thus, as we have seen, to waste the goods of the community and perpetuate the division into classes, which means continual war and waste.

From *The Political Writings of William Morris*, edited by A.L. Morton
(Lawrence & Wishart, 1979)

Sidney Webb and Beatrice Webb
EXTENDING SOCIALISATION (1920)

But our present failures are to be ascribed, not merely to deficiencies in knowledge, but also to the impossibility, with our existing institutions, of bringing into play such knowledge as is available. The House of Commons and the Cabinet, as they exist today, are as incapable of organising the industrial and social life of Great Britain, so as to make a decent social order, as the capitalist system has proved itself to be. It is for this reason that thoughtful socialists lay so much stress on quite a different conception of government. They are insistent, for the new social order, not only on a varied and highly developed organisation of knowledge, and of an 'adult education' far transcending the present imagination of the Board of Education, but also on such a transformation of administrative institutions, from the House of Commons to the trade union, as will provide an environment of free initiative and personal activity, which are now so much restricted, and without which there can, in the long run, be no full social efficiency. It is with this object that, far from heaping up all government on a centralised authority, they propose the widest possible variety in the forms of socialisation – calling in aid a far-reaching reorganisation of the vocational world, a vast extension of the consumers' co-operative movement, a great development of local government and even the splitting into two of the powers of Parliament itself. The same sense of the need for much more detailed knowledge and much more widely disseminated personal interest in production and distribution than the capitalist system has been able to afford, lies at the back of the proposals for a constantly increasing participation of employees of all kinds and grades in the management of the enterprise. We ourselves lay equal stress on the freedom of the independent professional, and even on the continuance, unabsorbed, of individual producers themselves owning the instruments with which they labour. What we visualise is a community so variously organised, and so highly differentiated in function as to be not only invigorated by a sense of personal freedom, but also constantly swept by the fresh air of experiment, observation and verification. We want to get rid of the 'stuffiness' of private interests which now infects our institutions; and to usher in a reign of 'Measurement and Publicity'. It is to a free democracy, inspired by the spirit of social service, and illumined by ever-increasing knowledge, that we dedicate this book.

A Constitution for the Socialist Commonwealth of Great Britain
by Sidney Webb and Beatrice Webb (Longmans, Green & Co, 1920)

G.D.H. Cole
CONTROLLING THE MACHINE (1941)

Socialism, however, though it involves a generous approach to economic equality, is not wholly a bread-and-butter question. As I have said, it is also, and ultimately, a question of the spirit of man. As giant power spreads over the world, as the units of production grow larger and the units of business control much larger still, the mass of men pass more and more under the domination of the machine. Immensely greater power to control the lives of the many passes into the hands of the few – as long as the few are allowed to own and manipulate the machines. This is true not only of industry, or of warfare: it is true of propaganda also, with its new techniques of psychological approach. Individualism and *laissez-faire* quite change their practical meaning when the individual comes to mean in practice a great capitalist trust or a newspaper syndicate with unlimited capital at its back. It is useless to wish these giants away, or to sigh for the joys of an age of little things. There can be no peace for the soul of man, and no space for the individual to live his own life, till we have learnt by collective action to subordinate these monsters to our needs . . .

Socialism is, in the last resort, simply the means to this control. A socialist civilisation is one in which the past victories of humanity are not thrown away, or bombed into unrecognisable fragments because they have been misapplied, but are used as a basis for further conquests in the interests of ordinary, decent people. The trouble is that these ordinary, decent people, who claim for the most part nothing better than to be let alone, cannot be let alone until the world has settled its fate anew. The bombs will fall upon them, the giant machine will bind them to the will of its masters, the megaphones will blare propaganda at them, and they will live unquiet lives, until they themselves realise that, for very peace and quietness, they must do for themselves what no political sect can do without them – claim their right to be free, not by turning their backs on the juggernauts that ride over them, but by facing manfully the task of bringing these monsters under collective, democratic socialist control.

From 'A Socialist Civilisation' by G.D.H. Cole in *Programme for Victory* (1941)

Anthony Crosland

AIMS OF DEMOCRATIC SOCIALISM (1960)

I start with three assumptions. First, while British socialists may differ about particular policy issues (for example, the exact form and extent of future public ownership), they would all subscribe to the following basic socialist values:

(1) An overriding concern with social welfare, and a determination to accord a first priority to the relief not merely of material poverty, but of social distress or misfortune from whatever cause.

(2) A much more equal distribution of wealth, and in particular a compression of that part of the total which derives from property income and inheritance.

(3) A socially 'classless' society, and in particular a non-élite system of education which offers equal opportunities to all children.

(4) The primacy of social over private interests, and an allocation of resources (notably in the fields of social investment and town and country planning) determined by the public need and not solely by profit considerations.

(5) The diffusion of economic power, and in particular a transfer of power from the large corporation (whether public or private) both to workers (either directly or through their unions) and consumers (through the co-operative movement).

(6) Generally, the substitution of co-operative for competitive, and other-regarding for self-regarding, social and economic relations.

(7) In foreign affairs, the substitution of disarmament, international action and the rule of law for nationalism and power politics.

(8) Racial equality (both at home and abroad), the right of colonial peoples to freedom and self-government, and the duty of richer nations to give aid and support to poorer ones.

(9) An increase in the rate or economic growth, both for the sake of a higher standard of living and as a pre-condition of achieving other objectives.

(10) A belief, not merely in parliamentary democracy, but in the rights and liberty of the individual as against the State, the police, private or public bureaucracy, and organised intolerance of any kind.

These ten values, or aspirations, constitute the basic principles of democratic socialism. There may be legitimate disagreement about their precise interpretation, and about the exact means – the particular institutional changes or forms of economic organisation – through which they can best be realised in our society. But no one can call himself a socialist who does not assent to the basic values.

From *Can Labour Win?* (Fabian Tract no. 324) by Anthony Crosland (1960)

John Maynard Keynes
THE END OF LAISSEZ-FAIRE (1926)

Let us clear from the ground the metaphysical or general principles upon which, from time to time, *laissez-faire* has been founded. It is *not* true that individuals possess a prescriptive 'natural liberty' in their economic activities. There is *no* 'compact' conferring perpetual rights on those who Have or on those who Acquire. The world is *not* so governed from above that private and social interest always coincide. It is *not* so managed here below that in practice they coincide. It is *not* a correct deduction from the principles of economics that enlightened self-interest always operates in the public interest. Nor is it true that self-interest generally *is* enlightened; more often individuals acting separately to promote their own ends are too ignorant or too weak to attain even these. Experience does *not* show that individuals, when they make up a social unit, are always less clear-sighted than when they act separately.

From *The Collected Writings of John Maynard Keynes*, Vol. IX (Macmillan, 1972)

Michael Young
ECONOMIC DEMOCRACY (1948)

Underlying the economic problem of the next decade is a vitally important question: what is going to be the spiritual driving force of the mixed economy? It is a question which must be asked even in a chapter whose main concern is with economics. No doubt the practical completion of Labour's great measures for the expansion of the social services will change the quality of the lives of very many people. The improvement of education, in particular, will at last make a reality of Labour's aim to give everyone a fair start in life; in ten or twenty years the great majority of key jobs should be filled by those whose sheer merit has been their only qualification. Ability which in previous generations has been untapped will be at the nation's service. The emergence of the classless society will be one source of inspiration.

But this will not be enough. The full answer must be found in the extension of democracy. There are unfortunately still too many people who talk about the reconciliation of planning and democracy, as if we already had as much democracy as necessary and as if the only problem was to introduce planning while preserving the democracy which we have got. On the contrary, the point is that to make planning work, in the early part of the second half of the twentieth century, there must be more democracy. Too many people have thought of democracy as a form of State alone. It is much more than that: it is a way of life. 'Government of the people by the people' is not an ideal reserved for Parliament. It is the most effective method of social co-operation wherever people are combined together for common purposes. Socialists have never been content that democracy should be restricted to politics. They have always wished to match political democracy with an economic democracy which would give every worker the same kind of rights in his work as he possessed in politics.

What holds our society, or any society, together is man's instinctive urge to contribute to the good of his own family and, beyond his family, to the good of his fellow men. Frustration is the universal child of restrictions which prevent people from making a contribution to the welfare of the community. Men who can do nothing of significance for their fellows seldom get respect from others and, what is worse, seldom feel the self-respect which is one of the secrets of individual happiness. The growing scale of organisation in our more and more complex modern society throws higher and higher obstacles in the path of the individual. He finds it more and more difficult to see where he fits in. His life is controlled by remote and impersonal forces. He cannot apparently contribute to the welfare of other members of society outside his own family group in a way that is any longer meaningful.

The extension of democracy is in essence the extension of opportunity for people to contribute to society. It means that people should do things for themselves instead of having things done for them. How little do people do for themselves now! Their foreman and managers are appointed from above. Do they help to choose their parsons or their bishops, headmasters or the site for the new school? Do they have any share in the running of their hospital or their housing estate? How rarely, and how few. Social scientists today are showing that democracy does not (as so many people so dangerously believe) reduce efficiency but instead promotes it. Social science can be of the utmost value in carrying democracy into practice – in industry, social services, the school, leisure, and even in the home.

Men who influence the activities of the social groups of which they are a part are inspired with the spirit of community service. The man who at his work has a voice in the way his working life is organised is far more alive and incid-entally far more enthusiastic than one who is still treated as a passive hand, as a factor of production or as an awkward chap whose goodwill can be coaxed by a display of paternal benevolence. He who has responsibility, feels a sense of responsibility. So the extension of democracy, mammoth task as it is when it comes to detail, is the best hope of providing the inspiration which will carry Britain through the years of trial. But it will be far more than a means to the end of a higher standard of life. After all it is well known that in the right circumstances countries can become rich. But in no country has a place been found for the small man, and we are all small men, in a society dominated by hugeness. Find that place in Britain, as the Labour Party will have the chance to do in the next ten years, and the whole world may change its course. No country is better fitted for this pioneering task than Britain with its tradition of democratic action and its deep-seated habits of tolerance. We must seize our historic opportunity.

From *Socialism: The British Way* edited by Donald Munro (Essential Books, 1948)

Aneurin Bevan
DEMOCRATIC CONTROL OF THE ECONOMY (1950)

You only have to open any of the newspapers any morning, read the leading articles, and you will find always that before you come to the end of it, the Government, which means Parliament, at some time or another will be blamed for something it has done or not done. In fact it is an endless cacophony of blame and derision and nagging day by day.

That is all right in a wholesome democracy like ours. But you must remember that if an elected Parliament goes on denying itself powers of effective economic intervention in order to prevent these evils from occurring, if it goes on continuously divesting itself of powers, then it will undermine parliamentary democracy itself, because people will throw away an institution which is useless to remedy their wrongs. If government by discussion is infertile, then men who think with their blood come on the scene.

So I regard it as an absolute prerequisite for the defence of all the principles of democracy, for the maintenance of the best of the liberal inheritance, that elected governments in the modern world should arm themselves with effective economic powers; because unless they do that, then the people who complain, and properly complain, will cut out the roots of democracy themselves. That is the reason why no democracy in the modern world is safe unless it becomes a socialist democracy. There is no halfway house here at all. It may be that we are moving towards an eclectic society; we are not going to have a monolithic society, we are not going to have a society in which every barber's shop is nationalised. But we must have a society in which the democratic institutions and the elected representatives of the people have their hands on the levers of economic power and where the massive movements of economic affairs are under central direction and control. Unless that happens democracy itself will perish. That is why it is so very important for us to see the argument about public ownership from that particular angle.

From 'Democratic Values', the Fabian Autumn Lecture 1950, by Aneurin Bevan

James Keir Hardie
CONTROL OVER PROPERTY (1907)

We have seen how in our own country the boundaries of freedom have been widening with the progress of the ages. The slave of a thousand years ago, with no more right than the swine he tended, has fought his way upward through serfdom to citizenship. The modern workman is theoretically the equal in the eye of the law of every other class. His vote carries equal weight in the ballot box with that of the millionaire who employs him; he is as free to worship when and how he pleases as the noblest baron; his rights are in all respects the same as theirs. Combination and energy have raised him to where he now stands. But his task is not yet finished; the long-drawn-out struggle is not yet over. There is one more battle to be fought, one more fortress to be assailed ere he stands within the charmed circle of perfect equality. He has yet to overcome property and win economic freedom. When he has made property his servant, not his master, he will literally have put all his enemies under his feet.

From *From Serfdom to Socialism*

G.D.H. Cole
SELF-GOVERNMENT IN INDUSTRY (1917)

What, I want to ask, is the fundamental evil in our modern society, which we should set out to abolish? There are two possible answers to that question, and I am sure that very many well-meaning people would make the wrong one. They would answer POVERTY, when they ought to answer SLAVERY. Face to face every day with the shameful contrasts of riches and destitution, high dividends and low wages, and painfully conscious of the futility of trying to adjust the balance by means of charity, private or public, they would answer unhesitatingly that they stand for the ABOLITION OF POVERTY.

Well and good! On that issue every socialist is with them. But their answer to my question is none the less wrong.

Poverty is the symptom: slavery the disease. The extremes of riches and destitution follow inevitably upon the extremes of licence and bondage. The many are not enslaved because they are poor, they are poor because they are enslaved. Yet socialists have all too often fixed their eyes upon the material misery of the poor without relating that it rests upon the spiritual degradation of the slave . . .

Inspired by the idea that poverty is the root evil, socialists have tried to heal the ills of society by an attempt to redistribute income. In this attempt, it will be admitted that they have hitherto met with no success. The gulf between rich and poor has not grown an inch narrower; it has even appreciably widened. It is the conviction of Guild-Socialists that the gulf will never be bridged, as long as the social problem is regarded pre-eminently a question of distribution . . .

It is the pride of the practical reformer that he deals with 'the average man in his average moments'. He repudiates, as high-falutin nonsense, every attempt to erect a new social order on a basis of idealism; he is vigilantly distrustful of human nature, human initiative and human freedom; and he finds his ideal in a paternal governmentalism tempered by a preferably not too real democratic control. To minds of such a temper, collectivism has an irresistible appeal. The idea that the State is not only supreme in the last resort, but also a capable jack of all trades, offers to the bureaucrat a wide field for petty tyranny. In the State today, in which democratic control through Parliament is little better than a farce, the collectivist State would be the earthly paradise of bureaucracy.

The socialist in most cases admits this, but declares that it could be corrected if Parliament were democratised. The 'conquest of political power' becomes the alpha and omega of his political method: all his cheques are postdated to the Greek Kalends of the first socialist Government. Is, then, his ideal of the democratic control of industry through Parliament an ideal worthy of the energy which is expended in its furtherance?

The crying need of our days is the need for freedom. Machinery and capitalism between them have made the worker a mere serf, with no interest in the product of his own labour beyond the inadequate wage which he secures by it. The collectivist State would only make his position better by securing him a better wage, even if we assume that collectivism can ever acquire the driving power to put its ideas into practice: in other respects it would leave the worker essentially as he is now – a wage slave, subject to the will of a master imposed on him from without. However democratically minded Parliament might be, it would none the less remain, for the worker in any industry, a purely external force, imposing its commands from outside and from above. The postal workers are no more free while the Post Office is managed by a State depart-ment than trade unionists would be free if their executive committees were appointed by His Majesty's Minister of Labour . . .

The collectivist is prepared to recognise trade unionism under a collectivist regime. But he is not prepared to trust trade unionism, or to entrust it with the conduct of industry. He does not believe in industrial self-government; his 'industrial democracy' embodies only the right of the workers to manage their trade unions, and not their right to control industry. The National Guildsman, on the other hand, bases his social philosophy on the idea of function. In the industrial sphere, he desires not the recognition of trade unions by a collectivist State, but the recognition of a democratic State by National Guilds controlling industry in the common interest . . .

I have dwelt . . . upon the socialism of William Morris because I feel that he, more than any other prophet of revolution, is of the same blood as National Guildsmen. Freedom for self-expression, freedom at work as well as at leisure, freedom to serve as well as to enjoy – that is the guiding principle of his work and of his life. That, too, is the guiding principle of National Guilds. We can only destroy the tyranny of machinery – which is not the same as destroying machinery itself – by giving into the hands of the workers the control of their life and work, by freeing them to choose whether they will make well or ill, whether they will do the work of slaves or of free men. All our efforts must be turned in that direction: in our immediate measures we must strive to pave the way for the coming free alliance of producers and consumers.

This is indeed a doctrine directly in opposition to the political tendencies of our time. For today we are moving at a headlong pace in the direction of a 'national' control of the lives of men which is in fact national only in the sense that it serves the interests of the dominant class in the nation. Already many of the socialists who have been the most enthusiastic advocates of State action are standing aghast at the application of their principles to an undemocratic society. The greatest of all dangers is the 'Selfridge' State, so loudly heralded these twenty years by Mr 'Callisthenes' Webb. The workers must be free and self-governing in the industrial sphere, or all their struggle for emancipation will have been in vain. If we had to choose between syndicalism and collectivism, it would be the duty and impulse of every good man to choose syndicalism, despite the dangers it involves. For syndicalism at least aims high, even though it fails to ensure that production shall actually be carried on, as it desires, in the general interest. Syndicalism is the infirmity of noble minds: collectivism is at best only the sordid dream of a businessman with a conscience. Fortunately, we have not to choose between these two: for in the Guild idea socialism and syndicalism are reconciled. To it collectivism will yield if only all lovers of freedom will rally round the banner, for it has a message for them especially such as another school of socialism has had. Out of the trade union shall grow the Guild; and in the Guild alone is freedom for the worker and a release from the ever-present tyranny of modern industrialism.

From *Self–Government in Industry*

Aneurin Bevan
PUBLIC AND PRIVATE PROPERTY (1951)

Thus, judged from any angle, the relations between public and private enterprise have not yet reached a condition where they can be stabilised. That is why it is so foolish for certain Labour men to preach 'consolidation' at this stage. Before we can dream of consolidation, the power relations of public and private property must be drastically altered. The solution of the problems I have been discussing cannot be approached until it becomes possible to create a purposive and intelligible design for society. That cannot be done until effective social and economic power passes from one order of society to another.

At the moment we are between two worlds. We have lost the propulsions of one and we have not yet gained the forward thrust of the other. This is no place in which to halt.

That is not to say a halting place cannot be reached. I think it can. It is clear to the serious student of modern politics that a mixed economy is what most people of the West would prefer. The victory of socialism need not be universal to be decisive. I have no patience with those socialists, so called, who in practice would socialise nothing, while in theory they threaten the whole of private property. They are purists and therefore barren. It is neither prudent, nor does it accord with our conception of the future, that all forms of private property should live under perpetual threat. In almost all types of human society different forms of property have lived side by side without fatal consequences either for society or for one of them. But it is a requisite of social stability that one type of property ownership should dominate. In the society of the future it should be public property. Private property should yield to the point where social purposes and a decent order of priorities form an easily discernible pattern of life. Only when this is accomplished will a tranquil and serene attitude take the place of the all-pervading restlessness that is the normal climate of competitive society.

From *In Place of Fear* by Aneurin Bevan (MacGibbon & Kee, 1961)

George Orwell
CENTRALISED OWNERSHIP (1941)

It has become clear in the last few years that 'common ownership of the means of production' is not in itself a sufficient definition of socialism. One must also add the following: approximate equality of incomes (it need be no more than approximate), political democracy, and abolition of all hereditary privilege, especially in education. These are simply the necessary safeguards against the reappearance of a class system. Centralised ownership has very little meaning unless the mass of the people are living roughly upon an equal level, and have some kind of control over the Government. 'The State' may come to mean no more than a self-elected political party, and oligarchy and privilege can return, based on power rather than on money.

From *The Lion and the Unicorn: Socialism and the English Genius*
by George Orwell (Secker & Warburg, 1941)

Anthony Crosland
PUBLIC AND PRIVATE OWNERSHIP (1956)

Is it then not clear that the ownership of the means of production has ceased to be the key factor which imparts to a society its essential character? Either collectivism or private ownership is consistent with widely varying degrees of liberty, democracy, equality, exploitation, class-feeling, planning, workers' control, and economic prosperity. And it is surely the degree to which these attributes are present or absent which makes people differentiate between societies.

This does not of course mean that ownership can have no influence whatever on the character of a society, or on what decisions are taken in these various spheres. It leaves open the question of whether nationalisation is a good or bad thing. It might be that private ownership was either a help or a hindrance to the attainment of certain goals, such as income equality, or the diffusion of power, or a higher status for the worker. What it does mean is that the pattern of ownership, although it may influence, is unlikely to *determine* the extent to which such goals are attained, and the presence or absence of the basic attributes mentioned above. And even as an influence it is now much less important than other factors, such as the managerial structure of industry, the level of employment, the strength of the trade unions, the general social climate, and above all the character of the political authority . . .

The ideal (or at least my ideal) is a society in which ownership is thoroughly mixed-up – a society with a diverse, diffused, pluralist, and heterogeneous pattern of ownership, with the State, the nationalised industries, the co-operatives, the unions, Government financial institutions, pension funds, foundations, and millions of private families all participating. Since this is still a long way off, we need heavy taxation to limit profits and dividends. And it may be an unpopular solution amongst the traditionalists of the Left, who still want (or will be made to want by *ad captandum* speeches) the steady creation of State monopolies.

But it is too late to settle these matters now by evocations of the spirit of Keir Hardie. We no doubt want more nationalisation than we now have. But I at least do not want a steadily extending chain of State monopolies, believing this to be bad for liberty, and wholly irrelevant to socialism as defined in this book. State ownership of all industrial capital is not now a condition of creating a socialist society, establishing social equality, increasing social welfare, or eliminating class distinctions. What is unjust in our present arrangements is the distribution of private wealth; and that can as well be cured in a pluralist as in a wholly State-owned economy, with much better results for social content-ment and the fragmentation of power.

From *The Future of Socialism* by C.A.R. Crosland (Jonathan Cape, 1956)

John Strachey
LAST-STAGE CAPITALISM (1956)

The methods by which last-stage capitalism encroaches upon democracy are subtle rather than direct . . . What is to be apprehended is not, then, a direct attack. What is not only likely but inevitable – indeed it is taking place without ceasing – is an attempt, largely unconscious, on the part of capital, highly organised and integrated in the oligopolies, to manipulate and distort, and if necessary frustrate, the workings of contemporary democracy to its own advan-tage. Again, there is no need to postulate a high degree of conscious intention. It is often an error to attribute to social forces much self-consciousness. It is rather that the oligopolies, working quite naturally to further their own interests, come into conflict with this or that aspect of democracy and seek to modify it to suit themselves. But the sum of those modifications and manipula-tions, if they did not encounter successful opposition, would spell out the end of effective democracy.

This is another important 'special case' of the process we have been studying throughout this volume; a special case of the consequences of the reduction of the units in any sphere of the productive system to a small number of large firms. It will be recalled that this process has exceptionally far-reaching con-sequences in the case of banking . . . a reduction in the number of banks to the typical handful of oligopolies transformed the very nature of banking from being a humble handmaid of industrial production and commerce, useful for storing and pooling spare surpluses, into a mighty engine of control, capable, if acting in step with the State, of modifying the whole economic climate of the society in question. Now we must note other cases in which the process of 'oligopolisation', spreading from the strictly economic field into every part of contemporary society, has critically important consequences. The first of these examples is afforded by the press and the other media of mechanised expression, such as broadcasting and television . . .

Here we have a cardinal instance of how the development of capitalism in its last stage automatically encroaches on democracy. The dissemination of news and opinion has become a branch of big business and, like other big business, has passed into the oligopolistic stage. As such it becomes the quasi-monopoly of a handful of great firms, just as does the manufacture of motor cars, or chemicals, or steel, or half a dozen other products. But the dissemina-tion of news and opinion is no ordinary productive process. It is closely bound up with the existence of effective democracy. Experience has indeed shown that in favourable circumstances it is possible for democracy to function even when almost all the media of mass expression are in the hands of only one of the main political tendencies. But there is a limit to the monopolisation of opinion which democracy can stand and yet continue to be effective. If *all* the effective media of expression come into the hands of one political tendency – and it will be, of course, the pro big capital political tendency – then it is almost impossible for the electorate to make a rational choice. That is why such issues as the control of television are, and are felt to be, of immense importance. These issues – and not, in the main, constitutional forms, will be what really matter in the political struggles of the second half of the century.

From *Contemporary Capitalism* by John Strachey (Victor Gollancz, 1956)

Douglas Jay
ATTACKING UNEARNED INCOMES (1938)

Socialists should change the laws so as substantially to abolish inheritance. On the substance of this there should be no compromise whatever. For inheritance is at once the chief cause of inequality and of the resulting poverty, and the most indefensible of all the trappings of modern capitalism. The payment of inherited incomes is not morally justifiable, because the recipients make no real effort or sacrifice in return; and it is not economically justifiable, because the passive service of merely refraining from consuming one's capital is one that can be performed with equal efficiency by the State. Moreover, just because inheritance is associated with the family, it inevitably produces a propertied class, with all its attendant evils. The abolition of unearned incomes and the consequent social ownership of property must be the centre and the heart of socialism. The traditional socialist belief that unearned incomes are the main removable cause of poverty and inequality is true and of dominating importance . . .

Socialists have been mistaken in making ownership of the means of production instead of ownership of inherited property the test of socialisation . . . It is not the ownership of the means of production as such, but ownership of large inherited incomes, which ought to be eliminated. Indeed, the official Marxist definition of socialism, as propagated by Mr John Strachey for instance, denotes a state of affairs which would be perfectly compatible with all the most unbridled abuses of private capitalism. Socialism by this definition means the abolition of private ownership of the means of production. But supposing, as might happen in Russia, that the State owned all the means of production, but that at the same time there was a class of rich rentiers living entirely on the interest on Government securities, and handing them on freely up to 100 per cent to their children. It would be possible, on Mr Strachey's definition, to build up an entirely idle class of millionaire rentiers, and to say that 'socialism' had nevertheless been achieved. If we are to have the substance and not the shadow, therefore, we must define socialism as the abolition of private unearned or inherited incomes rather than of the private ownership of the means of production.

From *The Socialist Case* by Douglas Jay (Faber & Faber, 1938)

Alan Ryan
CAPITALISM AND AUTHORITY (1984)

It is remarkable how reluctant socialists have been to stress the one dimension in which capitalism is plainly deficient, that of industrial self-government. Capitalism has never mounted a convincing defence of itself in this area.

Consumers have often enough been said to be 'sovereign' in the marketplace, and this has provided a sort of defence against the idea that the capitalists themselves have exercised anything you could call industrial tyranny or dictatorship. If consumers are really sovereign all the capitalists can do is transmit the consumers' demands to the workers; they do not exercise an independent power, and their authority has nothing of what you might call a 'political' flavour about it. The intermediary role of the capitalist in the process of reflecting demand in supply raises no interesting moral questions. But this has always been a pretty unpersuasive story, not least because it simply begs the crucial question of why the ownership of the capital which a company employs in trading should entitle its owners to automatic and absolute authority over how the company is run. We do not think that the landowners who own the land on which London is situated should thereby obtain all the political authority which is actually located in borough and county councils. There is, therefore, a case to be made before we have to agree that the owners of the capital employed in commerce and industry may exercise all the authority exercised in commercial and industrial undertakings.

A simple answer would be that the capitalist is entitled to as much authority as is needed for the performance of his entrepreneurial functions. But this reply, reasonable as it is, too swiftly closes the gap between the capitalist as rentier and the capitalist as entrepreneur. The capitalist as rentier does only one thing, and that is advance the funds needed to enable production to proceed. He seems on the face of it entitled to no more authority than the investor in National Savings bonds can exercise over the way the Government spends the money he lends it. The rentier has a right to protection against mismanagement and speculation; it's not obvious that he has more rights than that. If anyone has a right to authority, it must be the entrepreneur. Whatever the pattern of ownership, he cannot do his job at all unless he can get others to do what he wants, the way he wants it and when he wants it. In that sense, he, like a political leader, needs authority to do his job; he has the same sort of claim to be given that authority, a claim based on the kind of job it is and the importance of its being done. Even so, it's worth noting that two distinct issues are at stake. Generals, prime ministers and entrepreneurs all *need* to be able to say 'go' with a confidence that he goeth. But this is a different issue from that of who it is who ought to bestow that authority upon them. What authority is needed and how it may legitimately be had are different questions.

Prime ministers need large but not absolute powers and should get them through the ballot box not through a military coup. The socialist view is surely that entrepreneurs need large discretionary powers but should get them from the votes of the workers instead of from the say-so of the rentiers. How socialist self-government can work without succumbing either to inefficiency on the one hand or erosion in the face of expertise and deference in the face of expertise on the other is a difficult empirical question. It is precisely the sort of question which socialist economists and sociologists ought to think about in a grimly realistic frame of mind. But the conceptual issue is simple enough. Capitalist management has been chronically non-democratic and non-participatory. The view that workers can sign away their industrial citizenship while they cannot sign away their political citizenship has needlessly gone unchallenged. Yet any defence of socialism's greater potential for *freedom* ought to make much of it.

From 'Liberty and Socialism' by Alan Ryan in *Fabian Essays in Socialist Thought*, edited by Ben Pimlott (Heinemann Educational Books Ltd, 1984)

David Marquand
THE PUBLIC GOOD (1988)

If we reject market liberalism and State socialism, we are left, in practice, with some variant or other of the mixed economy – of an economy in which resources are largely allocated through the market, but in which public power intervenes on a significant scale to supplement, constrain, manipulate, or direct market forces for public ends. That sentence, however, raises as many ques-tions as it answers. Public intervention implies a public purpose: otherwise, those who do the intervening cannot know what they are trying to achieve. But in a political culture shaped by the assumption that society is made up of separate, atomistic individuals, pursuing only their own private purposes, the notion of a public purpose which is more than the sum of private purposes is apt to seem dangerous, or meaningless, or both.

The result is an intellectual and moral vacuum at the heart of the political economy. Since the war, at the latest, Britain has had a substantial public sector and a large capacity for public intervention. But because the notion of a public purpose is alien to it, her political class has had no philosophy of public intervention or of what might be called the public realm. There are no agreed criteria for determining the ends which public intervention is supposed to serve, and no agreed procedures for deciding what the criteria should be; and the suggestion that there should be seems quaint, if not utopian. So does the suggestion that the public sector should be seen as the instrument of a public good, which the members of the public have agreed in common, and to the pursuit of which they therefore have a common obligation. Yet, without such a philosophy, it is hard to see how a political economy which depends on public intervention can command the support which it needs to function properly. In its absence, the public sector is apt to become a battleground for warring private interests, while its 'outputs' appear increasingly arbitrary and capricious. In good times, no obvious damage need result. Hard choices can be avoided, and predatory interests bought off. In default of active support, the system can make do with passive acquiescence. But in bad times, when passive acquiescence is no longer enough and when all decisions hurt, arbitrary ones are likely to undermine support for the system, at the very point when it is more needed. It would be wrong to suggest that this is a complete summary of the recent history of Britain's political economy, but few would deny that it summarises a good deal of it.

This has obvious implications for the problems we have been discussing. The questions of how to halt the decline in Britain's international competitiveness, of how to devise a satisfactory form of transnational power sharing and of how to respond to the growth of group power and the decay of traditional authority all pose hard choices. Except in the shortest of short terms, the answers cannot be imposed successfully from the top down. Yet none of the doctrines around which post-war British politics has revolved offers anything other than imposed answers, for none of them provides the moral basis for the sense of community and mutual obligation which would make it possible to look for answers in a different way.

From *The Unprincipled Society: New Demands and Old Politics*
by David Marquand (Jonathan Cape, 1988)

Will Hutton
A RETURN TO RESPONSIBILITY (1995)

For what binds together the disorders of the British system is a fundamental amorality. It is amoral to run a society founded on the exclusion of so many people from decent living standards and opportunities; it is amoral to run an economy in which the only admissible objective is the maximisation of shareholder value; it is amoral to run a political system in which power is held exclusively and exercised in such a discretionary, authoritarian fashion. These exclusions, while beneficial in the short term to those inside the circle of privilege, are in the long run inefficient and ultimately undermine the wealth-generating process.

Like a Russian doll, the task of reform has many layers. We need employment, which requires more capital stock and higher investment, which will be the most effective instrument for the social objective of bringing the margin-alised back into the fold. And that in turn will involve the redistribution of income, perhaps even of work. Yet all these measures depend upon a recogni-tion that rights – to consume now, to pay as little to the commonweal as possible, to satisfy desires instantaneously – must be accompanied by responsibilities if we are to live in a good society. Without lower consumption there can be no investment for the future; without taxation there can be no infrastructure of public support from which all benefit.

Corrective economic and social policies and institutions that embody them presuppose a system of values; and that demands a political constitution in which public values and common interests can be defined.

This implies nothing less than the root and branch overhaul of the Westminster version of democracy. If markets require boundaries and rules of the game, they must be set by public agency – but if such intervention is disqualified by the belief that any public action necessarily fails, then the initiative cannot even reach first base. The State must act to assert common purpose; but unless the State enjoys legitimacy and expresses the democratic will, it can make no such claim.

The constitution of the State is vital not only for its capacity to express the common good but also as the exemplar of the relationship between the individual and the wider society. The extent to which the State embodies trust, participation and inclusion is the extent to which those values are diffused through society at large.

What is needed is the development of a new conception of citizenship. If a well-functioning market economy requires skilled workforces, strong social institutions like schools and training centres, and a vigorous public infra-structure, these cannot be achieved if the governing class cannot understand the values implicit in such bodies. And if creative companies orchestrate the voices of all stakeholders into a common enterprise, embodying such a conception in company law is impossible if the State is genetically programmed to view the business of governance as the exercise of sovereignty, and the duty of the governed to obey. Unqualified shareholder sovereignty and parliamentary sovereignty are two sides of the same coin.

To break out of this cycle of decline and to build co-operative institutions, Britain must complete the unfinished business of the seventeenth century and equip itself with a constitution that permits a new form of economic, social and political citizenship. Economic citizenship will open the way to the reform of our financial and corporate structures; social citizenship will give us the chance of constructing an intelligent welfare state based on active solidarity; and political citizenship opens the way to political pluralism and genuine co-operation. This idea of citizenship could subsume differences of gender and race, and instil a sense of obligation to our natural environment – a victim of uncontrolled economic forces.

This national effort will have to be matched by an international economic and political architecture more conducive to such developments. The burgeoning international marketplace – destabilising currency flows, using offshore havens to avoid tax – is hostile to expressions of common and public interest. Private interests have too easily slipped the national leash and have used the ungoverned world beyond national frontiers to undermine what they regard as tiresome, inefficient and bureaucratic efforts to assert the moral and social dimension in human affairs.

This escape from responsibility cannot and should not be allowed to become permanent. Unless Western capitalism in general and British capitalism in particular can accept that they have responsibilities to the social and political world in which they are embedded, they are headed for perdition. Paradoxically, the most likely consequences will be the closure of the very open markets that business most needs as societies seek to protect themselves from the destructive forces that unregulated capital can release – a reprise in the early twenty-first century of the conditions Karl Polanyi described in the early part of this century. Societies were atomised by free markets that were then policed by centralised states and willed into being the supposedly protective forces of communism and fascism. That kind of breakdown, and those des-perate authoritarian attempts to repair it, must be avoided today. The demand for a moral economy is not simply the assertion of a different value system. It is a call to arms in a world in which time is running short.

From *The State We're In* by Will Hutton (Jonathan Cape, 1995)

Peter Shore

IN THE ROOM AT THE TOP (1958)

If socialists have been right to assume that private ownership of industrial property is the key to a capitalist society, they have been wrong in assuming that public ownership leads necessarily to a classless society. It does not. The power of industrial property remains, under public no less than private owner-ship, and the shape that it gives to society depends upon who controls it and the purposes for which it is used. It is not a natural pessimism but history and the evidence of our times that lead me to believe that those who control the community's wealth, whatever the legal forms of ownership may be, will use it to establish privileged positions and high rewards for themselves and to hand on such advantages as they can to their heirs. Where democratic counter-pres-sures are lacking, a 'new class' indeed seems unavoidable.

But the problems that this raises, though difficult, are not insuperable. If we develop and extend our democracy, we *can* make the corporate economy serve the community's needs; we *can* prevent managerial control leading to an excessive accumulation of advantages. We *can*, too, distribute decision-making power throughout industry and society. What stands in the way is not so much lack of techniques – although these are important – nor the inherent difficulties – and at times it does seem rather like separating a magnet from its field of force – but at root lack of will to further change. For the managerial society is not without its attractions. At least it is an advance on the past. It is more hygienic, more discreet, more efficient. It promises to supply us with an endless stream of new toys. If we lowered our sights sufficiently, might it not be possible to come to terms?

I know the answer I would give. I do not want a society in which an *élite*, viewing the world through boardroom windows, makes the big decisions, collects the big rewards, while the mass of men deprived of power and responsibility dig their gardens or watch the telly.

I want instead a society which shapes its institutions so that men may become self-determining, their own masters. For we are in the end what society allows us to be: adults or children, masters or men, apathetic or involved. Humanity can only develop if we have faith in its innate capacity, if we refuse to believe that men are what they are because they can be no different. This is to me the starting point of democratic socialism and the basic case for social change.

From 'In the Room at the Top' by Peter Shore, in *Conviction*, edited by Norman Mackenzie (MacGibbon & Kee, 1958)

DEVOLVING POWER

'I do not believe in dictators because I know from my experience and thinking and inner consciousness that world changes are not going to be the work of one man. They are going to be the work of toiling millions'

R.H. Tawney

THE DESIRE FOR RESULTS

The only sound test, in the first place, of a political system, is its practical effect on the lives of human beings. The war should have taught us one lesson, if it has taught us nothing more. It is idle for a nation to blazon Liberty, Equality and Fraternity, or other resounding affirmations, onto the façades of its public buildings, if to display the same motto in its factories and mines would arouse only the cynical laughter that greets a reminder of idealisms turned sour and hopes unfulfilled. What men demand is not merely paragraphs in constitutions, but results, in the form of arrangements which secure them the essentials of a civilised existence and show a proper respect for their dignity as human beings. Democracy must prove, if it is to survive, its faith by its works. It is unstable as a political system, as long as it remains a political system and little more, instead of producing, as it should, its own type of society and a manner of life in harmony with that type.

It is such a society and such a way of life that British socialists and their continental colleagues are labouring to create. They intend to create them, in the second place, not by jettisoning democratic institutions, but by using more assiduously the powers they confer. In the London of the 1930s, when Bloomsbury had just awoken to the recondite fact of the existence of a class struggle, and announced the discovery with bloodcurdling bleats, there were not wanting prophets who cried and cut themselves with knives at the alleged futility of political democracy. The rank and file of the Labour movement were then, and remain now, unmoved by these antics. They know the effects of the paralysis and perversions, to which, in the absence of a vigorous public opinion, democracy is subject, a good deal more intimately than the melodious intellectuals who harrow refined audiences with tearful cries of stinking fish; but they know also what they have gained from it. They regard democracy, not as an obstacle to socialism, but as an instrument for attaining it, and socialism, not as the antithesis of democracy, but as an extension of democratic principles into spheres of life which previously escaped their influence. Given the acceptance of that view, controversies may be bitter; but, once a political system has been put on a popular basis, the conflict takes place within the limits fixed by it. It turns, not on the merits or demerits of that system itself, but on the specific purposes for which, from time to time, opposing parties seek to use it.

From *The Radical Tradition: Twelve Essays on Politics, Education and Literature by R.H. Tawney*, edited by Rita Hinden (George Allen & Unwin, 1964)

E.F.M. Durbin

DEFENCE OF DEMOCRACY (1940)

Freedom of association, freedom from arbitrary arrest, power to count with others in the government of the nation – these are essential properties of any social order that can be described as good. They are fundamental requirements for any society claiming to provide an opportunity for the free development, and growing happiness, of the individuals composing it. An opposition between 'socialism' and 'the democratic method', if 'socialism' contains any reference to 'social justice', is meaningless to me. The relationship between the whole and the part. The democratic method, and the absence of terror, are an indispensable part of my conception of social justice.

It might, however, be suggested that while the method of political democracy, as defined by me, was one necessary characteristic of a just social order, it was not the only characteristic of it, and therefore no more fundamental than any other: for example, the existence of a just distribution of wealth. In that case it might be reasonable to sacrifice one of these characteristics – liberty – in order to obtain the other – equality.

Now it is perfectly possible for persons to prefer equality in the distribution of wealth to political liberty. They are then perfectly consistent – though in my view morally mistaken – to advocate a political terror in order to make the distribution of income less unequal. My point is not that such a position is untenable – since it is plainly logical – but simply that such a programme and such a strategy does not touch the problem of constructing a just society Economic quality can be fully achieved, and social justice remain as far away as ever, because one kind of injustice has replaced another – because one type of privilege (political) has been substituted for another (economic). The problem of a just society is not the single problem of economic equality, but the much more difficult problem of achieving simultaneously in one society both liberty and equality . . .

We reach then this final position – that the democratic method is not only essential for the achievement of socialism, but that it is part of that achievement. In so far as we are democratic we are already, in some degree, socialist; and to betray democracy is to betray socialism.

There is a complex and important sense in which socialism is necessary to democracy – the sense in which capitalism is incompatible with democracy. But there is a very simple and much more obvious sense in which democracy is necessary to socialism. It is not that democracy is the pleasantest, or most efficacious, or most certain method of achieving socialism, but that it is the only method; that all other hopes and all other programmes are mistaken and illusory. Democracy is not related to socialism as gilt to the gingerbread, or cream to coffee – a decorative addition or a great improvement; but as air to breathing, as coal to fire, as love to life – the indispensable means, the *fons et origo* of all our social hopes.

Democracy is a *method* of taking political decisions, of compromising and reconciling conflicting interests. The method is more important, more formative of the resulting social order, than the disputes so resolved.

When individuals or groups disagree – including nations and classes and parties within the State – the most important question is not what they disagree about, but the method or methods by which their disputes are to be resolved. If force is to be the arbiter between them, international war, civil war, cruelty and persecution are the inevitable consequences. Civilisation cannot be built upon these crises of destruction.

There are two great principles at struggle in the hearts of men – friendliness and aggressiveness, co-operation and struggle. The lives of us all, and the slow growth of reason and kindliness between us, depend upon the victory of the first principle over the second. It is only if men will agree at least in this, that their disputes shall not be resolved by force, that culture and justice can slowly develop in our midst. The vital question is the question of method. The method will determine the end . . .

The authoritarian architects of Utopia all start by building the upper floors of their buildings. They try to build insubstantial 'castles in the air'. Social justice is the spire and the crown of the human habitation. But there is only one foundation for it. Common security and common happiness can only be founded upon common consent – men must come freely to their own salvation – justice can only spring from liberty. Democracy is the foundation and cornerstone of the temple.

From *The Politics of Democratic Socialism* by E.F.M. Durbin
(George Routledge & Sons, 1940)

Neil Kinnock
DEMOCRACY AND POWER (1984)

In our society on every side we see things being torn apart. We see terrible wrongs done to the young and the old, we see wrongs done to the poor and the disabled; we see industries decimated, communities deprived, liberties lost. We see unjust laws – laws which are nothing more than prejudice made statute. And every fibre rages against the injustice and the waste of all that. And we ask ourselves; what we can do about it? For socialists that is the question of the ages – because it is in our very nature, in our conviction, that we want to do something. Especially when we are faced by injustice. It was a question faced by our movement in the 1930s; and they came back with the answer that the democratic road was the only route for British socialism. All other options, they said, were closed since socialism by insurrection was pure fantasy, and socialism without the ballot box would simply never secure the support and understanding of the

British people. They were right. They were right in times even more dangerous than ours, when fascism was pressing on every gate of liberty. Democracy is the first premise of our socialism; it is a matter of principle, not of convenience; it is a matter of common sense, not of tactics.

With its absolution, its dogmatism, its controls on local councils, its destruction of opportunities, its war on trade unionism, it is Toryism which defaces and relegates democracy in our country – not Labour, or the cause of Labour.

In saying that, we are not being smug and cosy, and giving in for the duration of the Tory Government, when we hold to our belief in democracy. We are upholding the only system which can give us power; the only system that we want to give us power; and the only system that we are prepared to wield when we have that power. Democracy is our cause at all times and in every respect. That is not a call to wait in idleness; it is not a call to relax until the election comes along. On the absolute contrary, it is a call to action – action to articulate and publicise the complaint of the people, for if they cry quietly, they will cry alone, action to break through the indifference to the scandals of social deprivation and industrial destruction in this country; action to pressure ministers and promote concessions, action to rouse and rally and resist; action to protect and promote the interest of the people that we are in politics to help; action that is continual; action that recruits and mobilises new people in our cause.

That is the action of democracy. We are democrats. At the earliest possible time we want to pass and enforce laws to redress grievances; to promote justice and opportunity, to punish race and sex prejudice; to change economic ownership and rewards. We want the power of the law to do that – so we cannot sharpen legality as our main weapon for the future, and simultaneously scorn legality because it doesn't suit us at the present time. To recognise that is not to be defeatist. It is to recognise the facts as they exist and as they are supported by the great mass of Labour people and Labour supporters in this country. To recognise that is not to bow down before a vague and variable idea called the 'sanctity of the law', because we all know how that can be built and bent to defend vested interests. It is to acknowledge that our greatest service to those who need our protection and provision from different laws, is to get power and turf out the authors of the present injustice.

We have to work for that incessantly, singlemindedly. It is a great cause but it is a careful and cool-headed cause. The people who need the support and safeguard of trade unionism and of public services, cannot afford to be part of any political 'Charge of the Light Brigade'. There is no glory in defeat for them; there is just nothing but extra miserable burdens of insecurity and insufficiency. In those circumstances, it is they – the poorest, the weakest, and the most needy – who are the martyrs. That's the fact.

From a speech to the Annual Labour Party Conference, in *Thorns and Roses: Speeches 1983-1991* by Neil Kinnock (Hutchinson, 1992)

Tony Benn

TECHNOLOGY AND DEMOCRACY (1979)

We can safely leave aside the scientific principles that have made technological advance possible and confine our attention to the result of their application. It is not how modern technology works that concerns us, as citizens, but what effect it has had on life. If we try to quantify the advances technology has made in the last fifty years, in terms of sheer machine capability, we can get an idea of the pace of that change, and what it has meant . . .

This is the scale of power the world is now attempting to cope with, using institutions that were largely devised before this power reached its present level. In this country our parliamentary, political party, civil service, trade union, educational and legal systems, all of them now under stress, were developed at a time when the machine capability was infinitesimal compared with what it is today. Many of our problems stem from institutional obsolescence. We live at a time in history when both the personal and collective material options open to us, and the expectations we have, are far greater than ever before. Yet a large number of people feel that they have progressively less say over the events that shape their lives, because the system, however it is defined, is too strong for them.

Many of the social tensions in Britain which we are now struggling to resolve actually derive from this feeling of waning influence. It is impossible to believe that the only liberation required can be achieved, as Conservatives suggest, by freeing a few thousand entrepreneurs from some government interference and providing them with higher material incentives by cutting personal levels of taxation. Nor can public ownership, economic planning and improved and more egalitarian social services, essential as all these are in providing the basis for further advance, alone provide the answer. There must be further fundamental changes to liberate people and allow them to lead fuller and more satisfying lives.

The process of re-equipping the human race with an entirely new set of tools, for that is what has happened, has produced two trends: the one towards interdependence, complexity and centralisation requiring infinitely greater skills in the management of large systems than we have so far been able to achieve; the other, going on simultaneously, and for the same reasons, towards greater decentralisation and human independence, requiring us to look again at the role of the individual, the new citizen, and his place in the community.

In sketching the changing relationship in democratic politics, of the huge new organisations on the one hand and the new citizen on the other, both created by technology, there is a common thread of argument. It is this. Authoritarianism in politics or industry just doesn't work any more. Governments can no longer control either the organisations or the people by using the old methods. The fact that in a democracy political authority derives from the consent of the electorate expressed at an election instead of by inheritance, as in a feudal monarchy, or through a coup d'etat, as in a dictatorship, makes practically no difference to the acceptability of authoritarianism. Except in a clear and local or national emergency when a consensus may develop in favour of an authoritarian act of State, or if imposed it is accepted, big organisations, whether publicly or privately owned, and people, whoever they are, expect genuine consultation before decisions are taken that affect them.

It is arguable that what has really happened has amounted to such a breakdown in the social contract, upon which parliamentary democracy by universal suffrage was based, that that contract now needs to be renegotiated on a basis that shares power much more widely, before it can win general assent again.

Modern democracy requires a revitalisation and reformulation of the philosophy of government enshrined in the idea of Parliament. Indeed unless we can develop such a framework we will never succeed in reconciling the twin realities of the age in which we live – on the one hand the need for supremely good national and international management of complex systems and on the other hand the need to see to it that the new citizen, who is also a potential beneficiary of much new power, is able to direct and control more effectively the uses to which technology is put.

From *Arguments for Socialism* by Tony Benn, edited by Chris Mullin (Cape, 1979)

Michael Meacher
EMPOWERING PEOPLE (1992)

So neither a remote, bureaucratic, centralised State nor an unfettered Thatcherite market system can release the power and opportunities for individuals to gain real control over their environment so as to develop their full potential as they choose. But there is a third and better way.Instead of the post-war socialist aspiration for the State to *supersede* market forces, which was not only over-ambitious but would raise as many problems as it resolved, the State should take the role of catalyst. Instead of seeking to be the universal provider, it should act, in different contexts, as regulator, advocate, enabler or protector.

It is linking the State to the cause of socialist individualism. No doubt for some for whom socialism is defined exclusively as State control over the commanding heights of the economy, this expression may seem a contradiction in terms. But that is to ignore that State versus markets is not so much an irreconcilable antithesis as a continuum where different trade-offs are possible. On the one side are the fundamentalist statists who pioneered the inflexible and bureaucratic 1940s nationalisations. On the other are the fundamentalist marketeers who currently champion untrammelled Thatcherite self-interest and want to roll back the State endlessly. In between are the advocates, on the one hand, of a much more flexible State regulation, and on the other of a much more constrained market system. Either of the two latter project a role for the State that is less heavy-handed, more innovative, more imaginative and indeed more of a stimulant if not directly entrepreneurial . . .

The facilitator role for the State is a key part of what should be the central theme of modern socialism. That theme is focused on the issue of power. Capitalist power lies in the concentration of control in a few hands of the main organisations that determine the future development of society. The essential characteristic of socialism by contrast is that control over people's lives is placed increasingly in their own hands.

Such a theme is not inconsistent with traditional formulations of socialism. These have centred round such ideas as the common ownership of the means of production, workers' control, welfare and equality, altruism and co-operative social relations, appropriating property incomes, and the brotherhood of man. These are all valid ideas in their own right, and there can be no question of reducing them to a single concept. Yet redistribution of power is at the heart of them all.It is what common ownership, workers' control and the appropriation of property incomes were precisely designed to achieve.

From *Diffusing Power: the Key to Socialist Revival* by M. Meacher (Pluto Press, 1992)

G.D.H. Cole
DIFFUSING POWER (1960)

I am neither a communist nor a social democrat, because I regard both as creeds of centralisation and bureaucracy, whereas I feel sure that a socialist society that is to be true to its equalitarian principles of human brotherhood must rest on the widest possible diffusion of power and responsibility, so as to enlist the active participation of as many as possible of its citizens in the tasks of democratic self-government.

From *History of Socialist Thought* by G.D.H. Cole (5 vols, Macmillan, 1953-60)

James Maxton
IF I WERE A DICTATOR (1935)

My criticism of the politician is not that he fails to keep order, but that he does it too well. He regards the suppression of discontent as his job, when his real duty is to analyse discontent, to find out the causes of discontent, to express discontent, and to establish a world order nearer to the heart's desire, more in keeping with the intelligence and the ethics of the men and women who live in the great age in which we are living.The two great problems confronting the peoples of the world, the problem of war and the problem of poverty – those two great things are in the minds of all.Those two great problems have to be solved by the men and women living now and they are not going to be solved by one man harrowing his fellows. Our age is a complicated and intricate one. We have wonderful specialists in literature, in art, in science, in technical affairs, in commerce – great experts, men who know and men who do. No politician, no dictator, is capable of controlling and directing every aspect of a complicated social and economic system. The brains of all have to make a contribution, and the driving force of the new social change has to come from the great mass of the people living in our big cities, in the crowded cities of America, of Europe, of Asia, Africa, and Australia, living in their millions, feeling themselves defrauded of a large proportion of what life ought to be able to give them, yet realising that there are opportunities being presented to mankind, more than ever before in human history. That mass, that huge, largely voiceless mass, will generate the driving force which is going to compel us to move out of our rather chaotic, sordid, squalid and unlovely way of living, into a new plane, a new richness, and a new beauty. I do not believe in dictators because I know from my experience and thinking and inner consciousness that world changes are not going to be the work of one man. They are going to be the work of the toiling millions.

From a speech at Foyle's literary luncheon at the launch of *If I Were a Dictator,* quoted in *James Maxton: Beloved Rebel* by John McNair (George Allen & Unwin, 1955)

Raymond Williams

POWER IN THE BASE (1983)

It is my belief that the only kind of socialism which now stands any chance of being established, in the old industrialised bourgeois-democratic societies, is one centrally based on new kinds of communal, co-operative and collective institutions. In these the full democratic practices of free speech, free assembly, free candidature for elections, and also open decision-making, of a reviewable kind, by all those concerned with the decision, would be both legally guaranteed and, in now technically possible ways, active. This is really the only road which socialists in these countries have left to travel . . .

The attraction of self-management, as now commonly foreseen, is its whole and direct democratic character. It is a conscious stage beyond representative democracy, whether in its post-feudal or bourgeois or social-democratic forms. Yet it is clear that most of its projections and experiments assume small-scale enterprises and communities, where its principles are more evidently practicable. What is then left beyond these, on larger scales, is either some vague and general goodwill or . . . the socialist command economy.

Some new definitions and principles need consideration. First, the problem of scale is more complex than the customary contrast of small and large. Thus certain industrial processes are necessarily complex, within both vertical and horizontal divisions of labour, and decision-making in them cannot in all respects be assigned to elements of the enterprise. Similarly, there is a range of social policies from those which affect only the inhabitants of a definable locality to those which affect much wider populations and the relations between localities. Self-management then cannot be confined to isolable enterprises and communities, for which some models exist, but must be taken, as a principle, into what are necessarily more indirect, more extended and therefore more complex forms.

This can be defined as the need for many new kinds of *intermediate* institutions, though we must be careful not to accept, uncritically, the received language of the intermediate between the dominant large and the locally autonomous small, which is evident in such terms as 'devolution' and 'decentralisation'. The condition of socialist democracy is that it is built from direct social relations into all necessary indirect and extended relations. This is expressed in received language as 'power from the base' or 'starting from the grass roots': each better than 'devolution' or 'decentralisation', with their assumption of authentic power at some centre, but in some ways affected by the continuing assumption of a 'centre'. The real emphases are better expressed as 'power *in* the base', *at* 'the grass roots'. In any event the principle is, and the practice should be, that all decisions are taken by all those who are directly concerned with them.

From 'Democracy Old and New' in *Towards Zero* by Raymond Williams
(Chatto & Windus, 1983)

Paul Hirst
THE PLURALIST STATE (1990)

The Left has been mesmerised by statism. Even moderate democratic socialists have constantly advocated giving more and more tasks to the State . . .

If socialists could accept the idea of a state that facilitated the work of democratically run associations in providing work and welfare, then they might have some chance of finding a more secure future for socialism. Democratic socialists seek to encourage co-operation, mutual assistance, fellowship and the greatest measure of equality attainable. They are not necessarily tied to particular social institutions like State ownership or central planning in meeting these objectives. Understood in this wider sense socialism can co-exist with a society of plural organisations and differing objectives. It could build its institutions of co-operative work and mutual assistance alongside other active groups of citizens and their projects; religious groups, ethnic communities, lifestyle communities, etc. A socialism committed to a pluralist society and to concentrating on organising social life through self-governing associations in civil society would pose less of a threat to others than a statist socialism, and might therefore expect to command more support. In particular it would be more open to Green conceptions of social organisation and to co-existing with Green associations.

A challenge to statist socialism does not mean a return to the Marxist illusions of 'smashing' the State. On the contrary, even if as many social activities as possible are devolved to self-governing associations in civil society, there will still be a need for a public power to regulate the actions of these associations and to ensure that they have the resources to carry out their tasks. A pluralist society with diverse social projects needs a public power to ensure order, but that public power need not be a 'sovereign state'; that is, a state claiming the exclusive control of power, asserting its primacy in every social domain, and imposing itself through a single centralised hierarchy. A pluralist state – as conceived by such English political pluralists as J.N. Figgis, G D H Cole and H.J. Laski – would be based on a quite different principle: that the State exists to protect and serve the self-governing associations. The State's powers would be limited by its function and such a State would recognise the inherently plural nature of all free social organisation. Pluralism requires that distinct locally and functionally specific domains of authority should have the autonomy necessary to carry out their tasks. This pluralist conception of the State is essential to a libertarian society, for 'decentralisation' and 'devolution' of power will accomplish little if all they do is to recreate centralised authorities at lower levels.

From 'From Statism to Pluralism' by Paul Hirst in *The Alternative: Politics for Change*,
edited by Ben Pimlott, Tony Wright and Tony Flower
(W.H. Allen & Co, 1990)

G.D.H. Cole
ACTIVE CITIZENSHIP (1920)

Guildsmen assume that the essential social values are human values, and that society is to be regarded as a complex of associations held together by the wills of their members, whose well-being is its purpose. They assume further that it is not enough that the forms of government should have the passive or 'implied' consent of the governed, but that the society will be in health only if it is in the full sense democratic and self-governing, which implies not only that all citizens should have a 'right' to influence its policy if they so desire, but that the greatest possible opportunity should be afforded for every citizen actually to exercise this right. In other words, the Guild Socialist conception of democracy, which it assumes to be good, involves an active and not merely a passive citizenship on the part of the members. Moreover, and this is perhaps the most vital and significant assumption of all, it regards this democratic principle as applying, not only or mainly to some special sphere of social action known as 'politics', but to any and every form of social action, and, in especial, to industrial and economic fully as much as to political affairs.

In calling these the fundamental assumptions of Guild Socialism, I do not mean to imply that they are altogether beyond the province of argument. They can indeed be sustained by arguments of obvious force; for it seems clear enough that only a community which is self-governing in this complete sense, over the whole length and breadth of its activities, can hope to call out what is best in its members, or to give them that maximum opportunity for personal and social self-expression which is requisite to real freedom. But such arguments as this, by which the assumptions stated above may be sustained and reinforced, really depend for their appeal upon the same considerations, and are, in the last resort, different ways of stating the same fundamental position. The essence of the Guild Socialist attitude lies in the belief that society ought to be so organised as to afford the greatest possible opportunity for individual and collective self-expression to all its members, and that this involves and implies the extension of positive self-government through all its parts.

No one can reasonably maintain that society is organised on such a principle today. We do, indeed, possess in theory a very large measure of democracy; but there are at least three sufficient reasons which make this theoretical democracy largely inoperative in practice. In the first place, even the theory of democracy today is still largely of the 'consciousness of consent' type. It assigns to the ordinary citizen little more than a privilege – which is in practice mainly illusory – of choosing his rulers, and does not call upon him, or assign to him the opportunity, himself to rule. Present-day practice has, indeed, pushed the theory of representative government to the length of substituting almost completely, even in theory, the representative for the represented. This is the essential meaning of the doctrine of the 'sovereignty of Parliament'. Secondly, such democracy as is recognised is conceived in a narrowly 'political' sense, as applying to a quite peculiar sphere known as politics, and not in a broader and more comprehensive sense, as applying to all the acts which men do in association or conjunction. The result is that theoretical 'democrats' totally ignore the effects of undemocratic organisation and convention in non-political spheres of social action, not only upon the lives which men lead in those spheres, but also in perverting and annihilating in practice the theoretical democracy of modern politics. They ignore the fact that vast inequalities of wealth and status, resulting in vast inequalities of education, power and control of environment, are necessarily fatal to any real democracy, whether in politics or in any other sphere. Thirdly, the theory of representative government is distorted not only by the substitution of the representative for the represented, but also as a consequence of the extended activity of political government falsifying the operation of the representative method. As long as the purposes of political government are comparatively few and limited, and the vast mass of social activities is either not regulated, or regulated by other means, such as the medieval guilds, it is perhaps possible for a body of men to choose one to represent them in relation to all the purposes with which a representative political body has to deal. But, as the purposes covered by political government expand, and more and more of social life is brought under political regulation, the representation which may once, within its limitations, have been real, turns into misrepresentation, and the person elected for an indefinitely large number of disparate purposes ceases to have any real representative relation to those who elect him.

It appears to the Guild Socialists, as to all real socialists, obviously futile to expect true democracy to exist in any society which recognises vast inequalities of wealth, status and power among its members. Most obvious of all is that, if, in the sphere of industry, one man is a master and the other a wage-slave, one enjoys riches and gives commands and the other has only an insecure subsistence and obeys orders, no amount of purely electoral machinery on a basis of 'one man one vote' will make the two really equal socially or politically. For the economic power of the rich master, or of the richer financier who is above even the master, will ring round the wage-slave's electoral rights at every point. A Press which can only be conducted with the support of rich capitalists and advertisers, an expensive machinery of elections, a regime in the school which differs for rich and poor and affords a training for power in the one case and for subjection in the other, a regime in industry which carries on the divergent lessons of the schools – these and a hundred other influences combine to make the real political power of one rich man infinitely greater than that of one who is poor. It is a natural and legitimate conclusion that, if we want democracy, that is, if we want every man's voice to count for as much as it is intrinsically worth, irrespective of any extraneous consideration, we must abolish class distinctions by doing away with the huge inequalities of wealth and economic power on which they really depend

. . .

The essentials of democratic representation, positively stated, are, first, that the represented shall have free choice of, constant contact with, and considerable control over, his representative. The second is that he should be called upon, not to choose someone to represent him as a man or as a citizen in all the aspects of citizenship, but only to choose someone to represent his point of view in relation to some particular purpose or group of purposes, in other words, some particular *function*. All true and democratic representation is therefore *functional* representation.

The structure of any democratic society must be in harmony with these essential principles. Where it employs the representative method, this must be always in relation to some definite function. It follows that there must be, in the society, as many separately elected groups of representatives as there are distinct essential groups of functions to be performed . . .

The Guild Socialist contends, then, that the internal management and control of each industry or service must be placed, as a trust on behalf of the community, in the hands of the workers engaged in it; but he holds no less strongly that full provision must be made for the representation and safeguarding of the consumers' point of view in relation to each service. Similarly, he contends that general questions of industrial administration extending to all industries should, where they mainly concern the whole body of producers, be entrusted to an organisation representing all the producers; but he holds equally that the general point of view of all types of consumers must be fully represented and safeguarded in relation to industry as a whole . . .

Men will never recognise or regard as self-government in any association a system which does not give to them directly as a group the right of framing their common rules to govern their internal affairs, and of choosing, by their own decisions, those who are to hold office and authority in their midst.

This being so, no solution of the problem of industrial government is really a solution at all unless it places the rights and responsibilities of the internal conduct of industry directly upon the organised bodies of producers. On no other condition will men who have risen to a sense of social capacity and power consent to serve or to give of their best. Any other attempted solution will therefore break down before the unwillingness of the workers to produce, and will afford no way of escape from the *impasse* to which we have already been brought by the denial under capitalism of the human rights of Labour. It is our business, then, to accept unreservedly this claim of the producer, and at the same time to reconcile it with the consumers' claim that his voice shall also count. We shall see that there is nothing impossible or even difficult in this reconciliation.

From *Guild Socialism Re-Stated* by G.D.H. Cole (Leonard Parsons Ltd, 1920)

Sheila Rowbotham

THE WOMEN'S MOVEMENT (1979)

I am not trying to assert against this that the women's movement has found *the* answer about how we should organise. Though it is certainly worth noting that the women's movement *has* found a means of remaining connected while growing for a decade, and that shifting and spontaneous initiatives have been taken by an extremely large number of women within the movement. But I *am* arguing that the form in which you choose to organise is not 'neutral', it implies certain consequences. This has been a growing recognition on the Left since the late Sixties. If you accept a high degree of centralisation and define yourselves as professionals concentrating above everything upon the central task of seizing power, you necessarily diminish the development of the self-activity and self-confidence of most of the people involved. Because, for the women's movement, the development of this confidence and ability to be responsible for our own lives was felt to be a priority, this became part of the very act of making a movement.

From *Beyond the Fragments: Feminism and the Making of Socialism*
by Sheila Rowbotham, Lynne Segal and Hilary Wainwright (Merlin Press, 1979)

Louis MacNiece

THE NEXT DAY I DROVE BY NIGHT (1938)

The road to Oxford; *Qu'allais-je faire* tomorrow
Driving voters to the polls
In that home of lost illusions?
And what am I doing it for?
Mainly for fun, partly for a half-believed-in
Principle, a core
Of fact in a pulp of verbiage,
Remembering that this crude and so-called obsolete
Top-heavy tedious parliamentary system
Is our only ready weapon to defeat
The legions' eagles and the lictors' axes;
And remembering that those who by their habit hate
Politics can no longer keep their private
Values unless they open the public gate
To a better political system. That Rome was not built in a day is no excuse
For *laissez-faire*, for bowing to the odds against us;
What is the use
Of asking what is the use of one brick only?
The perfectionist stands for ever in a fog
Waiting for the fog to clear; better to be vulgar
And use your legs and leave a blank for Hogg
And put a cross for Lindsay.
There are only too many who say 'What difference does it make
One way or the other?
To turn the stream of history will take
More than a by-election.'
So Thursday came and Oxford went to the polls
And made its coward vote and the streets resounded
To the triumphant cheers of the lost souls -
The profiteers, the dunderheads, the smarties.
And I drove back to London in the dark of the morning, the trees
Standing out in the headlights cut from cardboard;
Wondering which disease
Is worse – the Status Quo or the Merc Utopia.
For from now on
Each occasion must be used, however trivial,
To rally the ranks of those whose chances will soon be gone
For even guerrilla warfare.
The nicest people in England have always been the least
Apt to solidarity or alignment
But all of them must now align against the beast
That prowls at every door and barks in every headline.

From *Autumn Journal*

William Morris
LOOKING FORWARD (1890)

Our business, I repeat, is the making of socialists, i.e., convincing people that socialism is good for them and is possible. When we have enough people of that way of thinking, *they* will find out what action is necessary for putting their principles in practice. Until we have that mass of opinion, action for a general change that will benefit the whole people is *impossible*. Have we that body of opinion or anything like it? Surely not. If we look outside that glamour, that charmed atmosphere of party warfare in which we necessarily move, we shall see this clearly: that though there are a great many who believe it possible to compel their masters by some means or another to behave better to them, and though they are prepared to compel them (by so-called peaceful means, strikes and the like), all but a very small minority are not prepared *to do without masters*. They do not believe in their own capacity to undertake the management of affairs, and to be responsible for their life in this world. When they are so prepared, then socialism will be realised; but nothing can push it on a day in advance of that time.

Therefore, I say, make socialists. We socialists can do nothing else that is useful, and preaching and teaching is not out of date for that purpose; but rather for those who, like myself, do not believe in State socialism, it is the only rational means of attaining to the New Order of Things.

From 'Where Are We Now?' in *Political Writings of William Morris*, edited by A.L. Morton (Lawrence & Wishart, 1979)

COPYRIGHT ACKNOWLEDGMENTS

The editors and publisher would like to thank the following for permission to reproduce extracts from copyright material:

Cambridge University Press for John Stuart Mill: *On Liberty and Other Writings*, edited by Stefan Collini; Jonathan Cape for *The Future of Socialism* by C.A.R. Crosland, *The State We're In* by Will Hutton, and *Arguments for Socialism* by Tony Benn, edited by Chris Mullin; Chatto & Windus for *Culture and Society 1750–1950* by Raymond Williams, *The Long Revolution* by Raymond Williams, and *Towards 2000* by Raymond Williams; Faber & Faber Ltd for *The Socialist Case* by Douglas Jay, *Comrades* by Bill Douglas, and Dennis Potter: *Seeing the Blossom – Two Interviews and a Lecture*; The Fabian Society for the extracts from Fabian Tracts and pamphlets; Victor Gollancz Ltd for *The Labour Party in Perspective* by Clement Attlee; Gomer Press for 'The Angry Summer' and 'Tonypandy' in *The Collected Poems of Idris Davies*, edited by Islwyn Jenkins; Harper Collins Publishers Ltd for *Freedom Under Planning* by Barbara Wootton, *The Peaceful Revolution* by Herbert Morrison, *The Attack and Other Papers* by R.H. Tawney, and *Conviction* edited by Norman Mackenzie; David Higham Associates for *Socialism in the New Society* by Douglas Jay, *In Place of Fear* by Aneurin Bevan, and *The Unprincipled Society* by David Marquand; Hodder and Stoughton Ltd for *Looking Ahead* by Herbert Morrison; Institute of Public Policy Research for *Social Justice, Strategies for National Renewal, the Report of the Social Justice Commission*; The London School of Economics and Political Science and Cambridge University Press for *A Constitution for the Socialist Commonwealth of Great Britain* by Sidney and Beatrice Webb; Lemon, Unna & Durbridge Ltd for *Boys from the Blackstuff* by Alan Bleasdale; The Merlin Press Ltd for *Beyond the Fragments: Feminism and the Making of Socialism* by Sheila Rowbotham, Lynne Segal and Hilary Wainwright, and *Writing by Candlelight* by E.P. Thompson; John Murray Ltd for *Religion and the Rise of Capitalism* by R.H. Tawney; *New Left Review* for *Working-Class Attitudes*, a conversation between Richard Hoggart and Raymond Williams; the Estate of the late Sonia Brownell Orwell and Secker & Warburg for the George Orwell extracts; Oxford University Press for *Change in British Society* by A.H. Halsey; Maggie Pearlstine for *Choose Freedom – The Future of Democratic Socialism* by Roy Hattersley; Penguin Books Ltd for *Christianity and the Social Order* by William Temple, and *Roots* from the Wesker Trilogy by Arnold Wesker; Pluto Press for *Diffusing Power: The Key to Socialist Revival* by Michael Meacher, and *Citizenship and Social Class* by T.H. Marshall and Tom Bottomore; Reed Consumer Books Ltd for *The English Journey* by J.B. Priestley; Routledge for *Equality* by R.H. Tawney, *Strategy of Equality* by Julian le Grand, *What Have We Done to Defend* by E.F.M. Durbin, and *The Politics of Democratic Socialism* by E.F.M. Durbin; the Society of Authors for *The Intelligent Woman's Guide to Socialism* by George Bernard Shaw; Charles Strachey and Elizabeth Al Qadhi for *Contemporary Capitalism* by John Strachey.

Every effort has been made to acknowledge copyright material which appears in this book; the publisher apologises if, by being unable to trace copyright holders, there are any omissions to the above list.